AF334061

Men with stakes

Manchester University Press

Men with stakes

Masculinity and the gothic in US television

Julia M. Wright

Manchester University Press

Copyright © Julia M. Wright 2016

The right of Julia M. Wright to be identified as the author of this work has been asserted by her in accordance with the Copyright, Designs and Patents Act 1988.

Published by Manchester University Press
Altrincham Street, Manchester M1 7JA

www.manchesteruniversitypress.co.uk

British Library Cataloguing-in-Publication Data
A catalogue record for this book is available from the British Library

Library of Congress Cataloging-in-Publication Data applied for

ISBN 978 0 7190 9770 6 hardback

First published 2016

The publisher has no responsibility for the persistence or accuracy of URLs for any external or third-party internet websites referred to in this book, and does not guarantee that any content on such websites is, or will remain, accurate or appropriate.

Typeset in Sabon by
Servis Filmsetting Ltd, Stockport, Cheshire
Printed in Great Britain by
TJ International Ltd, Padstow

Contents

Acknowledgments

I would like to begin by thanking the Social Sciences Humanities Research Council of Canada for its generous support of my research. Although this project was never proposed to SSHRC, it partly arose from and became intertwined with funded projects in ways that were mutually beneficial.

My thanks as well to everyone at Manchester University Press and the diverse audiences who generously responded to early rehearsals of parts of this work in various forms: conference audiences at annual meetings of the Northeast Modern Language Association, the Popular Culture Association, and the Canadian Association of American Studies; convention audiences at Hal-Con in 2012 and 2013; and online responses to an early version of Chapter 3, "Latchkey Hero: Class, Masculinity, and the Gothic in Eric Kripke's *Supernatural*," *Genders*, 47 (spring 2008). My presentations at the International Gothic Association have focused on the nineteenth century, but the generative exchanges at that always intellectually lively conference lie behind many of the pages here. The interlibrary loan department at my university continues to exceed expectations in its ability to quickly find and deliver the books I cannot find locally, and my research on all subjects would have ground to a halt long ago without it.

My gratitude as well to various colleagues in gothic studies generally for myriad helpful conversations, many on gothic film and television in particular. The list is long, but must start with Jason Haslam, who has generously re-watched and then re-discussed *Buffy*, *Angel*, *X-Files*, and other series with me, as well as newer ones from *American Horror Story* to *Being Human*; Joel Faflak, for very long conversations about *X-Files* and *Millennium* when they were still on the air (not knowing we would both soon be writing about popular culture), and many rewarding discussions since; as well as such eminently collegial scholars as Steven Bruhm, Lauren Goodlad, Karen Macfarlane, and Peter Schwenger, from whom I have learned so much in conversation and from their published work. I would also like to thank the television writers who keep me watching, especially Ben Edlund and Darin Morgan; their work is not extensively represented here because of the specific concerns of this study, but if this were a work of fan-writing there would be whole chapters on Edlund's "Smile Time," "Night Shifter," and "The French Mistake," and Morgan's "Blood," Jose Chung episodes, and "Somehow, Satan Got Behind Me."

Finally, my personal thanks to Jason Haslam. This book, more than any other I have written in our years together, would not have been possible without him.

Introduction

"Popular folklore would have us believe that deep in the underworld there are ruthless men who fear nothing – this story should debunk that myth."[1] So begins the second episode of the influential gothic television series, *Kolchak, the Night Stalker* (1974–1975), in which Carl Kolchak (Darren McGavin), a reporter for the Independent News Service, uncovers various supernatural phenomena including, in this episode, zombies. But this opening monologue is not about zombies. The episode deals extensively with the criminal "underworld" and aired two years after *The Godfather* (1972) was released, a film known for its realism and its depiction of powerful (outlaw) masculinity. Kolchak's zombie story will "debunk" such representations of "ruthless men who fear nothing" as "popular folklore," directing against realism what is a common charge against the gothic, namely that its characters and monsters are extravagantly impossible. If "fantasy is the impossible made probable," as Rod Serling famously intoned in 1962, then Kolchak's opening monologue counters that realism is the improbable made plausible. And, of course, it is.

Televisual realism regularly asks its viewers to accept the improbable – that everything significant happens to a small group of characters, that someone will accidentally overhear exactly the worst part of a conversation, that one small group will produce a long series of romantic-couple combinations, and so on. I start here with *Kolchak* not only because of its critique of realism (a critique that, as I shall argue, is typically gothic in US television), but also because of its particular target: the representation of an extreme form of masculinity as commonplace. In the gothic television series on which I focus here, such masculine types are exposed as cultural constructs; they are neither natural nor inevitable, but part of the artificial language of realism as an artistic mode. The strong father, the rebellious son, the self-sacrificing hero, the self-indulgent villain, and so on are the stock figures of dramatic narrative, and gothic television series draw attention to these clichés as such through parody or hyperbole or simply, as the saying goes, by hanging a lantern on them.[2] There are no "real men," but myriad conventional characters through which masculinity and traditionally related ideas – about reason, about order, about society – can be explored and discussed. This introduction will establish the framework for the chapters that follow by considering first the relationship between the gothic and realism, then the construction of masculinity, and finally the larger tradition of exploring gender in US television gothic.

"Reconnoitering the Rim": starting points

The identification of the gothic with fantasy is not only a matter of scientific epistemology (ghosts do not exist) but also of foundational definitions of it, even as early as Edmund Burke's assertion in 1757 that such narratives "affect minds" because "none can form clear ideas" of "ghosts and goblins."[3] The tension between televisual realism and gothic fantasy has conventionally been the crux of much discussion of gothic television, dividing critics into two camps: the modes are incompatible and therefore gothic television fails; gothic television is masterful because it resolves this incompatibility, offering, to take two scholarly examples from twenty years apart, a "reconciliation" between "reality" and "fancy," or "an effective bridge between the two."[4] Both of these positions are predicated on the nineteenth-century argument – derived from such sources as Samuel Taylor Coleridge's *Biographia Literaria* (1817) – that organic unity is key to artistic value. In other words, it is a critical position that has itself, like Kolchak's "ruthless men," become part of a general worldview that is largely left unquestioned. Helen Wheatley usefully refocuses the problem that "television [is] too 'literal'" to address the domestic emphasis of televisual realism and argue that the gothic responds to "domestic form," suggestively echoing the understanding of nineteenth-century sensation fiction as the "mixture of contemporary domestic realism with elements of the Gothic romance."[5]

Wheatley's emphasis on response rather than formal unity takes us closer to the larger gothic tradition that is of interest in the present study. Critiquing, parodying, and otherwise interrogating realism and its precursor, verisimilitude, is a well-established feature of the gothic from its very beginnings: discussing the first gothic novel, published in 1764 by Horace Walpole, David B. Morris argues, "In its marvels and terrors, *The Castle of Otranto* actively subverts the prosaic vision of the world implicit in novelistic conventions of probability and verisimilitude," and, further, that "Gothic sublimity does not depend upon judgments concerning the truth or reality of supernatural agents and events – judgments which lead critics into bored denunciations of claptrap machinery."[6] Clichéd monsters aside, the gothic has, at its core, traditionally offered a challenge to the worldview promulgated in superficially "realistic" texts – as does *Kolchak*. This challenge is facilitated by relatively recent developments in special effects and other technological elements, offering what Wheatley terms "a more 'realistic' representation of the supernatural."[7] Wheatley's ironic punctuation is worth stressing, however. The "supernatural" is depicted on "realistic" terms not because of the verifiability of a depiction – we cannot judge the accuracy of a depiction of a non-existent being on the terms mandated by realism because, as Burke notes, we cannot even "form clear ideas" of them – but because the detail and probability of the televisual representation approaches the detail and probability expected of realism. To the extent that they "blur," gothic fantasy and televisual realism do so largely on aesthetic terms, at the level of "stylishness" and technical advances.[8] Realism is thus an aesthetic mode rather than the vehicle of a credible representation.

A key concern of this study is the ways in which attention to realism as an aesthetic facilitates critiques of the "folklore" promulgated by realism, especially on the subject of masculinity. *Kolchak*, with a crumply dressed, awkward, and middle-aged protagonist confronting the monsters of 1950s B-movies, rarely allows such fantasies to stand – and neither do the more recent series discussed in this study. This is not to suggest that gothic television programmatically follows a particular ideological agenda or gender model,[9] but that it has an insistently aesthetic framework and larger cultural history that enables discussions of culture as a construct; the gothic is, in fundamental terms, less about what is represented than about representation itself – including aesthetic mode – and thus often extends beyond simple horror. For instance, David Milch's *Deadwood* (2004–2006) is fundamentally gothic in its concern with tyranny, fakery, and cruelty – and in its overall concern with "debunk[ing]" the "myth" of the West and of the men who founded it.[10]

If, as scholars have argued, patriarchal power is reinforced by its cultural invisibility – by the uninterrogated, naturalized depiction of particular kinds of masculinity as inevitably in control, a depiction that is reinforced by representations of other kinds of masculinity as monstrous or comic – then that reinforcement relies also on the use of realism as a mode which seeks to elide the artificiality of its representation.[11] Realism is highly selective, as scholars have widely discussed, but a key part of its conventionality is its masking of literary device as objective representation on terms that René Magritte mocked in his painting of a pipe and the phrase, "Ceci n'est pas une pipe" (this is not a pipe).[12] The gothic, from its inception in Walpole's *Castle of Otranto: A Gothic Story*, has tended to call attention to its written-ness, to the constructedness of its representations, and not merely through such extravagant devices as vampires, ghosts, and demons. The literary–gothic joke, "it was a dark and stormy night," is predicated on the setting's recognizability as a literary device associated with the gothic. The phrase is not a weather report, nor is it designed to elicit the reader's concern that the heroine doesn't have a coat or umbrella – it is designed to elicit concern that she doesn't have a weapon. It is an allusion, and one recognizable as conventional foreshadowing that something scary is about to happen. In building on this tradition, the gothic television of interest here makes visible what many other televisual modes leave invisible: it foregrounds textual debts, for instance, through the repetition of well-known lines; its characters are widely conversant with popular culture, creating in-jokes for the viewing audience; and it often "goes meta," commenting on its own form.

In focusing on masculinity in gothic television I do not aim to be comprehensive or frame what follows as symptomatic, but to facilitate a detailed examination of such gothic commentary on cultural norms and debates as well as to supplement the significant body of work on the domestic gothic in television by looking at its masculinist correlates. In the chapters that follow, I examine such gothic commentary in recent television series, especially *American Gothic* (CBS, 1995–1996), created by Shaun Cassidy; *Millennium*

(Fox, 1996–1999), created by Chris Carter; *Angel* (WB, 1999–2004), created by Joss Whedon and David Greenwalt; *Carnivàle* (HBO, 2003, 2005), created by Daniel Knauf; *Point Pleasant* (Fox, 2005–2006), created by Marti Noxon; *Supernatural* (WB, 2005–2006; CW, 2006–), created by Eric Kripke; and the first season of *American Horror Story* (FX, 2011–), created by Brad Falchuk and Ryan Murphy.[13] As part of a longstanding gothic tradition, these series' interrogation of masculinity is intertwined with larger examinations of social institutions, cultural assumptions, and established forms of knowledge, particularly science and religion. In other words, in interrogating masculinity, these series explore, and sometimes take apart, patriarchy and related forms of traditional order – what "realism," in broad terms, would have viewers accept as natural or inevitable. The plots may sometimes seem absurd or cliché, especially to viewers and readers unfamiliar with the genre's conventions, but it is the dialogue, allusions, and patterns of imagery that are the vehicles of much of these series' commentary. Such series as *Walking Dead* (AMC, 2010–) and *True Blood* (HBO, 2008–2014) are not considered in this study primarily because of their refusal of such elements of the gothic tradition; *Walking Dead* does not even use the term "zombies," let alone refer to well-known zombie narratives. The characters in such series seem never to have watched a television episode or film, read a book, or heard a song, not only because they never refer to gothic precursors but also because they almost never refer to television of any mode or genre, or film, books, songs, paintings, or even cultural icons such as store chains or celebrities – *True Blood* does often depict characters watching television, but only for fictive news and advertisements of the fictive product of the title. The characters in such series are radically separate from cultural as well as physical elements of our "reality." The series that are considered here not only use but also stress such cultural reflexiveness.

For instance, in a late-season episode of *Supernatural*, the lead characters Sam Winchester (Jared Padalecki) and Dean Winchester (Jensen Ackles) are thrown into an alternate universe in which they are the actors Jared Padalecki and Jensen Ackles working on a television show called *Supernatural*, so that the "real" Padalecki and Ackles have to perform Sam and Dean trying to pretend to be Padalecki and Ackles acting the roles of Sam and Dean. Sam and Dean act the parts of Padalecki and Ackles acting the roles of Sam and Dean very badly. While they *are* Sam and Dean, they are not the technically accomplished actors Padalecki and Ackles: they flub lines, miss their marks, and move awkwardly. "Being" the character is not only insufficient, but also counter-productive, because acting is a technical performance, guided by aesthetic requirements such as lighting, blocking, script integrity, and timing. The episode is named "The French Mistake" (6.15) after a dance number in Mel Brooks' *Blazing Saddles* (1974),[14] a musical extravaganza performed in the midst of a series of metafictional moves which expose the hidden devices of televisual and filmic realism: buildings are revealed to be mere façades, background townspeople are cardboard cutouts, and then the camera reveals movie lots and sound stages, lights and crew, as Brooks breaks down the walls between sets and exposes the fakery of it all, ending with the heroes riding off into the sunset, then getting into a chauffeur-driven car, and driving off into the sunset. As Rose Zimbardo suggests, "*Blazing Saddles* is designed to expose the fictionality of cultural inscriptions that are altogether empty yet are powerful enough to move us to kill one another. There is no 'nature,' no 'reality' in such a satire."[15] The *Supernatural* episode goes one step further because it is framed as an allusion to the ending of *Blazing Saddles* – this is *another* "French Mistake." Operating within this kind of *mise en abyme*, representation in gothic television is necessarily a comment *on* representation, and on the absence of a "real" ground to representation. Moreover, in "The French Mistake," Sam and Dean discover that, in a world where *Supernatural* is just a television show, there are no demons or vampires or ghosts: the gothic there is always fictive, so that the "fake" television show depicts precisely what cannot exist in this world's reality. The real in such gothic works is always "real" – a quotation to be discussed rather than a ground to be assumed and taken for granted.

Masculinity in this context is thus necessarily quite different from the sorts of damaged white male bodies that have been so widely discussed in literary and film criticism, from the "wounded" bodies that "signal a crisis," to the injured "hard body" "that can overcome pain to achieve a goal," to the tortured body that, in response to dominant notions of masculinity in terms of reason and self-discipline, finds that "pain – grueling, physical pain – offers the only permissible medium of feminized feeling."[16] While there are certainly elements of such representations in some of the series discussed here, they are more likely to appear as allusion or discussed as a pathology and hence rendered non-normative and non-natural, or "unreal." Masculinity, like other elements of style, is rendered meaningful but not representational: it *signifies*. This is the other side of the counterfeit coin discussed by Jerrold Hogle in his influential work on the literary gothic. Hogle argues, drawing on Jean Baudrillard, that the gothic registers anxiety about "a pervasively counterfeit existence: the fact of signifiers referring back to signifiers, none of which contain or connect to their own meanings in the ways their users and observers assume they do or wish they would."[17] This subversion of dominant views is key to the gothic. While Hogle is concerned with disconnection at a semiotic level, Morris finds it at a formal level as well. Writing of "the narrative principle of repetition in the gothic," he suggests, "While absurd by the standards of realist fiction, such instabilities also serve to call into question received ideas of character and of social relations," specifically "challeng[ing] the concept of a world where everything and everyone is unique, marked by intrinsic differences, possessing a singleness which makes them exactly and only what they appear."[18] The gothic has a long history of challenging Enlightenment notions of the individual that undergird modern ideas of masculinity, and of fictional character as such. In the series discussed in the chapters that follow, the gothic operates to offer such a wide-ranging unsettling of "received ideas."

"A Lie Agreed Upon": proliferating masculinities in *Angel*

Take, as an example, *Angel*, a spinoff from *Buffy the Vampire Slayer* (1997–2003). The series focuses on a repentant vampire with a soul, Angel (David Boreanaz), and one of its creators contends that the series is "about how hard it is to be a man."[19] But the show constantly troubles the idea of "a man," even down to the non-unitary identity of its protagonist, "his body a site where masculinity is openly re/constructed," as Lorna Jowett has discussed.[20] In the show's mythology, vampirism is effected by a demon that Angel's soul must, with constant vigilance, suppress; "perfect happiness" through sexual consummation with the heroine, Buffy, or drugs, or magical hypnosis are mechanisms by which that soul's vigilance is compromised, allowing the demon to control Angel's body once again. The soulful Angel has to deny his own desires to stay "good" and so fight monsters and protect the vulnerable; the soulless demon Angelus torments and slaughters for his own pleasure. Superficially, then, *Angel* juxtaposes two conventional sorts of masculinity, one ideal and the other horrific: the self-sacrificing chaste hero, who submits to torture on a semi-regular basis, and the self-serving licentious villain, who tortures others. The hero is socially isolated, his "brooding" repeatedly the subject of comment by other characters; the villain is intensely social, part of an extended vampire "family." In this regard, the series draws on fairly conventional gender paradigms discernible as far back as Homeric epic: masculinity is most heroic when it is in a purely masculine context, removed from the world of women and domesticity, like the Greek camp at Troy in Homer's *Iliad*; women in this view weaken (heterosexual) men, rousing their sensuality and so distracting them from their self-sacrificing mission, the threats posed by Circe or the Sirens in Homer's *Odyssey*. But vampirism, as it is represented in *Angel*, also frames masculinity in relation to sovereignty. Virtue must discipline desire, and it is consciousness – a self-awareness that is compromised by sex, drugs, and hypnosis, but furthered by "brooding" – that exercises that discipline. But, in this model, masculinity is complete unto itself: it is the self-determining, self-governing fantasy of the Enlightenment and its narrative expression, the *Bildungsroman* (the coming-of-age story). Any man with self-control can become a hero, and the series entangles "how hard it is to be a man" with how hard it is to maintain self-control. Against the *Bildungsroman*, however, the series pits other narrative genres which complicate its vision of the autonomous individual hero, especially *film noir*, in which masculine position is often determined through brutal competition between men in morally ambiguous worlds, and medieval romance, where the competition between men is just as brutal but the morality much clearer.

In an influential discussion of *noir* and masculinity, Frank Krutnik argues that

> *noir* "tough" thrillers reveal an obsession with male figures who are both internally divided and alienated from the culturally permissible (or ideal) parameters of masculine identity, desire and achievement. Regarded in this light, *film noir* – or at least a significant proportion of the films so termed – emerges as a particularly accentuated and pressurised mode of hero-centred fiction. These films will frequently offer an engagement with problematic, even illicit potentialities

> within masculine identity, yet at the same time they cannot fully embrace or sanction such "subversive" potentialities.[21]

There are significant ways in which gothic television adapts *film noir*, especially through its appropriation of the detective genre, and consequently inherits this troubled vision of masculinity – at once an "accentuated and pressurised mode of hero-centred fiction," and an acknowledgment of yet hesitation to endorse "illicit potentialities within masculine identity."[22] *Angel*'s use of genre and juxtaposition of different masculine types serves to call attention to the conventionality – as narrative convention, as cultural construction – of masculinity. Moreover, both *film noir* and romance stress the relativism that determines masculinity, not just in terms of homosociality, as defined by Eve Kosofsky Sedgwick, but also in terms of dominance and what James Eli Adams terms "styles of masculinity."[23] Patriarchy might empower men, but men are not equally powerful or powerful in the same ways. Consider the conventional popular representations of two male types: a university football coach and a scientist who runs a lab at the same university. Both represent men in positions of authority over others who are well-paid professionals in a university setting, but who is more macho – the jock with the whistle or the nerd in the labcoat? Much of the on-screen analysis of Angel's masculinity similarly proceeds through comparisons with other male character types.

From early in the first season, which heavily invokes *film noir* and its history of brooding but stoically macho detectives, Angel, for instance, is juxtaposed with Wesley (Alexis Denisof), who somewhat awkwardly tries to mimic Angel's heroic masculinity. In the second season and later, Angel is regularly compared to the Host (Andy Hallett), his name later revealed to be Lorne. Lorne is a karaoke nightclub owner who is glibly sociable, sings R&B songs traditionally associated with female vocalists, dresses in brightly colored shimmery suits (in contrast to Angel's insistently black, matte clothes), and is generally "metrosexual" with only occasional heteronormative assertions of his sexual desire for women.[24] In the final season, with Angel now the CEO of the Los Angeles branch of the demonic law firm Wolfram & Hart, Spike (James Marsters) voices the centuries-old lament that masculinity is compromised by the sensual luxury that, as a CEO, Angel now enjoys. But, far beyond the main characters, the series regularly plays out on-screen multiple possibilities for masculinity, from the nerdish CEO of a software company who plays Dungeons and Dragons to a slick lawyer who is revealed to be class-passing, more comfortable in cowboy boots and an old truck than expensive loafers and limousines. Moreover, masculinities change: Wesley begins the series as incompetent, clumsy, and submissive, but gradually becomes more confident and serious, so that by season 4 those who knew him before are struck by the change in him (see "Salvage" 4.13); Gunn (J. August Richards) is introduced as a street kid who has organized a team to fight vampires in the poorer part of the city, but becomes a ballet-loving boyfriend and later the lawyer of the group.[25] As Jowett puts it, "*Angel* offers not just one monolithic version of masculinity but a continuum of masculinities, and at any time any character may occupy a position along this continuum."[26]

Lorne's home, Pylea, the only multi-episode setting for the series that is outside of LA, offers a revealing contrast to this contemporary vision of multiple and shifting masculinities. Pylea is a Monty-Pythonesque medieval world, with knights, a castle, a princess, and oppressed human beings not only forced to do unpleasant forms of physical labor but also comically coming into contact with excrement of various types. In trying to explain to Angel why he does not want to return to Pylea, the Host describes it:

> Talk about screwed up values. A world of only good and evil, black and white, no gray. No music, no art, just champions roaming the countryside, fighting for justice. Boring. You got a problem, solve it with a sword. No one ever admits to having actual feelings and emotions, let alone talks about them. Can you imagine living in a place like that?
>
> ("Belonging" 2.19)

Later in the episode, his cousin accuses him of cowardice, and Lorne replies, "For the last time – not a coward. I just saw both sides of the joust. How are you supposed to joust someone when you partially agree with their point of view?" Pylea, then, allies heroic masculinity with a world of absolutes – "good and evil, black and white" – enforced with violence, refusing interiority ("actual feelings and emotions") and complicated ethical perspectives in which it is possible to "partially agree." In a later episode in the Pylea arc, "Through the Looking Glass" (2.21), the series returns to the implications of enforcing only one kind of masculinity. Angel is heralded by the Pyleans as a champion among champions:

LORNE: Nice to be seen as a hero without all the pesky moral ambiguities you get back home, isn't it?

ANGEL: Yeah, maybe it is a little.

LORNE: They see you a certain way. You start to see yourself that way. You become that image. I get it – I do. Because I know how *they see me*. Can we *go*?

This, of course, is Angel talking about his "actual feelings and emotions" with Lorne, as Lorne sets in motion the very process of identification that led to his being labeled a coward: he sympathizes with Angel's position ("I get it – I do"), and then, on that basis, invites Angel to sympathize with his perspective. Moreover, Lorne highlights what a number of *Angel* episodes explicitly address: masculinity is constituted in a sociocultural space, and is not prior (or "natural") to that constitutive process. Hence, first "They see you a certain way," then "You start to see yourself that way," and, finally, "You become that image." Angel is not born that way.

Lorne articulates a view of gender consistent with current gender theory, particularly that body of work influenced by Judith Butler's idea of gender as performative: that is, gender roles are not only performed but also, in being performed, become consolidated as gender roles, and so gender is "performative" in the sense defined in J. L. Austin's *How to Do Things with Words*.[27] Austin defines as performative those speech acts which accomplish what they describe, such as "I do" as a legal commitment in a marriage ceremony:[28] "They see you a certain way. You start to see yourself that way. You *become that image*." The performative is transformative, not transient like simple performance. In the depiction of Pylea, moreover, this gender performativity is inextricable from genre. Angel, as champion, is associated with the quest: as Fred (Amy Acker) puts it after he rescues her from Pylean warriors, the "handsome man saved me from the monsters" (2.21). At the end of the narrative arc he is to fight the rulers' champion on behalf of the oppressed. This is romance, a mode whose medieval origins are highlighted by the medieval appearance of Pylea (that is, its use of televisual cues associated with medievalism rather than its authentic depiction of medieval life), and it is supposed to end with a death. Lorne, however, is associated with music – intervals of sound, the harmonization of difference, and female performance. In Pylea, he sings "Stop! In the Name of Love," first recorded by the Supremes in 1965, and "Somewhere over the Rainbow," famously sung by Judy Garland in *The Wizard of Oz* (1939).

The multi-episode narrative arc thus comments extensively on the conservative gender politics borne by romance, the ur-genre from which detective fiction, the gothic, science fiction, and other non-realist forms derive, and the inextricability of gender from all that was covered by the eighteenth-century term "moral philosophy" – structures of knowledge, political organization, culture, and economic systems, as later chapters of this study will explore in more depth. Masculinity in *Angel* both buttresses and tropes different moral orders: on the one hand, power through dominance, strict morality, and a violent struggle between good and evil that brooks neither political nor gendered dissent; on the other, aesthetics, color, and the capacity to inhabit a gray space in which opposed perspectives can be grasped and diversity is at least possible as an aspiration. Lorne's karaoke nightclub, for instance, welcomes demons and human beings of all backgrounds, as Lorne counsels all of them on their "actual feelings." Through Pylea, then, *Angel* explores not only different "styles of masculinity" and the performative constitution of masculinity but also the profound ties between gender and genre, both ideologically and formally.

The performative is not incidental to the generic in this context. Austin includes among "primitive devices in speech," that is, idiomatic phrasing that is not explicitly and precisely performative, the category of "Connecting particles" in which "we use 'therefore' with the force of 'I conclude that'; we use 'although' with the force of 'I concede that,'" and then adds, "A very similar purpose is served by the use of titles such as Manifesto, Act, Proclamation, or the sub-heading 'A Novel.'"[29] In other words, genre designations are as performative as gender identities. Just as the title "Act" indicates that the text under that heading will change the law of the land, so the title "Novel" *does* something, even if it is to nullify any speech acts which follow by enjoining the reader not to take them, again in Austin's terms, "seriously" – that is, as legally binding acts or promises.[30] In the gothic, this non-seriousness – this open inauthenticity – is fundamental. As Hogle has argued in a series of essays, central to the gothic is the "ghost of the counterfeit," a counterfeit of a counterfeit which implies that there is no authenticity to be found in signification, as in Baudrillard's theory of contemporary media: Baudrillard suggests the signifier is "fundamentally a 'simulacrum' ... able to be industrially reproduced on the basis of a pattern or mold that is itself a counterfeit of the counterfeit."[31] Baudrillard has been a key thinker for another major theorist of the gothic, Fred Botting, providing a framework for gothic scholars' exploration of the ways in which the gothic, over the last 250 years, has persisted in calling attention to frauds, fakes, counterfeits, masks, disguises, and all the myriad ways in which identity is not natural or authentic but is wrought out of cultural performance – a counterfeit of a counterfeit, in which "you become that image." Jowett and Abbott suggest that "mix[ing] horror with action, comedy, and melodrama" is a sign of "increased genre hybridity" on US television,[32] but the gothic has traditionally mixed these elements – certainly this is an apt description of such early gothic narratives as Walpole's *Castle of Otranto*, Matthew G. Lewis's *The Monk* (1796), and Bram Stoker's *Dracula* (1897), forward to Richard Matheson's blending of science and gothic in the mid 1900s, and beyond. The mixing of modes and genres in the gothic is part of its attention to its own constructedness – it is not natural or authentic (as realism purports to be), but is built out of and on top of prior texts, established conventions, and stock devices. This brings us back to the *Supernatural* episode, "The French Mistake." The representational *mise en abyme* of that episode is exemplarily gothic precisely because it depicts representation as not merely counterfeit, but as a counterfeit of a counterfeit that alludes to another counterfeit which exposes representation as counterfeit: in Hogle's phrase, a "refaking of what is already fake."[33]

"Advances, None Miraculous": gothic roots

US television gothic more specifically has also had a long-standing interest in gender, spoofing the presentation of the "normal" television family since the 1960s. The first gothic series in the USA to follow a single set of characters, *Bewitched* (1964–1972), has been read as reactionary in this context, part of a 1960s sitcom pattern in which "super-powerful women ... efface their potential in return for the 'rewards' of family life."[34] Drawing on such movies as *I Married a Witch* (1942) and *Bell, Book, and Candle* (1958), *Bewitched* focuses on not the love story but the witch's post-courtship desire to be domestic, though the earliest episodes stress the new couple's sexual desire, Samantha Stevens (Elizabeth Montgomery) using her witchcraft to speed along domestic chores so that she can get to the marriage bed more quickly. With nearly infinite power at her fingertips, Samantha repeatedly asserts her desire to be a homemaker, wife, and mother, a choice contrasted by the lifestyles of her partying cousin Serena (also played by Montgomery) and her high-society mother, Endora (Agnes Moorehead).[35] The central problem of many episodes, however, is not Samantha's power as a witch or her lack of it as a homemaker, but rather the powerlessness of her husband, Darrin (Dick York in the first five seasons). As Lynn Spigel indicates, this powerlessness is often corrected by the end of the episodes. But an emphasis on the episodes' narrative closure obscures the seriality of television: Darrin's powerlessness (as an advertising executive, as a husband, as a father) will be resurrected again in the next episode, because these corrections are never a cure and much of the dramatic tension as well as comedy of the series require his powerlessness.

Instead of disappearing into a hidden workplace, like so many fathers of early television, Darrin Stevens is regularly represented as being at the mercy of the arbitrary authority of a self-serving boss and the need to placate willful, arbitrary clients (arguably, variants on the arbitrary authority of the standard gothic villain); when he is rewarded, it is often because of an accident arising from his inability to manage his domestic space and family. He has an office at home and his in-laws bother him at work, and his boss regularly requires him to turn his home into a space for courting clients, transgressing the work-home divide so crucial to the maintenance of the norms entrenched in the family-centered sitcoms and drama series of the era. The Stevens' home is even surveilled by a busybody neighbor, who refuses her husband's pleas to stop watching the Stevens' family in yet another repetition of the series' guiding trope in which the patriarchal male is unable to control his domestic space and the women in it.

The series is also intertwined with 1960s subtexts on class and race: Samantha's father objects to what he terms "mixed marriages," and both parents are represented as somewhat aristocratic, particularly when they deplore Samantha's home and clothing.[36] But the series' exploration of gender relies heavily on the examination of work. Darrin is good at his job, but that is not enough to succeed: clients must be courted, complimented, and conciliated. Moreover, the debate between Samantha and her mother over the "drudgery" of housework needs to be recognized as groundbreaking in the mid-1960s for representing housekeeping *as work* – it is neither invisible, as it so often was (and is) in nominally realist television depictions of domestic life, nor is it represented as the natural activity of any adult woman. From the first episodes of *Bewitched*, it is represented as hard work that is time-consuming, physically difficult, and endless.

Just as the series makes visible that which so many family-centered series take for granted, namely "women's work," it also pursues the broader education of men in women's experiences. In "It Shouldn't Happen to a Dog" (1.3), Samantha is sexually harassed by one of Darrin's clients. Darrin refuses to believe her, until he sees her being attacked at the end of the episode – the point not being the punishment of her attacker, but rather Darrin's new awareness of women's endangerment. In "A Very Special Delivery" (2.2), Endora is angry about Darrin's assumption that physical activity, such as that burdensome housework again, is healthier for a pregnant Samantha, concluding that if he knew what pregnancy was like he would be more sympathetic and do some housework to ease Samantha's physical burden. So, she gives him pregnancy symptoms, including backache, mood swings, strange food cravings, morning sickness, and a growing belly. In Darrin's fantasy sequence about the logical end of his symptoms, Samantha paces in the hospital waiting room and hands out cigars while Darrin gives birth; after the fantasy ends, Samantha arrives at the bar to which Darrin has retreated in order to comfort Darrin and assure him that his growing belly is "only a symptom – we'll be rid of them soon enough." The moral focus of the episode is not the pre-*Roe* v. *Wade* fetus, real or magically imagined, but rather that Darrin should understand how Samantha is being affected by her pregnancy and so be motivated to share in the housework – which is, in this episode as in so many others, represented as physically difficult. Once again, the point is not representation but signification. Samantha's situation is made a general one at the end of the episode when Endora hears a man brag that his wife has had five children and they are no trouble at all – so she gives him pregnancy symptoms as well. In such episodes, *Bewitched* offers a two-pronged attack on the assumptions of conventional family sitcoms: on the one hand, the "man of the house" has no real control over his home or his workplace, ineffectually asserting his will in the first and necessarily abjected in the second as well as unable to keep the two spheres separate; on the other, he is repeatedly instructed that he lacks knowledge of, and therefore proper sympathy for, women's material lives. Under the guise of the gothic, the series explodes the patriarchal fantasy of the conventional early sitcom's "realism" in which men's work reinforces their authority and women's work, and pregnancies, are unrepresented. If "Samantha's magic powers are harnessed in the service of the domestic," it is to point to the physical difficulty, if not the impossibility, of maintaining the domestic ideal of early sitcoms.[37]

Premiering at the same time as *Bewitched*, the shorter-lived series *The Munsters* and *The Addams Family* (both 1964–1966) more obviously parodied the norms of the family-centered sitcom but largely limited women's power to sexual power over their husbands: adoring their wives, Herman Munster and Gomez Addams are happily ruled at home by them. Nor are their working lives put at risk by their wives' power: Gomez does not work, and Herman's employment as a gravedigger is barely noted in *The Munsters*, and does not, like Darrin's, carry the requirement of "hid[ing] any kind of social deviance behind a strict veneer of allegiance to the corporate ideal."[38] *The Munsters* and *The Addams Family*, like early episodes of *Bewitched*, introduced sexuality to the sitcom screen in new ways, as Wheatley points out, but ultimately the direct parody keeps those two series focused on conventional gender roles and divisions – on "a comedic inversion of the all-American family sitcom."[39] In the pairing of Samantha's work at home and Darrin's in advertising, and the constant breaching of the boundaries between them, *Bewitched* concertedly undermines standard depictions of both spheres.

This ambivalence toward women's power and simultaneous undercutting of the myth of male power sets the paradigm for a number of more recent gothic television series associated with women- or girl-centered perspectives. *Buffy the Vampire Slayer*, *Sabrina the Teenage Witch* (1996–2003), *Charmed* (1998–2006), and similar series focus on girls and women with supernatural abilities who usually live in all-female households; if men are not entirely absent, they are largely ineffectual, like Darrin before them. This is crystallized in *Buffy*, where Xander (Nicholas Brendon) and Riley (Marc Blucas) repeatedly assert their sense of powerlessness in comparison to Buffy's preternatural strength and the former is, recalling Sigmund Freud's famous discussion of E. T. A. Hoffman's gothic tale, "The Sandman" (1816), metaphorically castrated at the end of the series when one of his eyes is destroyed by the misogynist Caleb.[40] Married couples, moreover, are almost entirely absent from these series, especially fathers: Xander's father appears only twice in *Buffy*'s seven seasons, and one of those appearances is in a dream sequence, and Tara's widower father appears in one episode, but these are rare exceptions.[41] Buffy's parents are divorced and her father increasingly an absentee one as the series proceeds; Willow's mother appears a couple of times, but never her father; Giles (Anthony Head), the central father figure of the series, is unmarried; teachers and principals are either explicitly unmarried or their marital status is unnoted; a recurring character, Amy (Elizabeth Anne Allen), was abandoned by her father; and so on.

The first gothic soap opera, *Dark Shadows* (1966–1971), turns from the beginning on absent fathers. The protagonist, Victoria (Alexandra Moltke), is an orphan, her parentage unknown; she arrives at Collinsport to be a modern-day governess to David Collins (David Henesy), about 10 years old. David's father, Roger Collins (Louis Edmonds), is cold and sardonic, and the first months of the series focus on the child's Oedipal efforts to murder him; and Victoria's employer, so the story goes, was abandoned by her husband when her daughter was still an infant. The first part of the series is sensationalist more than gothic. Gloomy settings, an antique home, the lonely governess – all of these are familiar gothic and sensational trappings from the nineteenth century forward. But murder, family secrets, absent parents, and corporate arm-twisting are all specifically sensationalist in that they focus on the breakdown of the moral order rather than the disruption of the natural order as well.[42] This breakdown is specifically a problem of masculinity: Roger is the only man in the house, and he is sophisticated to the point of effeteness and a failure as a father; his son is half mad; and when Burke Devlin (Mitchell Ryan) shows up, he is a breath of fresh macho air who recognizes, and works to correct, the son's violent hatred of his father, and offers a love interest for the young women, moving the various plots toward the restoration of patriarchal and heteronormative order.

But the series gradually turned toward the supernatural, most strikingly through Barnabas, sometimes credited with being the first remorseful vampire, tortured by his own monstrosity like

Anne Rice's Louis and Whedon's Angel after him (as well as Blade and numerous others).[43] Barnabas, turned into a vampire and then imprisoned in a crypt during the nineteenth century, is introduced narratively to solve the problem of the rapist Willie Loomis, whose sexual threat to women is frequently referenced, as in gothic works from *Castle of Otranto* forward, through ellipsis: it is Loomis who frees Barnabas from his crypt, so that the violent sexual offender releases the "monster" who will prey on women, allegorizing his crime. But Loomis becomes Barnabas's first victim and servant, very much like Stoker's Renfield, as the Victorian vampire turns the aggressive and sexually threatening modern-day Loomis into a submissive and quiet man who is intensely concerned about the safety of women. Through Barnabas, the series turns from absent and disdainful fathers to the ethically complicated patriarch who both reins in wayward male sexuality and preys on women himself, and who uses Victorian politeness to mask violence and exert control. Barnabas is embedded in the patriarchal history of the Collins family, introduced in the first weeks of the series as a long line of men of ability and action who built Collinsport and so are responsible for the wealth of the town as well as that of the family itself. One of these upstanding men buried Barnabas, his own son, conscious if not alive, in the family crypt to contain his monstrosity. With Barnabas, then, the series shifts from a sensationalist plot of a society gone awry without strong men to lead it, to a gothic plot in which predatory male sexuality is literally contained but figuratively displaced into vampirism. Hence, as striking a figure as Barnabas is, he is originally the personification of the danger that Loomis, in a more realist fictional world, represents, or would if such things could be directly represented in daytime 1960s US television.

The original *Kolchak, the Night Stalker* is perhaps the most directly influential program on the series discussed here. Preceded by two TV movies, *The Night Stalker* (1972) and *The Night Strangler* (1973), and later rebooted as *Night Stalker* (2005–2006), echoes of it can be found throughout gothic series of the last two decades. *Kolchak* is often cited as a source for *X-Files* (1993–2002), a series which spawned writers, directors, and actors who have worked in the series discussed in the chapters which follow; the third episode of *Kolchak*, "They Have Been, They Are, They Will Be," features aliens and various details familiar to *X-Files* viewers, from the mysterious stopping of watches at the same moment to government cover-ups.[44] Recent discussions of television gothic have largely ignored *Kolchak*, however: for instance, Eddie Robson discusses it only as a source for *X-Files*, while Wheatley includes it on a list of gothic television series but goes no further; Jowett and Abbott offer a rare exception in brief discussions of its structure and some episodes.[45] The series, as well as TV movies, follow the reporter, Carl Kolchak, as he deals with mostly supernatural threats that various male authority figures – his boss, the police, medical doctors, and so forth – refuse to recognize. He plays on his boss's machismo to manipulate him (for instance, belligerently refusing to go on an assignment he wants so that the boss will pick him for it), and is contrasted, in true *Odd Couple* style, with a smaller, more effete reporter named Updyke (Jack Grinnage). Kolchak is mentioned by name in some of the series discussed here,[46] and deals with unusual supernatural threats that appear in later television. For instance, one *Kolchak* episode features a Native American supernatural figure who can take on the shape of a coyote or a crow ("Bad Medicine" 1.8), a figure echoed closely in *Buffy the Vampire Slayer* ("Pangs" 4.8). Links are most evident in *Supernatural*. First conceived as a series about reporters, it shares with the only season of *Kolchak* a number of "legends," as they are termed in *Kolchak*: not only the staple fare of vampires, zombies, and werewolves, and the device of using fire to put ghosts to rest, but also such figures as the more obscure, to many Western viewers, Hindu Rakshasa (*Kolchak*, "Horror in the Heights" 1.11; *Supernatural*, "Everybody Loves a Clown" 2.2).

As this cursory survey of pre-1980 gothic television suggests, we can broadly organize US gothic television in relation to the twin poles of the domestic space and the work space, even as they complicate gender paradigms in more specific ways. The former, even into the twenty-first century, centers predominantly on female protagonists, from Samantha in *Bewitched* and the Collins' women in *Dark Shadows* to Buffy and the sisters on *Charmed*. The latter, even now, generally focuses on male protagonists, from *Kolchak* (in all its versions) to *Angel* and *Grimm* (2011–). But a number of recent series, on which I focus below, juxtapose rather than separate these spheres: *Millennium* focuses on a male protagonist, the profiler and supernatural seer Frank Black (Lance Henriksen), but places him in two juxtaposed, and increasingly overlapping, locations, the bright-yellow home and the bleak workspace of a consultant on murder cases, a conjunction echoed in *Carnivàle* through the contrast between the preacher's carefully controlled home and the carnival enterprise; *Supernatural* focuses on supernatural detective work as "the family business," one pursued, until late in the series, only by men, constantly calling attention to the lack of a stable family space that such "family" work entails. The first season of *American Horror Story* goes back to the domestic environment of *Bewitched*: the father has an office in the home, and housework is once again difficult, though it is solved here not by magic but by a ghost maid rather like *Bewitched*'s ever-fading Esmeralda (Alice Ghostley). But the house is the supernatural agent, as the season's narrative arc twists through various domestic crises – money problems, infidelity, teenage angst, domestic violence – in which the house bears the marks of all the other domestic crises to happen within its walls. In other words, recent television gothic, though not as obviously parodic as the more famous mid-1960s series, continues to call attention to and challenge the paradigms of television's domestic realism.

"Tell Him Something Pretty": gender, history, myth

This study thus takes as a key premise not only that masculinity is a cultural construction, with different versions in circulation at any given historical moment and in any given cultural milieu, but also that the construction of masculinity is itself thematized in many of the series considered here as part of a larger exploration of culture. If, as Peter Lehman suggests (tacitly academic) "men and women, straight or gay/lesbian, talk to each other about masculinity and the male body through film theory and criticism,"[47] then that conversation is related to a larger conversation in which, outside of academe, "men and women talk to each other about masculinity and the male body through" film, television, media reviews, and fan culture. The two conversations are not isolated from each other: the academic conversation is fundamentally possible because of what is going on in film and television, and film and television are in some measure shaped by film theory and criticism, most obviously, perhaps, through all of the producers, directors, writers, actors, and other film and television creators who took related courses in university,[48] but also because they, of course, read, even if they do not always assume that viewers do. Sera Gamble, then a writer for

Supernatural, addressed this issue in an interview with the flashy title, "Dealing with Gore!" posted on her network's promotional site during the series' third season:

> I think Eric [Kripke] pulls me back a little bit – you know, I go all the way to edge and go "And then, we can talk about Nietzsche!" "No, no we really, really can't." And I'm like, "But there's this really beautiful poem that Rainer Maria Rilke wrote about angels, and how they're terrifying!" He's like "That's great, but … " It's really good fodder for conversation in the room, and then you kind of go "OK, how is this a story about the boys, and how can you do it in a way that's disgusting and makes Standards and Practices call you and yell at you?"[49]

This is a pointed illustration of how mainstream media writers can perceive the gap between what they know, and what they can show – and how material still crosses that gap as "fodder for conversation in the room." From season 4, *Supernatural* moved toward precisely such a depiction of angels, but apparently has yet to cite Rilke overtly. *Millennium*, moreover, has an episode that openly mocks "Standards and Practices" ("Somehow, Satan Got Behind Me" 2.21), television's internal censors, to address other ways in which industry assumptions about viewers constrain creative production – in an episode that deals extensively with the sort of lurid violence that such censors generally permit while fussing over scatological language and sexuality.

This wider cultural exchange around and through media representation is alike part of the discourse of the "crisis of masculinity" discussed by Brenton J. Malin and others: with no assurance through realism of a "natural" masculinity, the meaning of "masculine" is disputable and hence uncertain. Moreover, "Because masculinity is a social construction, every discussion of manhood stakes a claim in its potential meaning."[50] Masculinity, in other words, is symbolic – even mythic, on Barthesian terms (and Kolchak's) – as well as ideological. Masculinity's long-conventional association in Western thought with order, reason, and self-governance means that to challenge masculinity is to challenge those other concepts key to the naturalized vision of modernity. Thus, a central concern of this study is the ways in which the interrogation of "styles of masculinity," to use Adams' phrase, is implicated in the interrogation of the dominance of social institutions (such as corporate America) and epistemologies (such as science) associated with modernity.[51]

At stake here, then, is not just solving the mystery or ending the threat – though those are the focus of the plots for many episodes in these series – but how meaning is produced. Following Butler's argument, every representation of masculinity is performative in that it alters the cultural field in which various options for masculine behavior are offered to individuals. In nineteenth-century England, to take one example, cultural mores tipped back and forth on whether a beard was manly or not. In the 1980s, hairy chests hung in the balance, and lost; now, most white under-40 "masculinist" heroes in twenty-first-century US film and television are depicted with shaved chests. This might seem a trivial example – a matter of fashion rather than substance – but it speaks to the ways in which masculinity can be invented and then perpetuated through media representation until, as Malin puts it, it becomes "invisible" and we cease to notice the artificiality of it, and cease to notice the constant labor necessary to keep all those acres of chests smooth until parody comes along to call attention to it, as in the chest-waxing scene of *40-Year-Old Virgin* (2005).[52]

But juxtapositions of different masculine "styles" in *Angel*, discussed earlier, undo such transparency, and the self-conscious attention to form – genre, mode, and medium – in the gothic provides a ready vehicle for such juxtapositions. Wheatley finds a resurgence in the gothic on US television in the 1990s and attributes it, following a number of commentators, to cultural angst – to "the 'reality' of lives lived in fear."[53] This misses, however, the playfulness of much gothic television, especially its allusoriness, its "in-jokes," and its refusal of doctrine. Whedon's feminist critique, and its limits, in *Buffy the Vampire Slayer* are fairly obvious, and to focus only on that ideological work is to ignore the wittiness and constant genre references of the series, from Buffy being thrown out of a pop-culture class at university ("The Freshman" 4.1) to the pop-culture references in her first meeting with Dracula. Sarcastically, she asks, "This isn't just a fanboy thing, is it? Because I've fought more than a couple of pimply, overweight vamps who called themselves Lestat," and Xander later mocks him, "where did you get that accent, *Sesame Street*?" ("Buffy vs. Dracula" 5.1). Such gothic television is less about pessimism and fear than about exploring the potential of the gothic form to facilitate the analysis of culture itself. After all, in "Buffy vs. Dracula," Buffy stakes the vampire, he reconstitutes himself, and she stakes him again, wryly noting, "You think I don't watch your movies? You always come back" – an analysis of generic convention rather than defensive, or definitively conclusive, violence.

This might sound like the postmodern rather than the gothic, and with good reason: certainly there is much that the two modes share, as I shall discuss further in Chapter 4. But, as Wheatley demonstrates in her analysis of "allusionism" in *Twin Peaks*, allusions in the gothic "create *meaning*": "the 'horrid' is represented by references to the detective genre, horror movies, film noir and the Gothic, on the one hand, and, on the other hand, the 'normal' is found within allusions to the soap opera, the sitcom and the teen romance genre."[54] Moreover, these allusions forge a particular kind of audience, not just "a knowledgeable viewer, able to identify a plethora of references and parodies,"[55] but also a viewer trained to recognize popular culture as the site of intertextual play. Hogle has pointed to the importance of Shakespeare's *Hamlet* as a precursor to the gothic, partly through its counterfeiting of fathers as well as its dramatic representation of ghosts, midnight settings, and battles between good and evil.[56] But *Hamlet* is also a vital precursor for its staging of a play within a play, the inset play commenting on the action of the framing play, in an intertextual loop. Walpole's invocations of Shakespeare's five-act plays in his five-chapter *Castle of Otranto*, the repetition of the names Matilda and Manfred from *Otranto* to Lewis's *The Monk*, Byron's *Manfred*, and Mary Shelley's *Mathilda*, quotations from Coleridge's *Rime of the Ancient Mariner* in Shelley's *Frankenstein* – such allusiveness charts textual relationships that signify, indicating that there is interpretive value to thinking about the text in relation to those it references, and perpetually reminds the viewer (like Austin's designation "Novel") that the text is not "serious," or at least not transparently representational. Hamlet's play within a play is not intended to tell the audience what happened to the hero's father, but to provoke a reaction from the one audience member who *already knows* about the murder.

As Asbjørn Grønstad notes in a trenchant discussion of the ways in which film, and particularly filmic violence, foreground the artificiality of the medium, "Most films refer to other texts, thereby already adding to that 'intractable opacity of the visible' that is the work of the figural."[57] This feature, as I have already suggested, is foregrounded in much gothic television and film: film might regularly invoke, for instance, the downward shot over a staircase, used in Fritz Lang's *M* (1931) and then elaborated in the "vertigo effect" (or "trombone shot") in Alfred Hitchcock's *Vertigo* (1958), and some version of it has appeared in dozens of films since, but *The Rocky Horror Picture Show* (1975) is unabashedly dense in references to art, literature, and horror film, as Rolf Eichler has detailed.[58] This practice goes back to the early decades of the gothic, such as the 1797 play, *The Castle Spectre*, in which the author, Matthew Lewis, "rel[ies] on the audience's knowledge of Gothic traditions," as James Allard has noted, while the printed version includes explicit references to Shakespeare's plays, Walpole's *Castle of Otranto*, and other antecedents.[59] A more recent extension of this convention explicitly insists on the characters knowing US popular culture as well as the audience does. The first episode of *American Gothic*, for instance, establishes its gothic tweaking of another series' Carolinas sheriff and his young son by having Sheriff Lucas Buck whistle the theme song to *The Andy Griffith Show* (1960–1968). In an interview about the episode, the show's creator, Cassidy, remarks,

> One of the problems I have, and a lot of people have, with suspense movies is that the actors always act as though they have never seen these movies. ... I wanted to give them a sensibility that the audience would have. It always bothered me that every one in the audience knows not to open the door, except the leading lady. That awareness of pop culture is translated into 'American Gothic' with the sheriff whistling the theme to 'The Andy Griffith Show.' It's evil, and it is ironic. Buck sees the irony of the situation. Yeah, he grew up with that show just like the rest of us.[60]

A year later, Wes Craven's *Scream* (1996) offered a horror movie in which most of the characters are experts on the genre and its leading examples. Similarly, in an early episode of *Supernatural*, Dean Winchester berates Kat, the filmic cliché of a blonde teenager who walked into a haunted building because her boyfriend pressured her to do so:

> DEAN: Hey, I've got a question for you. You've seen a lot of horror movies, yeah?
> KAT: Yeah, I guess so.
> DEAN: Do me a favor. Next time you see one, pay attention. When someone says a place is haunted – don't go in.
>
> ("Asylum" 1.10)

It is not only viewers of gothic television who are expected to know the conventions of the genre – if televisual realism is to acknowledge the saturation of our daily lives by cultural materials, it must also expect that characters will know them too. The gothic is, in this sense, arguably more realistic than all of those realist series in which references to cultural materials are largely absent.

While most episodes of *Supernatural*, particularly in the early seasons, are readily characterized as 42-minute horrorfests, the series generally also demands that its viewers "pay attention," and episodes are peppered with cultural references from classic rock to pop culture to canonical literature. In "Sex and Violence" (4.14), to take just one example, Sam Winchester tells his brother that the demon-of-the-week is a siren and Dean replies, "Like in the *Odyssey*?"; to his brother's surprised look, he retorts, "Yes – I read." Literature is used to comment on the form of an episode itself, as the Winchesters meet Chuck, the author of *Supernatural* books, who thought that he had created the Winchesters and their stories until the brothers knocked on his door. They ask him about the book he is currently writing:

> CHUCK: It's very Vonnegut.
> DEAN: *Slaughterhouse-Five* Vonnegut or *Cat's Cradle* Vonnegut? ...
> CHUCK: "Kilgore Trout" Vonnegut. I wrote myself into it. I wrote myself, at my house, confronted by my characters.
> ("The Monster at the End of this Book" 4.18)

This happens to Trout, for instance, at the end of Kurt Vonnegut's *Breakfast of Champions* (1973). Earlier, Chuck, thinking he has controlled their lives as their author, remarks, "The things I put you through ... all for what, all for the sake of literary symmetry"; on finding out that they lived his "ghost-ship" plot, he apologizes, "I am so sorry. I mean, horror is one thing, but to be forced to live bad writing. If I would have known it was real, I would have done another pass." *Supernatural* is also indebted to Goethe's *Faust* for some of its basic demon lore and regularly invokes Led Zeppelin; *Millennium* often cites Nostradamus and uses literary epigraphs for episodes, and season 2 includes a number of episodes that invoke the music of Bobby Darin and Patti Smith; *American Gothic* is broadly Faulknerian but also refers repeatedly to Elvis Presley and frequently invokes the central *Faust* trope of the bargain with the devil. The literary and wider cultural debts of these series are diverse, and they regularly – even insistently – cross the imagined "high" and "low" culture divide.

Gothic television invites its viewers to recognize not only that the world depicted is a fictive one but also that it is a deeply intertextual one at the level both of its own construction and what it represents – the gothic world is one in which characters read books, watch movies and television, and listen to music, and both understand and talk about their world in relation to those cultural materials, making its engagement with culture potentially more extensive than representation and more complicated than allegory.[61] In its referentiality, gothic television also interacts with its audience: for instance, fansites list allusions, registering audience expectation that such allusions will be present for them to find. Art Baltazar offers a nicely concise statement on this aspect of non-realist genres in a recent interview on his new comic-book series with Franco Aureliani, *Itty Bitty Hellboy* (a spinoff of Mike Mignola's *Hellboy*). In response to Aureliani's remark, "We're big fans of every project we've worked on. We research and read stuff," Baltazar adds, "It's true. It's kinda like when [they] say 'Write what you know.' This is all the stuff we know about."[62] "Write what you know," a mantra for writers who work in realism and the expectation of viewers trained in realism, is here displaced: it is not the material world that is "known," but culture. "We research and read."

"A Constant Throb": US gothic television, 1995–2013

Most of the series discussed in subsequent chapters have attracted significant cult followings, including *Millennium* and *American Gothic*. Some, notably *Point Pleasant*, did not. Some were aimed at cable-television audiences expecting complex and challenging writing; others aired on networks that seem to think its viewers primarily want to gaze for a few minutes on fat-free bodies and photogenic faces. Most were short-lived but have done well in DVD sales, their brief network histories apparently troubled by confusion over the series' demographic appeal and hence marketing difficulties. Part of this confusion perhaps arises from the gothic's longstanding interest in challenging norms and stereotypes even as it appears to rely on them – including conventional types of masculinity. All of the television series central here share a concern with masculinity not only through their male leads but also in content, particularly through father–child relationships, and all are gothic in mode rather than simply paranormal in content, insofar as (albeit to varying degrees): (a) they reimagine history, typically to reveal common historical knowledge as sanitized, that is, purged of its unsavory or inexplicable content (like US television itself through "Standards and Practices"); (b) they explore the limits of rationality and individual will, particularly through the trope of insanity, challenging the Enlightenment ideal of the individual as sovereign, self-knowing, and governed by reason; (c) they criticize the excesses of capitalist culture, particularly the pursuit of wealth as "the American Dream";[63] (d) they represent the fictive world as a deeply intertextual one, permeated by references to literature, television, film, music, and religion, often, but not exclusively, drawing on the larger gothic tradition.

These series are also linked by personnel: Ben Edlund has written episodes, and been a producer of one sort or another, for *Angel*, *Point Pleasant*, and *Supernatural*; Daniel Knauf, creator of *Carnivàle*, has written for *Supernatural*; John McLaughlin wrote for *Carnivàle* and *Point Pleasant*; Denise Pleune was post-production supervisor on *Millennium* and associate producer on *Point Pleasant*; Ron Milbauer and Terri Hughes have written for *Point Pleasant* and *Supernatural*; Sam Raimi, a major figure in the recent history of horror film, was executive producer for *American Gothic* and producer of a film written by Eric Kripke shortly before Kripke launched *Supernatural*; Marti Noxon, creator of *Point Pleasant,* worked as a consulting producer on *Angel*; Chris Carter series alumni such as John Shiban and Kim Manners worked on *Supernatural* in significant capacities; Thomas J. Wright worked as a director on *Angel*, *Millennium*, and an episode of Kripke's first television series, *Tarzan*; Michael R. Perry was a writer for *American Gothic* and *Millennium*; Bruce Seth Green directed episodes of *American Gothic* and *Angel*; James Wong co-wrote a number of episodes of *Millennium*, especially the second season which is of significant interest here, and wrote episodes for the first two seasons of *American Horror Story*. And so on. Such criss-crossing of writers, producers, directors, and other crew is not unusual in the television industry, especially within a particular mode or genre, but is noted here to highlight the extent to which these series arise from a shared body of knowledge about televisual genre, mode, technique, and history that cuts across various networks and demographic markets. Hence, Gunn's ironic reference to Angel's team as they flee Los Angeles as "the big bad free-will gang" ("Sacrifice" 4.20) resurfaces in the fifth season of *Supernatural* in Dean's equally ironic remark, "team free will: one ex-blood junkie, one dropout with six bucks to his name, and Mr. Comatose over there – awesome" ("Song Remains the Same" 5.13), highlighting the series' shared interest in autonomy as a central, and yet elusive, fundamental of proper masculinity.[64]

There are also shared gothic traditions. Jowett and Abbott suggest that, in the Kolchak movies, "producer/director Dan Curtis," of *Dark Shadows*' fame, "deliberately situates the fantastic within a very ordinary reality in order to blur the boundaries between the real and the fictional, with television serving as an effective bridge between the two."[65] But Curtis is only part of the picture: Richard Matheson had writing credit on both films. Matheson wrote extensively in gothic and science fiction, and was successful in both print and television; his novels include *I Am Legend* (1954) and *Hell House* (1971), both adapted into films, and he wrote for such gothic anthology series as *The Alfred Hitchcock Hour*, *Twilight Zone*, *Night Gallery, Circle of Fear*, and *The Outer Limits*, frequently marking and crossing the boundary between science and the supernatural. Echoes of Matheson's *Hell House* can be found in at least two of the series discussed here (see Chapter 4), and his influence on gothic television writing is broad – it is well established, for instance, that *X-Files* acknowledged its debt to *Kolchak* with a recurring character, Senator Richard Matheson. Another influential gothic work is Charlotte Perkins Gilman's "The Yellow Wallpaper" (1892), explicitly cited in *American Horror Story* and implicitly but heavily echoed in *Point Pleasant*. Edgar Allan Poe is frequently cited, and so is Mary Shelley – and so are other television series, from *X-Files* to *Buffy the Vampire Slayer* (both are mentioned, for instance, in episodes of *Supernatural*). Character names are also resonant in gothic television. As with the Faustian villain, Lucio, in *The Sorrows of Satan* (1895) by Marie Corelli, the identification of Lucifer with the root *luc* (from the Latin *lux*) for "light" is a gothic convention and it continues through the series here, including the Faustian Lucas Buck in *American Gothic*, Lucifer's agent, Lucas Boyd, in *Point Pleasant*, and the demonic Lucy Butler in *Millennium*. Another recurring name in television gothic is "Burke," recalling Edmund Burke's influence on the gothic and perhaps as well the notorious nineteenth-century grave-robber and murderer, William Burke: examples here include Edmund Burke and Juliet Burke in *Lost*, David Burke in *Point Pleasant*, Burke Devlin in *Dark Shadows*, Ralph Burke in *Night Gallery* (1969–1972), and so on.[66] The continuities which shape gothic television as such lie here – in the exchange of personnel, in the circulation of devices and allusions, in the repetition of the same sorts of questions and concerns – rather than in the depiction of particular sorts of monsters and villains.

While my focus is the gothic aesthetic rather than television series as marketed commodities, it is worth stressing the ways in which these gothic series demonstrate the inexactness of the industry's ideas of its audience's tastes and interests. The most long-lived of these series, *Supernatural*, airs on a network that explicitly focuses on young women viewers whom it seems to assume are centrally interested in romantic fantasies involving male characters who display both machismo (troped by tall, fit, but non-hirsute, physiques), and sensitive, moral natures – an audience of wanna-be Barbies in search of Ken dolls. But, despite its compliance with this mandate, particularly through its two lead actors, the series has, from the start, done well with older women and with male viewers, keeping it on the air year after year; a group of viewers resisted the network's pitch, asserting early on in a self-published volume, *Some of Us Really Do Watch for the Plot*. This claim has since been borne out by a substantive body of fanfic, websites tracing allusions and the series' mythology, discussion boards, and so forth, suggesting wide engagement with the series on terms that go far beyond narrow heteronormative fantasy and dated, arguably even misogynist, assumptions about the range of young women's interests. The feminist "Web Zine about the comics industry," *Sequential Tart*, has regularly reviewed episodes of *Supernatural*, for instance, and published interviews with women writers and actors who work for the series.[67] *Millennium*, to take another instance, despite being a Chris Carter creation on the heels of the success of Carter's *X-Files*, with a number of personnel transferred from *X-Files* to shepherd the new series, was reinvented season after season as they looked for the ratings boon promised by the topical theme of the series – millennial angst, including Y2K fears. It did not even make it to the millennium, and was cancelled in 1999, but still has a significant fanbase. The varying network success of these series and yet substantial fandoms speaks to a suggestive rupture between television-as-marketing-regime and television-as-cultural-production, their very unpredictability in ratings demonstrating the gothic in operation – a mode that conventionally highlights (rather than transparently accepts) dominant paradigms, and often resists the very structures on which marketing proceeds, such as the equation of identity with character, the dominance of Judeo-Christian belief, gender conservatism, and the self-correcting perfection of capitalism.

In *American Gothic*, *Point Pleasant*, and the first season of *American Horror Story*, for instance, tourist sites are revealed to be the locations of bleakly violent histories; in *Supernatural*, the religious origins of the USA emerge as heterogeneous, and Christianity itself is revised in the late seasons, while Samuel Colt, the nineteenth-century arms manufacturer, is reinvented as a weary demon hunter; in *Millennium*, especially in the second season, dominant Christianity is reframed as a patriarchal conspiracy, concertedly in an episode that focuses on an alternative women's Christianity and another that allies Christian mysticism with Nazi remnants; in *Carnivàle*, world history and events leading up to the first atomic bomb are reimagined. Such critiques of the public narrative are reinforced by various private narratives in which characters' awareness of the truths that the dominant myths conceal drives them into psychological distress: *Angel* has an alternative timeline episode in which Angel sits straitjacketed, chained to a wall, driven mad by his crimes as a vampire, and Fred, a recurring character for most of the series, is introduced at the end of season 2 as a woman driven to a nervous breakdown by her experiences in a demon dimension; *Point Pleasant* features a leading character with a history of mental illness, confined again to a mental hospital because her husband will not believe what she tells him is happening; in *American Gothic*, Caleb's sister Merlyn, while alive, was driven to madness by watching Sheriff Buck rape her mother, and is only sane again as a ghost; *Millennium* begins with Frank Black having recently recuperated from a breakdown, a season-2 episode has a long sequence depicting Lara Means (Kristen Cloke) going insane to a Patti Smith soundtrack, and season 3 begins with Frank's recovery from a second breakdown; and *Supernatural* returns to this theme even more persistently, with a number of madhouse episodes, including one in which the brothers are diagnosed as borderline insane ("Sam,

Interrupted" 5.11), and, less dramatically but more persistently, the frequent reiterations of a scene in which one brother urges the other to talk about trauma. The myth of a known, commonly understood world and history is deeply intertwined in the gothic with the myth of the individual as a stable subject, self-governed through free will and reason.

The first two chapters here focus on father figures who are implicated in these two myths. Chapter 1 focuses on father figures identified by their sons with discipline, whether as morality (good versus evil) or as sociality. I begin with *Angel* because of its paradigmatic treatment of father–son competition, both the struggle for power within the family group (especially Oedipally) and the son's struggle to win the father's approval of his masculinity, and I end with a discussion of the only recurring fatherless male character in the series. In *American Gothic*, the subject of the next section, the proliferation of father figures shifts the competition to the adult men who stage various debates about what constitutes proper masculinity and what boys should be taught about it, reinforcing the premise that masculinity is constructed rather than natural. Through its supernatural features, it demonizes not only violence against women but also the father's desire to perpetuate himself through his son. Finally, I turn to *Point Pleasant*, where the critical lens is turned more fully on children who disappoint or overtly reject their fathers.

While Chapter 1 deals with fathers who are all too present, Chapter 2 focuses on fathers who are all too absent – an absence that highlights their iconic power. I begin here with *Carnivàle*, which juxtaposes the patrilineal quest to find the biological father with the patriarchal quest to supplant a male figure of power. Intertwined with these quests are competing views of history: the mythical vision of Avatars, the conflict-driven decades from World War I to the 1930s Dustbowl, and an evangelical vision of a Puritans' America that has strayed. Through it all, the series regularly puts wonder above fact – spirit above matter – in a critique of realism and Enlightenment thought as the "false sun" of the first atom-bomb test, a critique that extends to masculinity by having the patriarchal quest supersede the patrilineal one. In the next section, I turn to the first two seasons of *Supernatural*, also dominated by the quest to find the father. John Winchester is a godlike figure: his journal is treated almost as a Bible, his sons' central and unimpeachable source for solving supernatural problems; he gives commands from a distance that his sons instantly follow; and, early in season 2, he sacrifices himself to save one of his sons. In later seasons, the parallel between John-the-father and God-the-Father is made explicit. But the mythic father is also undone by televisual realism, particularly in a set of episodes that depict him captured, beaten, and defeated. In the final section of this chapter, I turn to the more complicated case of *Millennium* where the idealized 1990s father figure, Frank Black, is juxtaposed with various other paternal types – they all fail. At the same time, undomesticated masculinity fails more spectacularly, whether serial killers or solitary men who retreat from a world they cannot engage. The conservative domestic ideal in particular is revealed to be a fantastic surface that deflects attention from a much messier reality.

The next two chapters explore gothic subversions of the dominant worldview promulgated through mainstream television. Chapter 3 focuses on *Supernatural* as a series that, on the face of it, centers on two extreme but Hollywood-conventional masculine types: both Winchesters are over 6-foot tall and hyper-fit, smart, good with kids, attractive to women, self-sacrificing, and so on. But the series almost constantly calls attention to class and specifically the heroes' alienation from the norms of televisual realism: a clean and spacious home with an enormous kitchen (somehow available to nearly every TV family this century) that reflects a stable home life and financial ease. As in an earlier movie by the show's creator, Eric Kripke, a lower-class background instantiates a deep vulnerability and uncertainty – an alienation from the Leave-It-to-Beaver conventions that televisual realism insists are both "normal" and desirable. The next chapter turns to gothic television's suspicion of three grounds for the empirical certainty depicted through realism: science, media, and Hollywood itself. Focusing on two episodes of *Millennium* in which scientific profiling fails, dramatically, I address the series' interrogation of the Enlightenment ideal of the stable, self-knowing and self-disciplining subject. I then turn to *Supernatural*'s treatment of popular media, and specifically its interest in the way in which media produces, rather than represents, the material world. Finally, I delve into the first season of *American Horror Story*, where the darker history of Hollywood – of would-be actors who must peddle their own flesh, of lives lived in disappointment, of murders, and of the sensationalizing of murder – constantly erupts into what is in many respects a conventional narrative of domestic gothic. All of the episodes at the center of this chapter focus on, or are named for, houses, but not domestic spaces of the sort discussed by Wheatley, Ledwon, and others as domestic gothic: the "pest house," a term for a place for isolating the sick; "hell house," a malleable term used both for haunted houses and a Christian-focused Halloween variant that is designed to inculcate a horror of "sins"; and "murder house," where the domestic is supplanted by its violation.

In the Conclusion, I turn to the ultimate gothic challenge to the sovereign male subject: the conspiracy. In various series, the conspiracy emerges as a figure for, and vehicle of, interference with free will and, simultaneously, the hidden machinery of history that drives it forward in less-than-providential directions. In *Millennium* in particular, the conspiracy that erodes male sovereignty is also allied with the series' investigation of non-normative femininity, both in the demonic Lucy Butler and in angel-seeing visionaries of other episodes. The conspiracy, in other words, marks the failure of masculine autonomy. "Stakeholder" traditionally refers to the objective non-participant who holds the stakes while betting or other transactions take place to determine the disposition of the stakes. "Men with Stakes" hold power in order to properly dispose of it, like the hero-protagonists of many of the series discussed here. Conspiracy not only interferes with the operation of individual free will but also represents the failure of the stockholding principle – or, rather, its transformation into the modern meaning, where stakeholders merely seek to protect their own interests.

Notes

1 "The Zombie," wr. Zekial Marko and David Chase, *Kolchak* (ABC, September 20, 1974). Dates and crew information for series are taken from the Internet Movie Database (www.imdb.com). Transcriptions of dialogue throughout are my own, with each episode indicated by title and season and episode number (e.g., 6.3 indicates the third episode of season six, following the North American practice of using "series" to refer to a show and "season" to refer to all of the episodes in a particular television year, as per contracts).

2 In an episode of *Stargate: SG-1*, a character who is a television writer explains the phrase: "It's a writer's term. Another character points out how convenient it is. ... That way, the audience knows I intended for

it to be convenient, and we move on" ("200" 10.6). The explanation precisely draws the distinction between realism, where improbability is a mistake, and non-realist modes, where improbability can be the author's intention.

3 Edmund Burke, *Enquiry Concerning the Origin of Our Ideas of the Sublime and Beautiful* (1757), ed. Adam Phillips (Oxford: Oxford University Press, 1998), p. 54.

4 Lenora Ledwon, "*Twin Peaks* and the television gothic," *Literature/Film Quarterly*, 21:4 (1993), 268; Lorna Jowett and Stacey Abbott, *TV Horror: Investigating the Dark Side of the Small Screen* (London: I.B. Tauris, 2013), p. 37.

5 Helen Wheatley, *Gothic Television* (Manchester: Manchester University Press, 2006), 1; Patrick Brantlinger, "What is 'sensational' about the 'sensation novel'?" *Nineteenth-Century Fiction*, 37 (1982), 1.

6 David B. Morris, "Gothic sublimity," *New Literary History*, 16 (1985), 301, 309.

7 Wheatley, *Gothic Television*, p. 171.

8 Wheatley, *Gothic Television*, p. 173.

9 As Tosha Taylor suggests in a discussion of *American Horror Story*, the recycling of old gothic tropes can complicate "progressive discussion," "Who's afraid of the Rubber Man? Perversions and subversions of sex and class in *American Horror Story*," *Networked Knowledge*, 5:2 (September 2012), 149.

10 For a fuller discussion of some of the gothic dimensions of Milch's series, see Julia M. Wright, "The gothic frontier of modernity: the 'invisible hand' of state-formation in *Deadwood*," *The Last Western: Deadwood and the End of American Empire*, ed. Jennifer Greiman and Paul Stasi (New York: Continuum, 2013), pp. 42–61. Quotations in this chapter's headings are all titles of *Deadwood* episodes.

11 For an excellent overview of this, see Sally Robinson, *Marked Men: White Masculinity in Crisis* (New York: Columbia University Press, 2000), esp. the introduction.

12 René Magritte, *La Trahison des images* ("The Treachery of Images") (1929).

13 Except for *Supernatural* and *American Horror Story*, all of these series appear in Wheatley's useful list of US television gothic series (*Gothic Television*, p. 5).

14 *Blazing Saddles*, dir. Mel Brooks, wr. Mel Brooks, Norman Steinberg, Andrew Bergman, Richard Pryor, and Alan Uger (Warner, 1974).

15 Rose Zimbardo, "The semiotics of Restoration satire," *Cutting Edges: Postmodern Critical Essays on Eighteenth-Century Satire*, Tennessee Studies in Literature, vol. 37 (Knoxville: University of Tennessee Press, 1995), p. 35.

16 Robinson, *Marked Men*, 9; Susan Jeffords, *Hard Bodies: Hollywood Masculinity in the Reagan Era* (New Brunswick, NJ: Rutgers University Press, 1994), p. 50; Lauren M. E. Goodlad, "Looking for something forever gone: gothic masculinity, androgyny, and ethics at the turn of the millennium," *Cultural Critique*, 66 (2007), 109.

17 Jerrold Hogle, "'Frankenstein' as neo-gothic: from the ghost of the counterfeit to the monster of abjection," *Romanticism, History, and the Possibilities of Genre: Re-forming Literature, 1789–1837*, ed. Tilottama Rajan and Julia M. Wright (Cambridge: Cambridge University Press, 1998), p. 181.

18 Morris, "Gothic sublimity," 304.

19 David Greenwalt, quoted in Lorna Jowett, "'Not like other men'?: the vampire body in Joss Whedon's *Angel*," *Studies in Popular Culture*, 32 (2009), 38.

20 Jowett, "'Not like other men'?" 38.

21 Frank Krutnik, *In a Lonely Street: Film Noir, Genre, Masculinity* (New York: Routledge, 1991), p. xiii.

22 On the detective genre and *Angel*, as well as some attention to the series' use of *film noir*, see Brendan Riley, "From Sherlock to Angel: the twenty-first century detective," *Journal of Popular Culture*, 42 (2009), 908–22.

23 Eve Kosofsky Sedgwick, *Between Men: English Literature and Male Homosocial Desire* (New York: Columbia University Press, 1985); James Eli Adams, *Dandies and Desert Saints: Styles of Victorian Masculinity* (Ithaca, NY: Cornell University Press, 1995).

24 For a useful overview of Lorne's representation as sexual but sexually ambiguous, see Stan Beeler, "Outing Lorne: performance for the performers," *Reading Angel: The TV Spin-off with A Soul*, ed. Stacey Abbott (London: I.B. Tauris, 2005), pp. 88–100. For a suggestive treatment of the subject, see also Lorrie Palmer, "Ruby red and emerald green: the queer demon diva of my dreams," *Camera Obscura*, 23 (2008), 194–99.

25 For examinations of the racial and gendered dynamics of Gunn's transformation, see Michaela D. E. Meyer, "From rogue in the 'hood to suave in a suit: black masculinity and the transformation of Charles Gunn" (*Reading Angel*, pp. 176–88); David Buchbinder, "Passing strange: queering whiteness in Joss Whedon's *Angel*," *White Matters*, ed. Susan Petrilli (Rome: Athanor, 2007), pp. 229–35.

26 Jowett, "'Not like other men'?" 49.

27 See Judith Butler, "Imitation and gender insubordination," *Inside/Out: Lesbian Theories, Gay Theories*, ed. Diana Fuss (New York: Routledge, 1991), pp. 13–31.

28 J. L. Austin, *How to Do Things with Words*, 2nd edn (Cambridge, MA: Harvard University Press, 1962), p. 5.

29 Austin, *How to Do Things with Words*, p. 75.
30 See, e.g., Austin, *How to Do Things with Words*, p. 27.
31 Hogle, "'Frankenstein' as neo-gothic," p. 191; Hogle cites Jean Baudrillard, "The structural law of value and the order of simulacra," *The Structural Allegory: Reconstructive Encounters with the New French Thought*, trans. Charles Leven, ed. John Fekete (Minneapolis: University of Minnesota Press, 1984), pp. 54–73, but see also Jean Baudrillard, *Simulacra and Simulation*, trans. Sheila Faria Glaser (Ann Arbor: University of Michigan Press, 1995). For Hogle's other discussions of the counterfeit, see Jerrold E. Hogle, "The ghost of the counterfeit – and the closet – in *The Monk*," *Romanticism on the Net*, 8 (November 1997), http://erudit.org/revue/ron/1997/v/n8/005770ar.html?lang=en; "The struggle for a dichotomy: abjection in Jekyll and his interpreters," in *Dr. Jekyll and Mr. Hyde after One Hundred Years*, ed. William Veeder and Gordon Hirsch (Chicago: Chicago University Press, 1988), pp. 161–207; "Stoker's counterfeit gothic: *Dracula* and theatricality at the dawn of simulation," *Bram Stoker: History, Psychoanalysis and the Gothic*, ed. William Hughes and Andrew Smith (New York: St. Martin's Press, 1998), pp. 205–24; "Gothic," *Handbook to Romanticism Studies*, ed. Joel Faflak and Julia M. Wright (Oxford: Wiley-Blackwell, 2012), pp. 195–212.
32 Jowett and Abbott, *TV Horror*, p. 9.
33 Hogle, "'Frankenstein' as neo-gothic," p. 189.
34 Lynn Spigel, *Welcome to the Dreamhouse: Popular Media and the Postwar Suburbs* (Durham, NC: Duke University Press, 2001), p. 128. See also Rachel Moseley, "Glamorous witchcraft: gender and magic in teen film and television," *Screen*, 43:4 (2002), 403–22; Wheatley, *Gothic Television*, who builds on Spigel and Moseley (p. 141). Before *Bewitched*, gothic television was limited to anthology series of stand-alone tales, from what is often cited as the first dramatic television series, *The Television Ghost* (1931–1933), to *Lights Out* (1949–1952), *Suspense* (1949–1954), and *Boris Karloff's Thriller* (1960–1962), a format that continued from *The Twilight Zone* (1959–1964) into the early 1970s with such series as *Night Gallery* and *Circle of Fear*.
35 Spigel, *Welcome to the Dreamhouse*, pp. 129–30. On Darrin's powerlessness, discussed here, see pp. 132–33.
36 On the series' containment of gender transgression through class politics, see Spigel, *Welcome to the Dreamhouse*, p. 130.
37 Moseley, "Glamorous witchcraft," p. 421. Suggestively, a number of writers from *Bewitched* and other domestic gothics later worked on the socially conscious series of the late 1960s and early 1970s. Richard Baer, for instance, wrote for *The Munsters* and penned over twenty episodes of *Bewitched*, and then eleven episodes of the career-woman

series *That Girl* (1966–1969) and an early episode of *M*A*S*H* (1972–1983). Another *Bewitched* regular, Michael Morris, wrote episodes for such series as *All in the Family* (1971–1979), *Maude* (1972–1978), and *Chico and the Man* (1974–1978).

38 Spigel, *Welcome to the Dreamhouse*, p. 130.

39 Wheatley, *Gothic Television*, pp. 142–43, 144.

40 See Sigmund Freud, "The Uncanny," in vol. 17 of *The Standard Edition of the Complete Psychological Works of Sigmund Freud*, trans. James Strachey (London: Hogarth Press, 1955), pp. 219–52.

41 Xander's father appears in a dream in "Restless" (4.22) and in "Hell's Bells" (6.16); Tara's father appears in "Family" (5.6). Anthony Bradney suggests that Buffy depicts the failure of the "traditional biological family unit," but what is specifically failing or absent is fathers – Bradney's counter-examples of functional partial families are all women only and Janet Halfyard, in citing Bradney, also stresses estranged fathers; see Anthony Bradney, "Choosing laws, choosing families: images of law, love and authority in 'Buffy the Vampire Slayer,'" *Web Journal of Current Legal Issues*, 2 (2003), http://webjcli.ncl.ac.uk/2003/issue2/bradney2.html; Janet K. Halfyard, "The dark avenger: Angel and the cinematic superhero" (*Reading Angel*, p. 150).

42 I refer here to sensation fiction as it was developed from the 1860s onward by such writers as Mary Elizabeth Braddon and Wilkie Collins, but Charlotte Brontë's *Jane Eyre* (1847) is also clearly relevant as well.

43 Anne Rice, *Interview with the Vampire* (1976); *Blade* (1998), written by David S. Goyer and directed by Stephen Norrington. Arguably the title character of *Varney the Vampire* (1845–1847) is the first cultural example of the remorseful vampire, but *Dark Shadows*' influence is more relevant for the instances mentioned here. For a brief overview of the reception of Barnabas, see Abbott and Jowett, *TV Horror*, pp. 48–49.

44 As Eddie Robson notes, the non-anthology form posed a problem – "a sense of absurd coincidence" that Kolchak found supernatural mysteries every week – that the *X-Files* writers tried to solve; see "Gothic television," *The Routledge Companion to Gothic*, ed. Catherine Spooner and Emma McEvoy (New York: Routledge, 2007), p. 247.

45 Robson, "Gothic television," pp. 246–47; Wheatley, *Gothic Television*, p. 5; Jowett and Abbott, *TV Horror*, esp. pp. 44–46.

46 See, e.g., "Awakening" (*Angel* 4.10) and "Free to Be You and Me" (*Supernatural* 5.3).

47 Peter Lehman, Introduction in *Masculinity: Bodies, Movies, Culture*, ed. Peter Lehman (New York: Routledge, 2001), p. 2.

48 Consider, for instance, the creators of the series on which I focus here:

Daniel Knauf and David Greenwalt have English degrees; Eric Kripke and Joss Whedon have film studies degrees; Chris Carter has a journalism degree; Marti Noxon has a degree in theatre arts.

49 "Exclusive: *Supernatural*'s Sera Gamble on old and new characters, plus dealing with gore!" (posted November 15, 2007). The CW Source, http://blogs.trb.com/network/cwsource/2007/11/exclusive_supernaturals_sera_g.html . She is likely referring to one of Rilke's *Duino Elegies* (1922).

50 Brenton J. Malin, *American Masculinity under Clinton: Popular Media and the Nineties' Crisis of Masculinity* (New York: Peter Lang, 2005), p. 4.

51 Adams, *Dandies and Desert Saints*.

52 Malin, *American Masculinity*, p. 3.

53 Wheatley, *Gothic Television*, p. 162.

54 Wheatley, *Gothic Television*, pp. 167–68.

55 Wheatley, *Gothic Television*, p. 167.

56 Hogle, "'Frankenstein' as neo-gothic," pp. 179–81. As Hogle notes, the first explicitly "gothic" novel, Walpole's *Castle of Otranto*, reworks elements of *Hamlet*; Ann Radcliffe is another early gothic writer to make the connection between the gothic and *Hamlet*, in "On the supernatural in poetry," *New Monthly Magazine*, 16 (1826), 145–52.

57 Asbjørn Grønstad, *Transfigurations: Violence, Death, and Masculinity in American Cinema* (Amsterdam: Amsterdam University Press, 2008), p. 16; Grønstad is quoting D. N. Rodowick's *Reading the Figural, or, Philosophy after the New Media* (Durham, NC: Duke University Press, 2001).

58 See Rolf Eichler, "In the Romantic tradition: *Frankenstein* and *The Rocky Horror Picture Show*," *Beyond the Suburbs of the Mind: Exploring English Romanticism*, ed. Michael Gassenmeir and Norbert Platz (Essen: Verlag Die Blaue Eule, 1987), pp. 95–114.

59 See James Allard, "Spectres, spectators, spectacles: Matthew Lewis's *The Castle Spectre*," *Gothic Studies*, 3 (2001), p. 256.

60 Justine Elias, "Television; 'American Gothic' settles in on the dark side," *New York Times*, October 22, 1995, www.nytimes.com/1995/10/22/arts/television-american-gothic-settles-in-on-the-dark-side.html

61 Take the counter-example of *True Blood*, an instance of soap-opera gothic beyond the purview of this study: the series allegorizes Hebdigean subcultures through supernatural categories, signaled by the opening credits' depiction of the sign, "God Hates Fangs," and the emergence of bikers as werewolves, inbred hill-folk as werepanthers, and so on, but largely eschews cultural referencing (for the foundational work on subcultures, see Dick Hebdige, *Subculture: The Meaning of Style* [London: Methuen, 1979]).

62 Dave Scheidt, "Talking about Itty Bitty Hellboy with Art and Franco: an illustrated interview," August 29, 2013, HuffPost, www.huffingtonpost.com/dave-scheidt/itty-bitty-hellboy-comic_b_3819676.html
63 See Wheatley, *Gothic Television*, for a discussion of *Twin Peaks* in this context.
64 The *Angel* episode quoted here was written by Ben Edlund, a producer of *Supernatural* and frequent contributor to it as a writer, though not credited as such on this episode.
65 Jowett and Abbott, *TV Horror*, p. 37.
66 The list is much longer in film, with characters named Burke from *London after Midnight* (1927) to *Scream* and *Tale of the Mummy* (1998).
67 See *Sequential Tart*, www.sequentialtart.com

1

Bedeviling paternal discipline: fathers from *American Gothic* to *Point Pleasant*

> [*Major Briggs to his son at the dinner table*] Rebellion in a young man your age is a necessary fact of life, and, candidly, a sign of strength. In other words, Robert, I respect your rebellious nature. However, being your father, I am obligated to contain that fire of contrariness within the bounds established by society as well as those within our own family structure. Robert, I note your reluctance to enter in a dialogue with me, your father. There are times when silence is golden. Silence can be taken many ways, as a sign of intelligence. The quieter we become, the more we hear ... [*Bobby defiantly puts a cigarette in his mouth; Major Briggs slaps Bobby so hard that his cigarette is knocked halfway across the table and lands in the food on his mother's dinner plate*].
>
> *Twin Peaks* ("Traces to Nowhere" 1.1)

Jerrold Hogle argues compellingly in a series of articles for the centrality of the counterfeit to the gothic. He takes the trope of the counterfeit back to the ghost of Hamlet's father to trace the ways in which the gothic is allied with an anxiety over the industrial age's emphasis on reproduction as copying, replacing the longstanding model in which identity and property are transmitted patrilineally from one generation to the next.[1] The gothic as a mode, or aesthetic style, thus emerges in tandem with an anxiety about genealogy – part of early gothic's concern with history, a subject to which I shall turn more concertedly in Chapter 4.[2] For early gothic poetry and fiction, as in *Hamlet* (1602), the genealogical concern is framed more specifically through aristocratic paternity as the determiner of status and identity: the originary gothic novel, *The Castle of Otranto*, has for its villain a man who has usurped an aristocratic title and property. This is, as in the usurpations of *Hamlet*, a disruption of the patrilineal exchange of power, a trend that reaches its limit in Mary Shelley's *Frankenstein* (1818) where a man usurps god's power to create life. In early gothic works with a subversive political bent, the aristocrat is technically legitimate but morally illegitimate – a tyrant who abuses his power, typically in violence against women under his guardianship, as in William Godwin's *Caleb Williams* (1794) and P. B. Shelley's *The Cenci* (1819), or a colonist who has dispossessed the indigenous landowners, as in Charles Robert Maturin's *Melmoth the Wanderer* (1820).[3] This aristocratic emphasis continues into twentieth-century gothic literature and film, generalized into figures of high socioeconomic status in the US context – *Dark Shadows* focuses on a rich family that has economically dominated the town for over a century, a painting of the patriarch over the fireplace in the main setting, while Anne Rice's Louis is a southern estate and slave owner before he becomes a vampire[4] – but is often deflected into the romance tradition of the chosen hero from a special (rather than a specifically aristocratic) family. The fifth season of *Supernatural*, for instance, sets aside its early depiction of hunters as everyday, working-class people who are drawn into hunting by a supernaturally provoked trauma to create an elaborate divine plot in which the two main characters, Sam and Dean Winchester, are part of a unique bloodline that makes the brothers viable "vessels" through which the archangels Michael and Lucifer can stage their final battle. Genealogy – and specifically the patrilineal – is thus deeply embedded in the gothic tradition, even as it changes in response to shifting socioeconomic structures, and continues to play a role in the television series discussed here.

The determinisms of genealogy offer an uncomfortable fit with modern ideas of the hero as an autonomous subject. In the recent reboot of *Spider-Man* (2012), the writers' decision to give Peter Parker a scientist-father makes Peter's scientific accomplishments an effect of inheritance, emptying the character of much of his original significance in the comics and the cartoon television series as a working-class hero – a self-made man, whose hard work and devotion to school work not only give him extraordinary abilities but also authorize his role as moral arbiter. This new Peter Parker instead raises a central dilemma of the gothic: on the one hand, the paternal figure is the source of special qualities (in recent gothic, often supernatural abilities) that strengthen the leading character(s); on the other, that same figure is often linked to a fatalist vision of "destiny" against which those characters struggle, their autonomy and ability to refashion themselves alike compromised. In the series discussed in this chapter, the paternal figure's control is writ large: the satanic sheriff of *American Gothic* and the never-seen Lucifer of *Point Pleasant* want their children to become morally corrupt and supernaturally continue their fathers' work (in other words, do what their fathers tell them to do), while the narrative backdrops are populated by failed and failing fathers. The so-called "Buffy-verse" has few major characters who are fathers, and yet *Angel* returns again and again to stern and emotionally distant fathers – a suggestive pattern, particularly given Greenwalt's remark that "*Buffy* is about how hard it is to be a woman, and *Angel* is about how hard it is to be a man."[5] In *American Gothic*, *Point Pleasant*, and *Angel*, fathers are disciplinary, trying to shape their children in their image and negate their children's autonomy, especially through their desire to fashion their own sense of self. The critique of controlling fathers is further elaborated by another set of concerns all three series share – child abuse and domestic violence, almost always perpetrated by patriarchal figures in the series.

"Daddy's home": *Angel*, masculine performance, and paternal disappointment

As with much of Joss Whedon's work, gender is on the surface of *Angel*: in the first season, the series examines the exploitation of women by Hollywood, domestic violence, and the machismo of policing, and uses Wesley as comic counterweight to Angel's more serious masculinity. Wesley in the first season is a "rogue demon-hunter" prone to mishaps, such as getting his axe stuck in a wall; Angel repeatedly has to take over from Wesley when Wesley fails at a task (for instance, during an exorcism in "I've Got You Under My Skin" 1.14), and rarely makes mistakes. Angel reads during his leisure hours, fights evil, and sacrifices personal happiness to pursue the greater good (explicitly in "I Will Remember You" 1.8) – and he makes breakfast for his team after a night of fighting, reassures Cordelia in non-judgmental tones when she finds herself pregnant after sex with someone she had only just met, and refuses to defend himself when Faith physically attacks him, instead comforting her when she collapses sobbing. In an episode that deals with a demon, Billy (Justin Shilton), whose supernatural ability is to intensify into violence what is represented as latent misogyny in men, Angel can defeat him because, Angel says, "that thing that Billy brought out in others – that hatred and anger – that's something I lost a long time ago" ("Billy" 3.6). Accepting of women, nurturing on occasion, and consistently intelligent and physically powerful, Angel simultaneously fulfills the action-hero ideal and a progressive gender politics. His one failing is a lack of sociability – an extreme form of masculinist autonomy – and the plot of the early seasons is devoted to tracing his progress in addressing that failure. And his one weakness is sex: "perfect happiness" through sex causes him to lose his soul, and turn into the evil, manipulative Angelus, figuring the danger of heteronormative sociability for the autonomous hero. A relationship with a starlet in the first season leads to the brief re-emergence of Angelus ("Eternity" 1.17); erotic dreams of his former lover, Darla, weaken him in the second season. So, the series overall suggests, Angel is a Renaissance man with a sensitive side who must be socialized through specifically non-erotic relationships, exercising his masculinity only to protect others. *Angel* thus reinforces a common message of the gothic: sexual desire turns men into predators. As one *Community* episode describes the "central insipid metaphor of those *Twilight* books," "Men are monsters who crave young flesh."[6] But, as *Angel* repeatedly argues to its viewers, masculinity is always created rather than biologically determined.

In the second season of *Angel*, for instance, the episode "Guise Will Be Guise" (2.6) deals at length with masculinity not as "natural," but as an artificial façade that is carefully and persistently constructed – as its very title, punning on "guise" and "guys," suggests. In the episode, Angel visits an assassin pretending to be a swami who tells him that his car and clothing create an ideal image which Angel would like to see reflected in others' perception of him:

ANGEL: It's just this way [wearing all black] I don't have to worry about matching. I don't have a reflection, so I

FAKE SWAMI: Sure you do.

ANGEL: I do?

FAKE SWAMI: You're reflected in the people around you – the way they see you. What do you think they see?

The episode then cuts to Wesley pretending to be Angel in the episode's comic plot. As Angel, Wesley tries to brood and be assertive, and wears a black coat, but in the opening of the episode, before his charade begins, he is depicted as decidedly un-masculine: he is ineffectual and clumsy, and the scene ends with Cordelia asking him, "Do you have any clothes a man would wear?" Clothes make the man – the guys need a guise. The very structure of the episode complicates the two characters' roles: the series' protagonist is at the center of the B-plot, in which very little happens as Angel talks about his angst with the fake swami; the sidekick is at the center of the A-plot, in which almost all of the action takes place, including the rescue of the (apparent) maiden in distress; and, most crucially, the B-plot explicates what is left unsaid in the action of the A-plot. Wesley's impersonation of Angel reproduces the image that the fake swami is talking about: a long black coat, a serious demeanor, and the threat that he will lose control and become dangerously violent.

While Wesley treats that image as if it has power, in the B-plot that power is compromised by Angel's curse, namely that he will lose his soul and become evil if he achieves "perfect happiness" through sex. During his rather macho encounter sessions with the fake swami – they fight, fish, talk about women – Angel's mention of his curse and its implications for his sex life leads to a derisive smirk from his would-be counselor. At the end of the episode, Angel learns that the supernatural underworld characterizes him as a "eunuch" because of it: "I'm not a eunuch," he protests. The B-plot, then, begins by highlighting the ways in which Angel works to perform one kind of public image for himself, and ends with Angel's distress that another kind of public image (in which he cannot, so to speak, perform) is circulating instead. Angel's heroic masculinity is thus countered, even compromised, by his inability to live up to another masculine ideal in which machismo is measured by sexual encounters with women.

At the same time, the episode critiques the corporate world as a pre-modern patriarchy in which men use violence – against each other, and against women – to jockey for power. The lead villain of the episode is a corporate tycoon who gets his wealth and power by worshipping a demon who demands the sacrifice of a virgin on his fiftieth birthday, so he has kept his 24-year-old daughter a near-prisoner from her mid-teens onward in order to ensure that she will be a fitting sacrifice. Two episodes after "Guise," Wesley reads a passage describing a ritual that requires the sacrifice of virginal young women. Cordelia (Charisma Carpenter) interjects, "Why is it always virgin women who have to do the sacrificing?" To Wesley's scholarly reply, "For purity, I suppose," she retorts, "This has nothing to do with purity. This is all about dominance, buddy. You can bet if someone ordered a male body part for religious sacrifice, the world would be atheist like that" and she snaps her fingers ("The Shroud of Rahmon" 2.8). "Guise Will Be Guise" is not only concerned with the multiple constructions of masculinity against which Angel is evaluated and through which he constructs his persona, but also with the ways in which the corporate world persists in a pernicious form of patriarchy that seeks to exploit and control women – a theme of numerous episodes in the series, most frequently in those that deal with aspiring actresses' treatment at the hands of Hollywood's executives, directors, and other power-brokers. In *Angel*, these figures are always male. (The series, however, does not stay "on message" on this point: the fifth season is dedicated to the more common cliché that modern corporate life and wealth are emasculating.)

While corporate culture allegorically figures patriarchy, fathers are the absent cause of much that happens in both *Buffy* and *Angel*.[7] Fathers are strikingly absent from the screen in *Buffy*, as if the feminist script of the series can only empower women in the absence of a functioning patriarchy: Xander's appears just once (twice if you count a dream sequence), but his alcoholism and fights with Xander's mother are otherwise referenced; Willow's father is also mentioned, but never appears; Buffy's father appears in only four episodes (in one of which he is part of an alternate reality), and is mentioned most frequently in the final seasons as an absentee father who cannot be reached or relied upon. The fathers who do appear are often monsters, so Ted (John Ritter) tries to become Buffy's stepfather, but turns out to be a killer robot, for instance ("Ted" 2.11), and the rhetoric of paternity is used most frequently to refer to vampire relationships, so the Master is "sire" to Darla, Angel to Drusilla and Spike (later altered to make Drusilla Spike's maker), and so forth.

In *Angel*, fathers are comparatively common and the vampire "family" more emphatic, particularly in a series of flashbacks which stress Angelus' role as patriarch-leader of vampire groups, most frequently depicting the late nineteenth-century group of

Drusilla, Darla and Spike – all explicitly or implicitly sexually connected to Angelus. Flashbacks establish Angelus, newly made, as a rebellious son, fighting with his father immediately before and after Darla makes him a vampire, and then challenging the authority of the male vampire, "the Master," that Darla has followed for centuries – Darla leaves that vampire group to join Angelus in a 150-year Bonnie-and-Clyde murder spree. In flashbacks to subsequent periods, Angelus acts as the leader to other male vampires, transforming and training Penn ("Somnambulist" 1.11) or directing James ("Heartthrob" 3.1) in the eighteenth century, and educating Spike in the nineteenth century (but not Drusilla). Collectively, dozens of flashback scenes establish Angelus as the center of various vampire groups, leading and training "sons" while the women seek to please him. Thus, in "Reunion" (2.10), an episode in which Drusilla is confused that Angel is not Angelus, she prophesies his physical arrival and return to evil by creepily announcing to Darla, "Daddy's home." Angelus thus follows a fairly straightforward Oedipal pattern: on the human level, he kills his father; on the vampire level, he marries his "mother" (Darla) and takes her away from the father figure, the Master. Once through the Oedipal stage, he becomes a father figure himself, effectively duplicating the Master, so much so that he even mimics the Master's language. And, of course, the vampire relationships crystallize a patriarchal formation in which men struggle with each other for power and women use sex to attach themselves to powerful men – even though Darla, as the eldest vampire, has greater supernatural force.

But in the series' present, Angel is no confident patriarch. Throughout the series, fathers are associated with their sons' sense of helplessness. Wesley most often articulates this view, but it is echoed by Angel as well. In "I've Got You Under My Skin" (1.14), Angel suspects a father is possessed:

> ANGEL: The father seemed kind of off – they were afraid of him.
> WESLEY: A father doesn't have to be possessed to terrorize his children; he just has to [*silences himself*]. We'll find out soon enough.

Later, the demon mocks Wesley as he tries to perform an exorcism: "You, do something? ... All those hours locked up under the stairs and you still weren't good enough, not good enough for daddy." The next episode, "The Prodigal" (1.15), deals with the relationship between Angel, when he was still human being named Liam, and his human father. The episode opens with their fight over Angel's profligate lifestyle:

> FATHER: Liam, you'll do as I say! … Defy me now you won't. Not as long as I live.
> ANGEL: You'll want to move away from the door now, father.
> FATHER: Go through it, and don't ever expect to come back.
> ANGEL: As you wish, father, always, just as you wish.
> FATHER: It's a son I wished for – a man! Instead God gave me you – a terrible disappointment.
> ANGEL: Disappointment? A more dutiful son you couldn't have asked for. My whole life you told me in words, in glance, what it is you required of me, and I've lived down to your every expectation, now haven't I?
> FATHER: That's madness.
> ANGEL: No, the madness is that I couldn't fail enough for you.

That night, he is turned into a vampire and he later returns to the house to slaughter his family, his father last: "You told me I wasn't a man, you told me I was nothing, and I believed you. You said I'd never amount to anything. Well, you were wrong [reveals he's a vampire]. You see, father, I have made something of myself, after all." His Oedipal triumph is then undercut by Darla:

> DARLA: The contest is ended, is it?
> ANGEL: Now I've won.
> DARLA: Are you sure?
> ANGEL: Of course. I proved who had the power here.
> DARLA: Do you think?
> ANGEL: What?
> DARLA: Your victory over him took but moments. … But his defeat of you will last a lifetime.
> ANGEL: What are you talking about? He can't defeat me now.
> DARLA: Nor can he ever approve of you, in this world or any other.

I quote this dialogue at length not only because it epitomizes the representation of fathers' effects on their sons in the series, but also because of how carefully it is written: Darla Socratically leads Angel along with questions, but the dialogue shifts to her statements and his questions as he begins to doubt that he has won, the actor's enunciation of the questions highlighting both their status as questions and Angel's confusion as he realizes that he will be forever undermined as "a man" without his father's approval.

Angel perhaps "jumped the shark" when Angel became a father in season 3,[8] but it offered the writers an opportunity to explore in some depth the father–son dyad that had long concerned the series. I return below to the depiction of Angel's and Wesley's relationships with their fathers, but Connor (Vincent Kartheiser) helps to illustrate the sorts of problems played out through such relationships. Connor was kidnapped as an infant by the vampire-hunter Holtz (Keith Szarabajka), and taken to a hell dimension where time passes more quickly, a device that makes it possible for Connor to leave a baby and return to LA after just a few episodes as a teenager approaching manhood. Holtz raised Connor to call him father and to hate Angel as the vampire who slaughtered Holtz's family. Holtz brutalizes Connor to make him a preternaturally skilled vampire-hunter, with the sole purpose of (again, Oedipus-like) killing his father. This is a series of substitutions in which nostalgic fantasy for hearth and home is always shadowed by violence and loss: Holtz takes Angel's son as revenge for Angel's murder of his own family, but Connor cannot replace the children he lost, and in the process Angel loses the infant son he cherished and gets back, in return, a nearly adult Connor who is filled with rage as he was toward his own father. These doublings are made explicit: for instance, Connor, in the episode of his return, says "Hi Dad" to Angel at the beginning of the opening scene and then, at the very end of the same episode, "Hi Dad" to Holtz ("A New World" 3.20). The introduction of Connor leads to various musings on father-son relationships, such as this one:

> ANGEL (as Angelus): I guess you just can't understand that special bond between dad and son, given that your own father's ashamed of you.
>
> WESLEY: And Connor's ashamed of you. The universe's way of maintaining order, I guess.[9]
>
> ("Soulless" 4.11)

Just as Holtz is exchanged for Angel, and Connor for Holtz's dead children, "that special bond" is replaced by shame as the glue that "maintain[s] order."

This exchange takes place after the group tricks Angel into becoming Angelus, as Connor confronts the caged demon:

> CONNOR: You think I care what you say? Angel told me how you'll try to hurt me – how you weren't my real dad, just some animal in a cage. Angel's my dad.

ANGELUS: I'm gonna cry.

CONNOR: That's what he told me, and he thought I believed him. The truth is, Angel's just something that you're forced to wear – you're my real father.

("Soulless" 4.11)

Guys will be guise – Angel-the-hero is "just something [he's] forced to wear." Connor has no real father, but a series of fathers, each father seeing Connor as the simulacrum of his own identity: Holtz shaped Connor into the instrument of his revenge; Angel tried to reshape Connor into the ideal projection of his own self-image (seeing in him, for instance, his own skills as a fighter, as is made explicit in "Benediction" [3.21] and myriad other episodes); and, for a time, Gunn, while Angel is missing, tries to discipline the wayward teenager. Later, he becomes precisely what evil-Cordelia and then Jasmine (Gina Torres) wish him to be, husband and then father. He is always defined provisionally and relationally, so that when Jasmine is killed he becomes a suicide bomber – threatening the physical dispersal of the self that he cannot stabilize. Connor is "unprecedented" ("Quickening" 3.8), the child of two vampires, and so unscripted – even before he is born, different cults debate his meaning, and this is carried through the series in the multiple roles into which Connor tries to fit. The only solution, the final episode of season 4 indicates (and season 5 bears out), is for Connor to have another father: a wizard creates an alternate reality in which Connor is not Angel's son, but the eldest in a middle-class, nuclear family in which the father is utterly mundane and so is the domestic world he inhabits. Connor does not need his "real" father, a common object of the romance quest back to the medieval period, but the right sort of "fake" one if he is to inhabit the real world – a gothic counterfeit (in Hogle's terms) of what is always already fake, the myth of the suburban dad who is so generic that the son can build his own properly generic identity, both self-governing and apparently self-determining. In season 5, Connor is an A-student who does not know how to fight and can even handle, calmly and with good humor, the revelation that Angel is his biological father. He is, in the fake universe, a "real boy" at last.

The series suggests, then, that masculinity is a style and patriarchy a specter; that is, characters assume the guise of various masculine performances, often unreflectively, while remaining haunted by paternal repudiation. This is not masculinity as over-compensation for childhood rejection – the series never causally links the performance to the trauma – but rather a *mise en abyme* of performances and fictions, the "pervasively counterfeit existence" of the gothic.[10] This reaches its apex in "Lineage" (5.7), as Wesley's disapproving father is revealed to be a cyborg disguised by magic: the father is never present but a mere simulation, as the cyborg calls attention to the ever-retreating horizon of patriarchal authenticity in the series. At the end of the episode, Wesley talks to his actual father on the phone and the father is once again absent from the televisual frame, except in the pained replies of the son which indicate that he is, again, being chastised for his inadequacies. The father-cyborg recalls the number of times that fathers appear in Whedon episodes as unreal figures: Xander's appears in a dream, Buffy's in an alternate reality, Ted is a robot, and Wesley's father only appears on-screen as a magically disguised cyborg. Fathers are phantasmatic, or, when present, performing particular roles to pressure their sons to behave in particular ways – Angel's father tries to badger him into good behavior, Holtz fakes his own murder to make Connor homicidal, Angel tries different strategies to solicit Connor's cooperation in a father–son relationship, and so on – and then those sons go on to perform, with varying degrees of success, various styles of masculinity. As Angel insists to his father, he has "*made* something of himself, after all."

Gunn is a suggestive counter-example: his father is never mentioned or depicted, and the earliest reference to Gunn's childhood is to a game he played in a children's shelter, contributing to the series' implication that he was parentless from a young age. Gunn's masculinity is uncompromised, and uncompromising: he wearies of being reduced to "the muscle," but he is always confident, physically powerful, and has equitable relationships with women. In the "Billy" episode, Gunn is infected by violent misogyny, too, but uses his last moments of self-control to beg Fred (Winifred) to knock him out before he can hurt her, making him the only infected, living man of the many depicted in the episode who does not physically abuse a woman. Wesley, conversely, physically threatens and verbally abuses her, on viciously misogynist terms, before she successfully knocks him unconscious, and the episode ends with him weeping over his guilt. Gunn is even typically masculine in an episode where Lorne supernaturally compels others to do his bidding: Angel has sex with a demon, Fred and Wesley become drunk without alcohol, and Spike becomes encouraging and cheery, but Gunn is told to "stake out [his] territory" and urinates on key sites in the office, including Angel's desk chair ("Life of the Party" 5.5). Gunn is arguably the closest the series gets to representing a masculinity that is neither explicitly performed nor encumbered by trauma, even though he has grown up fighting demons on the poorer streets of Los Angeles. Racially, this has problematic overtones because Gunn is the only major black character in *Angel*, recalling the first slayer in *Buffy*, who is also depicted as black and is called "the primitive." But his "natural" masculinity is socially functional: before joining Angel's team, he leads and implicitly raises a group of other homeless kids, keeping them safe and protecting the larger community by fighting vampires in the neighborhood. In "The Thin Dead Line" (2.14), Gunn is represented effectively dealing with teenage-male rebellion. He fails when he deals with traumatized boys – Connor, and earlier Gio (Khalil Kain) – but is generally able to lead young men to the right choices without using force or raising his voice. And he needs no father:

> GUNN: I don't need no Guardian Angel, and I don't need no talking to. It's not going to change the way things are down here, man. They're going to keep coming, and we're going keep fighting.
> ANGEL: I know.
> GUNN: That's it? You ain't going to talk at me, be all daddy figure?
> ANGEL: What am I going to tell you that you haven't already learned?
> ("War Zone" 1.20)

Healthy men – confident, capable, informed – have no fathers to disappoint or challenge, and need no "daddy-figure." *Angel* solves the Oedipal conundrum, the cycle of violence and betrayal that defines father–son relationships in the series, by removing the father entirely. For Gunn, there is no spectral or emotionally remote father, and no unresolved competition, precisely because he is, in the world of the series, no man's son.

Big Daddy in the new south: *American Gothic*

American Gothic was created by Shaun Cassidy and aired for one season on CBS. As with *Invasion* (ABC, 2005–2006), another Cassidy series, the canny exploration of genre conventions and slow build-up of a complicated plot perhaps contributed to the series' early cancellation, though *Invasion* was also likely impacted by especially unfortunate timing: it offers a narrative about an alien invasion that is launched under cover of a hurricane, and it premiered less than a month after Hurricane Katrina devastated New Orleans and much of the larger region. The slow pace of both, however, is integral to their engagement with Southern Gothic. *American Gothic* was arguably badly handled by the network, too. Episodes were aired out of order and many of those dealing most disturbingly with violence against women and children were left unaired: in "Potato Boy," the town psychologist is revealed to have molested child patients and a lead character, the teacher Selena Coombs (Brenda Bakke), initiates inappropriate contact with the 10-year-old protagonist, Caleb Temple (Lucas Black); in "Ring of Fire," a man is depicted burning a cigarette on his daughter's arm and beating his wife; in "Echo of Your Last Goodbye," an abandoned child is the center of a narrative of violent bullying at a school; in "Strangler," the Boston Strangler (Gareth Williams) is resurrected by Sheriff Lucas Buck (Gary Cole) and attacks a number of women in town. These episodes represent domestic violence through the bleakness of realism as well as attenuate it through the gothic. This is arguably the heart of the series' discomfiting tone. Tennessee Williams wrote of Southern Gothic that it shares "a sense, an intuition, of an underlying dreadfulness in modern experience,"[11] and *American Gothic* brings that vague "sense" into the harsh light of a well-lit televisual scene.

The series exaggerates some elements of the Southern Gothic, especially in its handling of the stereotype of the corrupt southern sheriff: on meeting Sheriff Buck for the first time, Dr. Matt Crower (Jake Weber) remarks, "I thought the southern sheriff was just a cliché" ("Pilot" 1.1). But the cliché is, in the series, a metaphor: police bribery is transmuted into Faustian bargains in which souls are traded for immediate desires; law and order are an illusion created by the sheriff's nearly absolute control of the community through his Faustian deals and supernatural power; and the corrupt sheriff is a figure for, and mask of, the corrupting devil. *American Gothic* in key respects gothically parodies a more pastoral vision of the south, *The Andy Griffith Show*. *The Andy Griffith Show* is set in Mayberry, a small town in North Carolina, and *American Gothic* in a small town in South Carolina. Both focus on a sheriff who works closely with a somewhat inept deputy and who has a young son who gets into various Tom Sawyer-ish scrapes. But the superficially genial demeanor of Sheriff Buck – giving townspeople chocolate on their birthdays and house loans when they need them – plays Andy Griffiths with a gruesome twist, his affability part of his manipulation of the townspeople into doing his bidding. And that affability is revealed as the veneer of a slick performance over profound evil from the first episode as Buck commits rape and murder on-screen.

The protagonist, Caleb Temple, grew up believing he was Gage Temple's son, but discovers in the first episode that his mother was raped by Lucas Buck and Buck is his biological father. Buck's arrival at the Temple home and the beginning of the assault are depicted on-screen, leaving no doubt as to the rape. After Buck kills Gage Temple and Caleb's sister Merlyn Temple (Sarah Paulson), again on-screen, leaving Caleb an orphan (his mother was killed by Buck soon after Caleb's birth), Buck tries to assert his parental rights and gain custody of Caleb. Caleb wishes to stay with Dr. Matt Crower, who cared for him after his sister's death, and another possible guardian is Gail Emory (Paige Turco), Caleb's cousin, a reporter, who has returned to Trinity to help Caleb. Enter a variation on Mayberry's Aunt Bea: Loris Holt (Tina Lifford), a single woman who runs a boarding house and takes custody of Caleb instead. They make soup together when they first meet, establishing Holt's home as a properly domestic space, its brightness and functionality a contrast to the bleak and run-down Temple household. The Judeo-Christian coordinates of the series are on the surface: it centers on Lucas Buck (his name evoking Lucifer) and the Temple family in a town called Trinity; Merlyn's appearance after her death is compared to that of an angel, and she wears a dress that could be a communion outfit; individual episodes deal with other religious topics, from a priest's misuse of the confession to a plague on the town's sinners in which a local river turns the color of blood. Mixed in with these biblical references, however, are more diverse notions of faith. Loris Holt's home is filled with African artwork representing her "dead ancestors" ("Eye of the Beholder" 1.3), for instance, and Holt gives Caleb information about a ritual to lay ghosts to rest ("Resurrector" 1.9).[12] And both Caleb's cousin, Gail Emory, and Lucas Buck are, the visuals imply, able to gather information by touching objects: at a number of moments in the series, their contact with an object leads to a series of quickly flashed contextual images that offer clues to the mysteries being investigated. *American Gothic*, though, is less concerned with the nature of faith than with its incompatibility with the role of money in US culture.

In the monologue that opens the series, Buck intones, over a bluesy musical background as clichéd images of the American South flicker by, "I've heard it said that the American Dream is a thing of the past, that the basic tenets of home, job, and family are slipping away. Well [laughs], not in my town. Where I come from that dream is still a reality. Of course you have to know who's boss. For those who follow my lead, life can be a paradise. But for those who don't – it can be a mighty rough road" ("Pilot" 1.1). As Wheatley has noted, this monologue is followed by "the establishing shot of the Temples' house," together "visualis[ing] both sides of the American Dream as presented in the American Gothic: the sunny façade and its dark underside."[13] But, while Wheatley emphasizes the series' gothic examination of the "American Dream" as domestic ideal, there are repeated references to masculinity in relation to a choice between money (and dominance) and faith (and care for others). This is laid out emphatically in "The Buck Stops Here" (1.17): Buck shows Caleb's class the front of a dollar bill and calls it a "buck," calling attention to the pun on his name, and then points out the Masonic temple on the back and calls attention to Caleb's surname, Temple. To close the lesson, Buck refers to the dollar bill as "the root of all evil." Lucas Buck and Caleb Temple are the two sides of that root. Buck's reading of "Temple" as a Masonic image associated with money is countered by the Christian imagery that surrounds Merlyn, the only biological "Temple" in the series. "The Plague Sower" (1.11) takes its central device from Exodus and has Merlyn turn a river to blood and bring down a plague on those working with Buck, as Dr. Crower develops religious mania and marks up passages in a Bible after describing the virus sweeping his town as "Old Testament." In the same episode, Selena warns Dr. Billy Peale (John Mese), "Look out for Sheriff Buck. … Have you ever looked into the face of evil? I mean, the pure, unadulterated thing." Later, Merlyn tells Caleb, "I was told to punish the wicked, and warn those that would sin." Merlyn's supernatural status is never clarified – she is sometimes referred to as a ghost, sometimes as an angel, and denies being either to Caleb in the first episode. Here, in "Plague Sower," she takes on the traditional role of the prophet, and of Moses in particular. Moses not only punished the wicked and warned the sinners, and through a plague that turned a river the color of blood, but also specifically punishes the worshippers of Mammon,[14] the golden calf, named for the Hebrew word for "money," bringing us back to Buck's dollar bill, a buck with a temple on the back. The Christian allegory is laid out across a number of episodes, with the central struggle between Buck and Merlyn, between Mammon and Temple, being focused on Caleb.

The superficial main plot of *American Gothic* evokes the standard *Bildungsroman* of various 1950s childhood television narratives: a young boy growing up must learn to separate right from wrong, like the boy protagonists of such series as *The Andy Griffith Show* and *Leave It to Beaver* (1957–1963). But this traditional theme is given gothic coordinates. On one side, there is Buck, encouraging Caleb to achieve dominance at all costs: to cheat in the science fair, humiliate his competitors at an archery competition to gain a psychological advantage, and so forth. On the other, there is Merlyn, chastising Caleb when he follows Buck's lead and smiling approvingly when he rejects Buck's advice. She is assisted by Crower, who gently advises Caleb, usually on terms that promote reason and education. This is explicitly about Caleb becoming "a man." In "Damned If You Don't" (1.4), for instance, Caleb has to compete in the school science fair but students are only allowed to use household objects. He wants to "make a tornado" and the standard household blender is not doing the job, he complains to Buck and Crower. Crower offers to loan him some books but Caleb refuses the offer:

> BUCK: Boy's right. Any sissy can do a book report. ... It's a sorry tornado comes out of a blender. ... Tell you what, a sheet of plexiglass, a big bunch of dry ice, and one of them one-horse motors, and you got yourself a tornado.
>
> CROWER: Well that's fine Caleb, but you need to know why things are – what makes them work. It's not as much fun but it's what separates the men from the boys.
>
> (1.4)

Caleb takes the special equipment from Buck, and Merlyn appears in order to lament his failure to do the right thing. Caleb withdraws from the science fair and, on prompting from Crower, delivers instead a lecture on tornadoes based on his reading of Crower's books. Merlyn appears a second time to praise his decision:

MERLYN: Caleb, you did real good. I'm proud of you. We're all proud of you.
CALEB: You was there, and mama?
MERLYN: We were all there, Caleb.
CALEB: I knew it. I could feel it, Merly. I was happy.

(1.4)

Throughout the series, Caleb's connection to women in his family – his cousin Gail, his half-sister Merlyn, his mother – leads him down a moral path, while Buck tries to drive him in the opposite direction, drawing a distinction between "family" and "father."

In the first episode, Merlyn gives Caleb a vision of Buck raping his mother because he "need[s] to know the truth." This brutal scene, made more disturbing by Caleb's very young age, is bracketed by two moments. In the first, Caleb sees the post-death Merlyn for the first time:

CALEB: Merlyn? Are you a ghost?
MERLYN: No.
CALEB: An angel?
MERLYN: I'm your family.

(1.1)

After the vision, Buck arrives at the house to claim Caleb as his son. Caleb flees to the attic and Buck pursues him:

BUCK: Look here, boy. There are only two roads in this world, and if you're listening to anyone but me, you're on the wrong one. ... Caleb, you're gonna have to trust me. [*enters attic, to find Caleb pouring liquor on the floor to start a fire*] That's good liquor you're wasting there, son.
CALEB: I ain't your son.
BUCK: Beg to differ.

(1.1)

This conversation, near the end of the episode, alludes directly to Buck's opening monologue: "For those who follow my lead, life can be a paradise. But for those who don't – it can be a mighty rough road." The pilot episode not only genders Caleb's ancestry but also represents it on gothic terms as a conflict between good and evil: on one side, there are the women who constitute Caleb's "family," centrally Merlyn and his (still living) cousin Gail; on the other, there is Buck, his biological father and representative of a patrilineal succession that becomes more significant as the series progresses. As with Connor and Angel, paternal connection is established through appearance. Connor in action moves like Angel in action, but the more Judeo-Christian *American Gothic* uses the language of "his image": in "A Tree Grows in Trinity" (1.2), Merlyn warns Caleb, "He [Buck] wants to raise you in his image"; in "Inhumanitas" (1.10), Caleb asks the priest who made a deal with Buck, "Does Lucas want to make you in his image too?" Later in "Inhumanitas," the implications of this are made clear as Caleb is revealed to be Lucas's next vessel if his current body is killed (there is a second *Rosemary's Baby* [1968] narrative involving Caleb's cousin Gail, who becomes pregnant with Buck's son). Like the angels in the late seasons of *Supernatural*, Lucas is looking for bodies to inhabit, in a deeply gothic nightmare of patrilineal succession. The father's desire to see his son as an echo of himself is gothically rendered as a tale of possession and of the negation of the son's agency in which the spirit of the father is transferred from one son's body to another. Supernaturally, Caleb is the son of the devil and will be his vessel after the current one is damaged; in the more realist narrative, Caleb must decide between not only good and evil, but also different versions of masculinity.

Caleb's connection to Buck is used throughout the series to explore the identification of masculinity with the impulse to dominate. In "Dead to the World" (1.5), as Caleb practices for an archery contest, Buck asks, "What about a man's target?" and tells Caleb to shoot a crow. Caleb replies, "I don't kill nothin' I don't eat" so Buck provokes masculine competitiveness: "He's a little too far for you, huh?" Caleb shoots the bird. Late that night, Merlyn appears in Caleb's bedroom:

> MERLYN: What happened today, Caleb?
> CALEB: Nothin'.
> MERLYN: Well, you're not sleepin'.
> CALEB: I didn't want to shoot that crow, Merly. I swear. I just – something came over me.
> MERLYN: Well, Lucas is a part of you, Caleb. …
> CALEB: Does that mean I gotta be like he is?
> MERLYN: No. But you can't run from him.
>
> (1.5)

The impulse to dominate is embodied in this episode by Waylon Flood (John Shearin), married to the Deputy's ex-wife, Barbara Joy (Helen Baldwin): Flood beats Barbara Joy and terrorizes his stepson, Benji (Lee Norris). The Deputy, Ben Healy (Nick Searcy), decides to put a stop to the abuse. He goes to Flood's house and asks Benji to leave so that he can discuss the matter with Flood alone; he then tells Flood to stop beating Barbara Joy, but Flood is unapologetic. He disables Healy with a kick to the groin and then beats him in front of his ex-wife and young son in an obvious display of dominance. The television viewer is given the same perspective as Benji and Barbara Joy, the camera frame limited largely to Flood's upper body so that the focus is on the beater and his power rather than the beaten and his pain. The scene indicates that Healy will not be the hero that the viewer, or his family, want him to be, as the episode refuses to provide a positive ending to the conventional narrative in which the hero challenges the villain to protect the victimized woman.

Instead, the writers shift the gender focus. In a scene that lies at the thematic heart of the episode, Crower goes to see Healy at the sheriff's station:

> CROWER: Your ex-wife came to see me again. She has some pretty serious bruises.
>
> HEALY: I'm gonna kill that son of a bitch.
>
> CROWER: Now, hold on, I'm not here to make the situation worse. Your wife is an adult. If she wants to change her life she will. Your son doesn't have any choice in this.
>
> HEALY: Did he hurt my boy?
>
> CROWER: Not physically, no. But if that man is his only role model he's going to think that kind of behavior's okay.

He then advises Healy to talk to his son and explain that spousal abuse is "wrong, and won't be tolerated," and Healy does so. The next time he talks to Flood, he asks Benji to stay. This time Healy is not beaten, cast down beneath the screen's field of vision, but dominates the frame, his head on a level with Flood's for much of the scene. But heroes never save the day in *American Gothic*. Buck shows up on the street behind Healy as Flood is about to hit him with a table leg and repeat the earlier beating; Flood, seeing Buck, backs down and then, implicitly as punishment for beating his Deputy, Buck triggers an accident with a table saw that severs one of Flood's hands. A final scene establishes that Benji and Healy are closer, however, and that Benji understands his father's lesson. While the traditional romance narrative in which the hero rescues the lady in distress motivates Healy's first visit to Flood, the scene with Crower invites a rejection of that narrative: the point is not to rescue the woman, who is an adult and makes her own decisions, but to train the next generation of men to end the cycle of (masculine) violence. At the same time, however, that training only proceeds after Buck's figurative emasculation of the tyrannical patriarch – establishing Buck's violent dominance, once again, over the people of the town.

Crower is not the center of the alternative view of masculinity promoted by the episode (and the series as a whole), but just one instance of many. In the same episode, Caleb's friend, Boone, for instance, encourages Caleb during the archery contest and replies, after Caleb asks, "Don't you want to win?", "Of course. But if I don't, your win's just as good." Buck, conversely, gives Caleb a top-of-the-line bow and advises him on "psychological warfare" to defeat Boone. The episode sets up an ideal in which men and boys talk – Crower and Healy; Healy and Benji; Boone and Caleb – to foster cooperation rather than competition, and to teach the rejection of violence. Sheriff Buck is the symbol of all that they must reject, and that includes not only his violence and will to dominate at any price, but also his abuse of women. The episode's third plot involves Buck's past with a woman named Holly: he courted her on old-fashioned terms, with flowers and flowery hyperbole about his devotion to her, and then drove her off a bridge when she refused to submit to his will, leaving her permanently mentally impaired and unable to think of anything but making herself pretty in case Buck will visit her. She is left a perfect pre-feminist doll, in the care of her beautician mother.

John Fiske noted in his discussion of *The A-Team* back in the 1980s that "The same qualities that enable the male to save the female are those that enable him to oppress (and rape) her."[15] This became a sort of televisual shorthand after depictions of attempted rape became admissible on mainstream television: in as little as 20–30 seconds of screen time, a new character can be introduced with clearly established heroic credentials just by saving a woman from a rapist. The modern equivalent of white and black hats in old Westerns, the device is used, for instance, in the first episode of *Carnivàle*, an early episode of *Angel*, and numerous action movies, and to opposite effect in the first episode of *American Gothic* to set up Buck's indisputable villainy. This filmic and televisual cliché is occasionally varied: in *Law-Abiding Citizen* (2009), written by

Kurt Wimmer, the opening scene depicts Clyde (Gerard Butler) injured and bound on the floor, doing nothing but make barely audible noises and grimace, as his wife is beaten and threatened with sexual violence, establishing early on Clyde's unheroic avoidance of direct confrontation. But its most important, and common, variation is the feminist one in which the woman is able to defeat her attacker, most emphatically in Whedon's transformation of the petite-blonde victim of horror movies into Buffy the Vampire Slayer, but the figure has antecedents in a number of action movies. For instance, Holly McClane (Bonnie Bedelia) might be the lady in distress that John McClane (Bruce Willis) must rescue and to whom she returns as wife at the end of *Die Hard*, as a number of critics have noted, but she punches the reporter that endangered her children in *Die Hard* (1988) and then, in the sequel, *Die Harder* (1990), after bragging that she knocked out two of his teeth, she knocks him out again for posing a threat.[16] But in *American Gothic*, this protector/attacker binary of conventional romance and adventure narratives (from gothic to horror and action film) is reworked to maintain the villainy of the attacker but imagine more long-term options for ending violence.

This is not even a one-episode theme, but one that continues throughout the series. In the unaired episode "Strangler," for instance, Healy tells a deputy to apologize to Gail Emory for mocking her account of a violent assault. After the apology, Healy tells Gail (echoing Crower's phrasing that spousal abuse "won't be tolerated" [1.5]), "I just can't tolerate disrespect for women when I'm in charge." The implication of the qualification – "when I'm in charge" – is precisely that Buck, who is usually "in charge," does allow it, a point the series makes in episode after episode, including one in which Buck gets his way by threatening a father with the molestation of his teenaged daughter. *American Gothic* thus repeatedly stages debates between adult men about masculinity and power that is left tacit in traditional televisual presentations of boyhood: being "a man" is not only about positive values such as stoicism and integrity, but also about recognizing patriarchal violence and challenging it before that power comes to them. Caleb does not learn that lesson. Supernaturally powerful because of his connection to Buck, he turns that power against Gail, becoming the monster from which she must try and defend herself – replaying any number of horror narratives. *American Gothic* refuses to defuse the threat, only showing strategies to move parts of its social world forward, and especially the strategy of conversations between men and boys about what being "a man" should mean.

"Do it, Daddy": dangerous fathers in *Point Pleasant*

While *American Gothic* explores what it might mean for a boy to become "a man," *Point Pleasant* follows the *Bildungsroman* of a girl who must, like Caleb, learn to make ethical choices before she becomes fully powerful. Her name a near-anagram of "Antichrist," as a late episode hints, Christina (Elizabeth Harnois), in her late teens, must choose between evil, represented by her father, who happens to be the Devil (also named as Satan and Lucifer in the series), and good, represented by her human mother, from whom she was separated at birth by her father's agents. The traditional television *Bildungsroman* typically involves young adults learning to make moral decisions, to discipline their behavior in order to secure not only their own futures but also the greater social good. For female protagonists, this has generally included controlling their sexuality. From eighteenth-century novels to contemporary horror movies, good girls say "no," partly to ensure that male characters remain on the right path, too, in the heteronormative logic of these works. Whedon's *Buffy* is nowhere more conventional than when it makes Buffy's consent to pre-marital sex the trigger that transforms Angel into a marauding monster. The guiding principle of *Point Pleasant* is consistent with this: Christina has to learn how to discipline her "power," overtly telekinetic but figured as sexual, or everyone will die. This apocalyptic threat is foreshadowed by various incidents in which her very presence intensifies the sexual feelings of those around her, destabilizing domestic and social order in the small resort town of Point Pleasant. The series, then, through Christina, hyperbolically yokes the control of adolescent female sexuality to the security of society as a whole on terms consonant with conventional horror film and television, from *Carrie* (1976), based on a 1974 gothic novel by Stephen King, to Whedon's usually feminist *Buffy*.

Point Pleasant's gender politics are quite different, as addressed in the "normal" families who come into contact with Christina after she is rescued from the ocean near Point Pleasant: while the Christina narrative espouses a conservative view in which women's sexuality is disruptive, these other characters' plots point to the disruptive effects, and near ubiquity, of men's violence against women. Logan Parker (Alex Carter) is so paranoid about his wife Sarah (Claire Carey) having an affair because she had sex with someone before she married him that he is emotionally abusive to her and physically abusive to others. The realtor Amber Hargrove (Dina Meyer) is a single parent, chasing rich men and often finding abuse at their hands – her daughter refers sarcastically to the signs of that abuse as "falling down the stairs again," while repeating her mother's behavior in seeking out powerful men. Lucas Boyd (Grant Show), Lucifer's agent in town, became immortal and started working for Lucifer after strangling his girlfriend Holly (Elizabeth Anne Bennett) during the Depression for prostituting herself to get money that the couple desperately needed – she became immortal too, but experiences her violent death over again every day at the same time, when the marks of his hands reappear around her neck. He gives her a pretty scarf, and she instantly recognizes it as a device to hide the marks of his violence on her body ("Waking the Dead" 1.9). Through Lucas and Holly in particular, the series deals with the survival of abusive relationships from the pre-feminist past into the post-feminist present.

The series is not without moral, unviolent men, but none of them is the adult man in a household. Jesse Parker (Sam Page) is Christina's counterpart, a lifeguard who was raised from the dead as a child and, it is implied, is a Christ figure who can stop Christina. But he is insistently non-violent and even resists the pressure to kill Christina-the-Antichrist. The priest that Christina seeks guidance from and the elderly servant she grew up with are also depicted as non-violent, caring men, and are killed to push her away from the "good" side. David Burke (John Diehl), bedridden for most of the series, conveys a message from God to Jesse, "Thou shalt not kill" ("Let the War Commence" 1.13). The series' cast of secondary characters, then, offers a contrast which serves to highlight the violence and abusiveness of the primary male characters. This is attenuated through Christina as well: she only has fathers (Lucas tells her that she had "plenty of fathers" ["Swimming with Boyd" 1.8]), and searches for her mother to find balance and morality, in a conventional gendering of good and evil used heavily in *American Gothic* as well. Moreover, the supernatural power she derives from her own father allows her to spur other father figures to rage, driving Ben Kramer (Richard Burgi) to beat a man for her on her command, "do it, Daddy" ("Who's Your Daddy" 1.3), and Father Matthew (Ned Schmidtke) to angrily condemn God from the pulpit for letting a younger priest die (1.9). While Christina on one level is a typical gothic rendering of female sexuality as dangerous, on another she is a conduit for male power, negatively defined – she gets her supernatural power from her father, and through it can both be violent and spur men to violence. Moreover, extending her iconic position as the representation of female sexuality, it is men actively in heterosexual domestic couples who are overtly violent in the series – not the widower Burke, the priests, or teenaged Jesse Parker. The series does not overtly connect the dots here and suggest that patriarchy invests female sexuality with power by representing it as dangerous to men, while using it to sanction violence against women. But it does consistently define Christina's potential for evil through the men around her, and especially fathers. This aspect of the series is most extensively explored through the family that takes Christina in when she arrives at Point Pleasant, the Kramers.

Ben Kramer is outwardly a calm and family-oriented man, his caring nature emphasized by his role as the family doctor in Point Pleasant. His wife Meg (Susan Walters), grief-stricken over the drowning of their elder daughter Isabelle (Audrey Marie Anderson) two years earlier, has visions – visions of Isabelle, of birds, of a man with his head on backwards (later revealed to be Lucas Boyd). Ben views the visions as symptoms that must be corrected through drugs, his management of her emotional excess and "hallucinations" consistent with his medical training. But his attempt to treat his wife is rendered insidious by the increasingly overt violence of his interventions: first gentle reminders that she take her medicine, then a raised voice, then administering injections and finally her forcible removal from her home and incarceration in a psychiatric ward. We can trace the origins of this kind of gothic narrative back to Charlotte Perkins Gilman's "The Yellow Wallpaper" (1892) and various Victorian novels with women incarcerated for madness, including Charlotte Brontë's *Jane Eyre* (1847) and Wilkie Collins' *The Woman in White* (1859). The *Point Pleasant* version of it is closely echoed in the first season of *American Horror Story*: in both, a character named Ben who has medical training responds to his wife's knowledge of supernatural events by pathologizing, medicating, and finally institutionalizing her and, in both cases, the woman's perspective is televisually validated. From the start, the viewer of *Point Pleasant* sees Meg's visions on-screen, encouraging the acceptance of them as being as real as other elements in the series. This visual validation is given scientific credence when Ben takes Meg in for an MRI: she has said that it feels like something is moving around inside her head and, as the MRI proceeds, the computer screen depicts a swirling motion in her brain, and then an increasingly bright light that appears to short-circuit the machine. Ben, his obstinacy countering the evidence within the scene and available to viewers, refers to this as a "malfunction" ("Swimming with Boyd" 1.8).

Ben, then, is not the calm voice of reason and of a "man of science" ("Mother's Day" 1.12). He is drugging and confining a healthy woman who sees the truth, refusing to listen to her. This is all the more to his discredit because it is revealed late in the season that he has been experiencing supernatural phenomena himself: a videotape of his daughter's suicide message, like the marks of Lucas's hands on Holly's neck, keeps reappearing. He marks the cassette with an X, then burns it in a fire on the beach; the next day, an envelope appears on his desk with the same cassette, including his scratched X on it. This has been happening, he tells Amber, for two years, ever since Isabelle's death ("Waking the Dead" 1.9). An argument between Meg and Ben after Meg gets a copy of the videotape reveals Ben's insistence on pathologizing the women in his life:

> BEN: I was trying to protect you …
> MEG: The only thing you've protected me from is the proof that I'm not crazy. I've known for a long time that Isabelle killed herself. She told me all about it afterwards. How could I possibly have known that if I was just imagining her? … Ben, don't you see? I have our daughter – you can too.
> ("Hell Hath No Fury Like a Woman Choked" 1.10)

Meg then points to the tape's continual return as further evidence that Isabelle is trying to communicate with them. Ben, however, persists in ignoring the tape's return and focusing instead on its contents, telling Meg, "Isabelle was sick, like you are sick. … That's what you should be getting from the tape. That's why she killed herself. I didn't know in time. I didn't see it, I didn't get her the treatment that could have helped." Meg tries one more time:

MEG: I know that you love me, and that you just want to take care of me, of us. I believe you, now you have to believe me. The things I see are real.

BEN: I can't.

The trope of vision for Ben's idea of rational understanding – "don't you see?" and "I didn't see it" – will become critical in the final episode, as I shall discuss shortly. Here, it is highlighted by the use of the television set in the background, moving in and out of the televisual frame. In the first part of this scene, it is frozen on Isabelle's image from her videotape as Meg repeatedly directs Ben's attention to it (staring at the screen when he first enters the room, gesturing toward it, walking up to the screen and pointing her hands at it). He either keeps his eyes directed away or only lets his eyes flicker onto it briefly. And, after he responds to Meg's plea, "let her in," with the remark, "stop with that," the screen comes into view again but is suddenly blank (Meg may have been within reach of the power button, but there is no indication that she has turned it off). In this, the scene visually reinforces the dialogue: Ben refuses to see. So he keeps trying to silence his daughter, destroying copy after copy of her videotaped suicide message, and to silence his wife, drugging her so that she will not speak of her visions. The scene can only end after the daughter's image has been removed from the field of vision.

While the dominant narrative involves Christina's struggle against, and then capitulation to, her father and her own potential for evil, another narrative takes place across the series – Meg's refusal of the medical paradigm pressed by Ben. In the first episode of the series, Meg stops taking her medication, and there are repeated references in the subsequent episodes to the drugs, making Meg's choice between medication and visions as much a continuous concern of the series as Christina's choice between evil and good. In the final four (unaired) episodes, Meg tries to stop Christina through non-violence and love, rejecting the Vatican group's plan to sacrifice seven Christians and send Jesse to kill Christina. Her only ally is David Burke, and to join her cause he has to stop taking his medication too. She tells him, as she shuts off his oxygen, "The thing about invalids is no one really notices us, do they? That's why we make the perfect soldiers. ... You were meant for more than this, David, but you can't do a damn thing from bed hooked up to these meds" ("Missing" 1.11). Drugs are represented as impediments to divine vision and participation, and hence as an obstacle to the one group that might solve the Christina–Antichrist problem without violence. Ben, as a medical doctor, is the key figure in this anti-medical thread. In the penultimate episode, Judy talks to her mother after Ben has her incarcerated in a psychiatric ward:

> MEG: I'm fine. I'm fine. You know that, right? Where's your father?
> JUDY: He's outside talking to some doctor. How could he do this to you? Doesn't he see what's really happening?
> MEG: I tried to tell him …
> JUDY: Let me talk to him.
> MEG: Honey, it's not that your father doesn't see. It's that he can't. He's a man of science and if he can't see it, touch it, and test it, then it's not real.
>
> ("Mother's Day" 1.12)

This empirical blindness is at the center of Ben's confrontation with Christina in the final episode, "Let the War Commence" (1.13). Having decided to abandon her quest to be good and give herself over to "the dark side" (*Star Wars* is another cultural work with the same trope), Christina turns on the Kramers, staging a family dinner in which she holds them telekinetically at the table. Although she has had little to do with Ben, he is the focus of her rage for much of these dinner scenes and the target of her opening volley as she walks into the house: "Still a doubter, Daddy?" She then orders dinner:

> CHRISTINA: Dinner. Now.
> MEG: Just do what she says, Ben.
> CHRISTINA: Your wife's got the right idea, again. You should try listening to her.

A few moments later, as they are all seated at the dinner table under Christina's coercion, Christina attacks Ben again:

> MEG: You're not an animal.
> CHRISTINA: Sure I am. We all are. Right, Dad?
> BEN: I'm not your father. … I don't know what you are, but I didn't make you. I want you out of this house, right now. …
> CHRISTINA: You think you understand.
> BEN: I do. I understand fine.
> CHRISTINA: You don't! You have no idea. You've been completely oblivious to what your family's been going through.

BEN: I knew something was wrong when you walked through that door. I knew!

CHRISTINA: I'm not the problem here. It's you. You've been blind. [*she supernaturally blinds him*] Blind as a bat.

(1.13)

When Judy begs Christina to heal him, Christina insists, "it's gonna be good for him, for all of you. He'll learn how to listen" (recalling my epigraph, above, from *Twin Peaks*). Deaf and blind to the women around him, Ben is "the problem here." Specifically, Ben's empiricism reduces those around him to "animals," as Christina's remarks stress: Meg's visions become symptoms to be treated with drugs, because there is no "ghost in the machine," in Arthur Koestler's phrase, just a physiological system governed by chemicals. And that view is blind to the spiritual and hence to "what [his] family's been going through," particularly all that Meg sees and he has refused to hear. Moreover, he has an overweening sense of his own power: to be a father is to "make" someone, and, despite everything, he is confident that he "understand[s] fine" and can take control of the situation by shouting at Christina, even as she supernaturally moves around objects and their bodies at will. And that control is allied with his governance of his house. He knows what is in his house, and can decide who gets to stay in it. This brief dialogue epitomizes the series' depiction of fathers: oblivious to what is really going on, and yet insistent on their authority to both declare what is truth and control, even "make," those around them.

The issue of control is emphasized later in the episode, as Christina talks with her other would-be father figure in Point Pleasant, Lucas, now her ally since she has decided to follow her father, Lucifer:

CHRISTINA: I'm not done here. People don't know how to act, what's good for them. They need to be trained.

LUCAS: And how's it going?

CHRISTINA: It'll take some time.

LUCAS: You see that's just it. You don't have enough time. You'll never get that dog to heel. Burn it down, Christina. The house, the town. This world was an experiment and it failed. Your dad sees that, and so do you. Let it end.

The transformation is dramatic: throughout the previous twelve episodes, Christina has been concerned with controlling herself, with disciplining her own desires and powers. Now that she is following her father, she only seeks to discipline others, taking on the traditional paternal role.

The main plot of the series, then, focuses on the conventional figure of the demonized and demonic sexual woman, with precursors from the apocryphal Lilith forward to Matthew Lewis's Mathilda and across various forms of gothic and horror including filmic clichés, her "evil" apocalyptic if she cannot properly discipline herself. But the rest of the cast of characters inhabit a more mundane world in which men hurt women in the name of discipline – not merely sexual, but also epistemological. The "man of science" will control his household, and anyone who does not think like he does will be expelled, while the supernatural plot resurrects pre-Enlightenment belief systems: prophecy, vision, and faith as forces that can do more than science and discipline to protect the material world.

All three series represent the father's rule over his children on gothic terms: domineering and psychologically (if not physically) violent, they are conventional gothic patriarchs, with precursors in Walpole's Manfred, P. B. Shelley's Cenci, LeFanu's Uncle Silas, and even Rice's Lestat. But while *Angel* focuses on the psychological effects of paternal discipline and idealizes the fatherless son as the man most directly able to access a socially productive and ethical masculinity, *American Gothic* and *Point Pleasant* raise wider questions about ethics and belief systems. *American Gothic* uses the gothic tyrant-as-devil to explore the ethics of masculinity, and specifically what makes a "good" son, a "good" husband, and a "good" community leader, with Buck as the recurring counterexample. If *Angel* renders fathers spectral, always off-screen or long dead but ever present to their sons as a monitoring (and admonitory) force, *Point Pleasant* disfigures them: they have a "tragic flaw," in the modern sense of a moral failing. Ben, the physician, "can't see" outside of a scientific worldview and so endangers his family; Logan, the sheriff, cannot imagine self-restraining female sexuality, and so his marriage breaks down and he uses excessive violence at work; and Christina's father, the businessman, puts the world on the fast-track to the apocalypse. Together, they represent male-dominated spheres of power – science, the law, high finance – and their flaws, like Sheriff Buck's, speak to a larger systemic failure. Patriarchy is represented in all three series as both pathological and destructive in its drive to control and discipline others.

Notes

1 See esp. Jerrold Hogle, "'Frankenstein' as neo-gothic: from the ghost of the counterfeit to the monster of abjection," *Romanticism, History, and the Possibilities of Genre: Re-forming Literature, 1789–1837*, ed. Tilottama Rajan and Julia M. Wright (Cambridge: Cambridge University Press, 1998), pp. 176–210.

2 See, e.g., Robert Miles, *Gothic Writing, 1750–1820: A Genealogy*, new edn (Manchester: Manchester University Press, 2002).

3 See, e.g., Kate Ferguson Ellis, *The Contested Castle: Gothic Novels and the Subversion of Domestic Ideology* (Chicago: University of Illinois Press, 1989).

4 "I was talking about the plantations. They had a great deal to do with it, really, my becoming a vampire. … I'd tell [my brother] my troubles, the difficulties I had with the slaves" (Anne Rice, *Interview with the Vampire*, 1976 [New York: Ballantine, 1997], pp. 6–7).

5 Qtd. Lorna Jowett, "'Not like other men'?: the vampire body in Joss Whedon's *Angel*," *Studies in Popular Culture*, 32 (2009), 38.

6 "Anthropology 101" (2.1), *Community*, wr. Chris McKenna, dir. Joe Russo. NBC, September 23, 2010.

7 See David Bordwell's discussion of the "absent cause" in *Vampyr* in his study, *The Films of Carl Theodor Dreyer* (Berkeley: University of California Press, 1981), esp. pp. 93–96.

8 The phrase refers to a notorious episode of *Happy Days* (1974–1984) in which a character waterski-jumped over a shark, and has come to mean that a series is struggling to reignite interest – the improbable addition of a new child is a common example.

9 In the first season, a flashback shows Angel's father yelling at him, "I am ashamed to call you my son. You're a layabout and a scoundrel and you'll never amount to anything more than that" ("The Prodigal" 1.15)

10 Hogle, "'Frankenstein' as neo-gothic," p. 181.

11 Tennessee Williams, *Where I Live: Selected Essays* (New York: New Directions, 1978), p. 42.

12 Episode numbers here follow the series DVD, which preserves the original order in which episodes were aired.

13 Helen Wheatley, *Gothic Television* (Manchester: Manchester University Press, 2006), p. 185.

14 See Exodus 32.

15 John Fiske, *Television Culture* (1987) (New York: Routledge, 2006), p. 212.

16 Gray Cavender suggests that the punch "perhaps violat[es] gender expectations, but restor[es] her place as mother" (p. 171) as part of the larger restoration of Holly to traditional feminine norms, but it is not clear how her maternal position is restored by punishing the reporter after the fact for exploiting her children – Cavender's point about her new acceptance of her married name seems much more on-point (pp. 171–72), though it is arguably a rejection of the multinational corporate life that required her to use her maiden name in the first place and that the film extensively condemns ("Detecting Masculinity," *Making Trouble: Cultural Constructions of Crime, Deviance, and Control*, ed. Jeff Ferrell and Neil Websdale [New Brunswick, NJ: Transaction, 1996; repr. 2009]).

2

Looking for daddy: *Carnivàle*, *Supernatural*, and *Millennium*

> Thomas Wolfe ... got a lot of help in organizing his novels from Maxwell Perkins, his editor at Charles Scribner's Sons. I have heard that Perkins told him to keep in mind as he wrote, as a unifying idea, a hero's search for a father.
>
> Kurt Vonnegut, *Breakfast of Champions* (1973)

If "a hero's search for father" was a cliché in 1973, it has now become a narrative convention so ubiquitous that it can pass without notice: narratives are driven by son's desires for the return of the father, whether as surrogate (say, *Live Free or Die Hard* [2007]), through a renewed relationship (*Super 8* [2011]), or to literally find him (*Indiana Jones and the Last Crusade* [1989]). It is difficult to recall many examples of "a hero's search for a mother," and the exceptions tend to be for warrior-girl heroes. In *Revolution* (2012–2014), the sword-wielding heroine finds her mother by accident while looking for her brother – but soon after mother and daughter are reunited, they are separated and the heroine continues on with her father-figure uncle (and possibly her biological father, the series hints), for whom she did search. Arya Stark in the early seasons of *Game of Thrones* (2011–) is another example, and she only looks for her mother because her father has been executed. In the gothic, this quest motif is complicated by the father's role as a representative of the larger social order – a patriarch in the domestic sphere, a ruler in the public sphere. His remoteness is allied with this power. Arguing for "obscurity" as productive of terror, Edmund Burke writes in 1757, in a work profoundly influential on early gothic and repeatedly invoked in television series, as I have already noted,

> Those despotic governments, which are founded on the passions of men, and principally upon the passion of fear, keep their chief as much as may be from the public eye. The policy has been the same in many cases of religion. Almost all the heathen temples were dark. Even in the barbarous temples of the Americans at this day, they keep their idol in a dark part of the hut, which is consecrated to his worship.[1]

This is not just an eighteenth-century view of the "barbarous," but one that Jean Baudrillard also finds powerful:

> the modern political imaginary goes increasingly in the direction of delaying, of concealing for as long as possible, the death of the head of the state. ... For a long time now a head of state – *no matter which one* – is nothing but the simulacrum of himself, and *only that gives him the power and the quality* to govern. No one would grant the least consent, the least devotion to a *real* person.[2]

Herein lies the value of the missing father in much television gothic. In what passes for televisual realism, fathers are conventionally fantastic, especially in the always calm and enlightened fathers that saturate the televisual field, from the 1950s and 1960s forward: consider *Leave It to Beaver*, *A Family Affair*, *The Courtship of Eddie's Father*, *My Three Sons*, *Eight Is Enough*, *The Cosby Show*, *Full House*, and so on. Endlessly patient, understanding, and gentle, they are what the fathers in *Point Pleasant* and *American Gothic* aim to imitate, but fail to reproduce – they are precisely unable, even uninterested, in understanding others. But the series at issue in this chapter are less concerned with the father's pathological drive to control, the subject of the previous chapter, than the symbolic power that the father wields over others. These fathers do not hector their children at the dinner table, but, by virtue of simply being fathers, are associated with the vague threat implied in the cartoon series title, *Wait Till Your Father Gets Home* (1972–1974) – such a father is "the idol in the dark part of the hut" who cannot be made "real" if he is to be powerful. The "hero's search for a father" in gothic television tends to be a quest to find this "idol" and expose it as such, particularly in *Carnivàle*, *Millennium*, and *Supernatural*, three series in which the "real" is exposed as a counterfeit or fake, particularly in relation to the place of the father as traditional authority and source of identity. Moreover, in these gothic series, the father is not only a "simulacrum of himself" but also the fulcrum through which narratives ask questions about the father's specialized knowledge and its status as "real" or "fake."

Carnivàle, fakery, and the man "in a dark part of the hut"

Carnivàle is fundamentally concerned with challenging realism through myth: from the first episode, bleakly detailed representations of the 1930s dustbowl are intercut with iconic and historical scenes (such as the detonation of an atom bomb, the trenches of World War I), as the realist narrative of the opening scenes is gradually taken apart and superseded by a mythic one that is, as Abbott and Jowett note, aesthetically allied with surrealism.[3] Daniel Knauf's "Pitch Document," released on the web after the series ended, details the myth of Avatars that defines both the protagonist, Ben Hawkins (Nick Stahl), and his antagonist, Brother Justin Crowe (Clancy Brown), through the series' unfolding narrative.[4] Both Ben and Justin have also been separated from their fathers at a young age, putting Ben in particular on an active quest to find his. In the carnival itself, the man called Management lies hidden from view in a wagon, never seen but by a select few of the carnival workers. When one of those select few invokes Management to authorize a decision it instantly silences all dissent in a dramatization of Burke's idea of the "idol in a dark part of the hut," even to Management's depiction as an indistinct figure hidden by shadows in the back of a carnival wagon. Jonesy (Tim DeKay) acknowledges the mythic power of Management in the life of the group when he begins to doubt: "Stop spinning these fairy tales. There ain't no Management" ("Pick a Number" 1.6). But there is. *Carnivàle* does not dispute the power of the idol; the series relentlessly suggests that it is the world of the Enlightenment, of science, the rational, and the bright light of day, that is false. This inversion, recalling my *Kolchak* example in the Introduction, is reinforced through the series' narrative arc: Ben replaces Justin's biological father, and Justin replaces Ben's biological father, refusing the determinisms of genealogy to serve instead a mythic order. Symbols matter, not bloodlines.

Hogle outlines the "fundamental neo-Gothic interplay of regression toward the counterfeit of a past, on the one hand, and the irreverent use of the counterfeit's images as cultural capital for 'free' circulation and profit, on the other."[5] This "interplay" is dramatized in *Carnivàle* through Ben, who works in a barter economy and investigates his family's past across the two seasons, and Justin, who plays on his status as a celebrity preacher to generate more power and profit. That Ben is increasingly identified as a Christ figure and Justin is his nemesis adds a further twist to the semiotics of the series. In much Christian practice, across a range of sects, an ordained minister is allowed to act *in persona Christi*, in the role of Christ, particularly in celebrating a sacrament. Justin as a minister is thus, by definition, a counterfeit Christ; Ben is a Christ-figure, with a mysterious absent father, the ability to heal, and so on, but one who unsettles the idealization of that figure. He commits murder to save the life of a woman he cares for; he has sex outside of marriage; and he worked as a petty thief in the years before the series' timeframe begins. And, in his search for the past, he finds only bloodshed, in his dreams of his father fighting in World War I, in his survey of his paternal grandmother's racist pictures of lynchings on her bedroom wall, and in learning about a mine cave-in that killed almost an entire town of men. While Justin offers his flock a nostalgic vision of a great America founded on grand principles, Ben uncovers an America built on violence and death – the real Christ-figure exposes "the counterfeit of [the] past" offered by Justin the counterfeit-Christ. These representations of the past are inflected by two critical visions of the present: in one, Justin inveighs from the pulpit against the corruptions of modernity; in the other, the series represents, on-screen, not only the bleakness of the Depression but also men who are physically compromised or non-normative in some way.

When they find Scudder, Ben's missing father and the mythical Usher, he is haggard and decrepit, resembling his mother "the Crone"; he is beaten and drugged by one of Justin's henchmen, and then easily killed by Justin. Justin's adoptive father is also weakened, his vulnerability as a paralyzed man who cannot speak stressed in the second season. The carnival includes various other male figures who are physically non-normative: Jonesy has a shattered knee; Management never leaves his bed; Samson, who runs the carnival, is a former dwarf strongman; the psychic Lodz is blind; the strong man is represented as childlike, not only because of an implied intellectual disability, but also because of his devotion to his mother and his asexual nature. Even Ben is regularly dressed in baggy clothes that accentuate his thinness, an image of 1930s hunger. (There are women invalids as well, most notably Sophie's mother, but secondarily so insofar as they are specifically injured by their contact with male Avatars.) The series' fertility myth thus focuses not on (feminine) generation but on a compromised masculinity in need of renewed potency.[6] Ben's healing of Jonesy – a former baseball player who leads the men who do the muscular work of running a carnival, from loading wagons to raising tents – exemplifies this concern of the series with the resurrection of a traditional US masculinity in which vigor and ethics are allied, nowhere more so than in the nostalgic vision of baseball as innocent, fair, and quintessentially American, despite the 1919 Black Sox scandal which Jonesy's backstory echoes.[7]

Justin, however, decries the modern age and argues for another kind of nostalgic return. In the final minutes of season 1, set in 1934 (less than a decade after the Scopes trial over the teaching of evolution in Tennessee schools), Justin preaches the failure of modernity:

> The clock is ticking, brothers and sisters, counting down to Armageddon. The worm reveals himself in many guises across this once great land, from the intellectual elite cruelly indoctrinating our children with the savage blasphemy of Darwin, to the craven Hollywood pagans corrupting them in the darkness of the local bijou, from the false prophets cowering behind our nation's pulpits, to the vile parasites in our banks and boardrooms and the godless politicians, growing fat on the misery of their constituents. The signs of the end times are all around us, etched in blood and fire by the left hand of god.
> ("The Day That Was the Day" 1.12)

Justin, in a kind of religious bricolage, mixes together a fundamentalist view of science ("savage blasphemy of Darwin") and a socialist critique of the economic elite ("vile parasites in our banks") with a gothic representation of new media: instead of Burke's "heathen" in the "dark part of the hut," he laments "pagans corrupting" in "the darkness of the local bijou," the symbol and vehicle of America's turn from religion. In season 2, Justin continues his apocalyptic vision of an America gone wrong:

> There is a dark lie festering in the heart of our nation today. Our founding fathers articulated the inalienable rights of every true American: liberty, equality, and the right to pursue happiness. And yet, and yet, somewhere along the way, we lost those glorious truths. And we have all been led to believe that through honest labor, industry, and optimism, we can achieve success and enjoy prosperity.

> What of you, what of you brothers and sisters, who have worked so hard, toiling and tending the land, only to see it snatched away. Not by God, brothers and sisters, but by Man, by the banks, by the craven men who run the banks. ... Is this our American Dream?
>
> ("Old Cherry Blossom Road" 2.4)

This is not to suggest that the banks are positively represented elsewhere in the series – the first episode condemns the banks' actions during the depression from an objective point of view – but to note that Justin is depicted, again and again, invoking ancient religious authority for a widespread condemnation of contemporary US culture, and especially the trappings of modernity – commerce, science, and media technologies (though he uses radio willingly enough). Justin gains his audience by inventing an idealized American past of natural bounty, deep faith, fair government, and the American Dream.

It is a specifically Protestant vision. Justin's public complaints about "Hollywood pagans" and "godless politicians" are juxtaposed with privately uttered slurs against Catholics: "papist hocus pocus" ("Day of the Dead" 1.11); "don't tell me you've become a papist" ("The Day That Was the Day" 1.12); "arrogance of the papists" ("Damascus, NE" 2.7). Justin, a Methodist preacher, echoes a long line of not only sectarian prejudice but also anti-Catholic gothic, identifying Catholicism with tyranny and superstition.[8] Ben, however, is Catholic, and his father, Scudder, is connected to the Catholic order of Knights Templar. Justin invokes the Protestant myth of America as the "City upon a Hill," John Winthrop's influential 1630 vision of a Christian and cooperative utopia:

> For this end, we must be knit together, in this work, as one man. We must entertain each other in brotherly affection. We must be willing to abridge ourselves of our superfluities, for the supply of others' necessities. We must uphold a familiar commerce together in all meekness, gentleness, patience and liberality. We must delight in each other; make others' conditions our own; rejoice together, mourn together, labor and suffer together, always having before our eyes our commission and community in the work, as members of the same body. ... For we must consider that we shall be as a city upon a hill.[9]

Ben's more quiet Catholicism – he participates in the ritual of confession, for instance – takes him not to nationalist myth but to a more material history. Ben's quest to find Scudder uncovers a past not of "glorious truths" and "honest labor" (or, in Winthrop's words, "mak[ing] others' condition our own"), but of the Klan, the exploitation of the poor, and war, most gothically in his discovery of his blind grandmother, "the Crone," in a room filled with pictures evocative of racism. Justin searches for a public myth, and Ben finds a dystopic reality in a hidden familial past.

Ben's quest to find Scudder is patrilineal; it delves into the past through the father, and understands identity genealogically. Justin's quest is patriarchal; he searches for Scudder to replace him as Usher of Destruction, repeating the mythic cycle rather than exploring the historical trajectory. The series' juxtaposition of the two quests proceeds aesthetically as well as narratively, with Ben in the midst of the dustbowls, looking hungry, sweaty, and dirty, while his well-fed counterpart, Justin, inhabits verdant rolling hills and a bright house.[10] Ultimately, the series ends mythically: Justin kills and replaces Scudder as the Usher, and Ben kills and replaces Management (Justin's biological father), taking his place in the "dark part of the hut." The patriarchal order supersedes the patrilineal, most strikingly in the switching of sons in this final rearrangement: the false Christ-figure Justin replaces Ben's father, and the Christ-like Ben replaces Justin's.

Ben's search reveals the racism and violence of the American past, while Justin's messianic sermons evoke early utopian visions of the "city upon the hill" amidst desperation and violence. The series thus critiques the national myth of "one Nation under God, indivisible, with liberty and justice for all,"[11] while offering a more pantheist myth as the hidden truth. In the series' opening monologue, Samson (Michael J. Anderson) intones,

> Before the beginning, after the great war between Heaven and Hell, God created the Earth and gave dominion over it to the crafty ape he called Man. And to each generation was born a Creature of Light and a Creature of Darkness. And great armies clashed by night in the ancient war between good and evil. There was magic then, nobility, and unimaginable cruelty. And so it was, until the day that a false sun exploded over Trinity, and man forever traded away wonder for reason.
>
> ("Milfay" 1.1)

The series, then, set a decade before the 1945 atomic bomb test at Trinity, defines itself in relation to the completion of the

Enlightenment project, when "man forever traded away wonder for reason," and in an episode whose name is an anagram for "family" as well as the name of a place. Both Justin and Ben are associated with spectacles designed to arouse "wonder": Ben travels with a carnival that offers sex shows, a contortionist, a snake charmer, and other marvels; Justin is a preacher who inspires thousands to follow and even idolize him. The two spectacles are ironic comments on each other, both with audiences looking for "wonder" in the decade before "a false sun exploded over Trinity." The series thus offers a critique of nationalist nostalgia for the "city upon a hill" alongside its own nostalgia for a pre-Enlightenment and global vision. The "false sun" ends the mythic narrative of the false sons.

Gothic mystery and the hidden father in seasons 1 and 2 of *Supernatural*

The television series *Supernatural* (2005–) was conceptualized, according to its creator Eric Kripke, as a way of exploring "urban legends" and "American folklore" through a narrative that combines elements of Jack Kerouac's *On the Road* (1957) and George Lucas's *Star Wars* (1977) in its two "blue-collar" heroes, the twenty-something Winchester brothers Sam and Dean (now in season 10, they are thirty-somethings).[12] The basic plot of most episodes in the first three seasons is this: the brothers get a call for help or uncover a local news story that suggests a supernatural phenomenon, they road-trip to the locale, and end the supernatural threat, putting ghosts and vengeful spirits "to rest," exorcising demons, and killing various monsters. This is all coded as "hunting"; the brothers are part of an extended community of "hunters," and tracking supernatural beings to end their threat is a "hunting trip." The Winchesters have been hunting for over twenty years, living on the road, staying in motels or with other hunters, propelled out of Middle America by the murder of the brothers' mother by "the Yellow-Eyed Demon" and their father's obsession with killing that demon, an obsession that Sam shares after his girlfriend, in the series' pilot, is killed in the same way as his mother. In the fourth season, this episodic structure turns epic: Dean is resurrected to serve God's will, with the angel Castiel as his guide, with the goal of stopping the breaking of 66 seals and hence the apocalypse. The Miltonic debts of the series from this point on are announced in a new recurring character, Anna Milton (Julie McNiven), as well as a multi-season plot about a war in heaven in which angels are soldiers divided by politics, as in John Milton's *Paradise Lost* (1674). In season 5, Lucifer has risen and the brothers are caught up in the angels' war as the apocalypse approaches: Michael, on one side, wishes to occupy Dean's body in order to act on Earth; Lucifer, on the other, wishes to use Sam's body; and, while Michael and Lucifer hunt the brothers, the horsemen of the apocalypse begin to appear. In season 6, Sam, back from hell, is soulless, and the quest continues in a search for Sam's missing ethereal essence, while season 7 deals with his trauma as internal threat and the Leviathans as the monsters-of-the-season. Season 8 takes the hunter mythology still further, introducing a group similar to *Buffy*'s Watchers' Council who supervise hunters, while season 9 returns to the Miltonic motif of a war in heaven – this time with angels who have fallen, and the ongoing quest to find God who might fix it all. Like Jonesy in *Carnivàle*, hunters represent an American blue-collar ground of muscularity and an unflinching work ethic, an ethic so grinding that the brothers rarely eat good food, or get a full night's rest, and even the party-hearty brother, Dean, chastises Sam for drinking while they are on a hunt ("Playthings" 2.11).

In a kind of hyper-bricolage, episodes cobble together romance motifs, conventions of blue-collar masculinity, dense pop-culture referencing, and what is often presented by the show's creator and producers in the early seasons as an "authentic" Americana. The term here evokes a specifically US oral and mythical culture that is, in the early seasons especially, insistently local. But this turns inside out as the early seasons of the series progress, as one episode makes clear that the United States, as a settler nation, was the site to which many such beliefs were brought. To date, the series has invoked supernatural creatures from Christianity and Islam to less globalized traditions in Europe, India, and pre-colonial America – all are found within the borders of the continental United States, though the series has steadily drifted toward an overarching Miltonic if not Christian myth. Kripke's well-documented awareness of cinematic and television genres, as well as the very conventionality of the gothic and horror modes in general, make it easy to identify typical features that link the series to other threads in popular culture, including a bevy of supernatural series to begin airing around the same time, such as *Medium* (2005–2011) and *Lost* (2004–2010),

Vancouver-made US fantasy from *X-Files* to recent science fiction series such as *Battlestar Galactica*, and the Route 66 tradition in literature and film (overtly in the *Supernatural* episode, "Route 666") as well as a very long tradition in the gothic of addressing national fears as a kind of haunting or possession by the "Other." So, the early seasons of the series operate at an unusual nexus: on the one hand, contemporary popular, globally distributed but Hollywood-centered culture; on the other, a global array of traditional beliefs that circulate not through electronic media but through the stories told for generations in locally defined communities, and specifically stories that migrate with populations, not digitally. The first-season episode, "Scarecrow" (1.11), for instance, deals with a pagan fertility myth: the myth and its rituals are sustained in a small town for centuries, transported from Scandinavia with settlers, but no one outside of the tightknit rural community is aware of it. Paganism is, however, equated with Puritanism, alike "imported" traditions:

> PROFESSOR: I'm afraid Indiana isn't known for its pagan worship.
> DEAN: What if it was imported? You know, like the pilgrims brought their religion over. Wasn't a lot of this area settled by immigrants?

Moreover, the tradition is sustained orally; the elders always meet face to face, and are never depicted with phones or other more modern vehicles of communication.

I want to stress this tension between two notions of the popular to explore some of the ways in which the series challenges distinctions and narratives in recent media theory. On the one hand, there is the kind of popular culture analyzed in contemporary cultural studies with nods to Adorno and Horkheimer as well as the Birmingham school and, from another vantage point, by Baudrillard.[13] Popular culture here is part of a US-centered capitalist machine, bolstering Gramscian hegemony while driving the masses to buy, with little reflection or even agency, more and more commercial products. On the other, there is the culture of the people: oral traditions that operate to a significant extent outside of the capitalist modernity that they often pre-date. Because they are oral or handwritten, they are not caught up in what Walter Benjamin dubbed "the age of mechanical reproduction" and so retain, in that argument, "The presence of the original [which] is the prerequisite to the concept of authenticity."[14] In the early seasons of *Supernatural*, the gothic is uncovered and understood through the latter form of the popular: the Winchesters' research consists of talking to local people, poring through town archives, and occasionally talking to university professors about the otherwise-forgotten past. If they use books, they are generally very old ones; if they use newspapers, they are local papers. Again and again, evidence lies outside of or on the low-volume edges of "mechanical reproduction." This interest in the singular cultural work is foregrounded in an early episode where tracking a painting's provenance is crucial to the solution of the mystery ("Provenance" 1.19). "Hunting" itself is depicted in the series as an almost entirely oral tradition: rumors circulate through the hunting community, they tell each other hunting stories over beer, and supernatural lore is gathered by phoning older hunters. Handwritten journals kept by hunters, most centrally the father John Winchester, remain the only written extensions of that tradition, and they are precious objects handed down from generation to generation.

This is not about a nostalgic return to the pre-technological, however (as Justin would have it in *Carnivàle*). While the brothers investigate local tradition through interviews and archival research, they also use Hollywood film, television and popular music to discuss their options as well as to provide a body of codewords through which they sometimes have to communicate. For instance, if the two brothers are separated, one goes to the first motel listed in the phonebook and registers as "Jim Rockford," the protagonist of the *Rockford Files* (1974–1980) ("The Usual Suspects" 2.7); "Funkytown," the title of a 1980 disco hit song, indicates that they are calling but cannot speak freely because a gun is pointed at them (see "Hunted" 2.10); rock musicians' and Hollywood actors' names are often used as aliases when they present themselves as officials to gain access to people they need to interview. The brothers, in other words, pivot smoothly between pre-electronic and electronic popular cultures on terms that I would like to suggest complicate the widely discussed phenomenon in which popular cultures are increasingly engaging, if not thematizing, the collapse into simulation addressed by Baudrillard, and by Hogle in relation to the literary gothic.

This collapse is explicitly addressed in a fourth-season episode, "The Monster at the End of this Book" (4.18). The brothers are mistaken for fans of a pulp series about two brothers who hunt the supernatural, their investigation of supernatural events legible to the owner of a comic-book store as their attempt to live-action role-play (LARPing). They pick up the books, and discover accounts of their own investigations, many book titles repeating the titles of early-season episodes. They track down the books' author, and discover that he is unaware that his visions are anything but the product of his own suddenly productive imagination; the angel Castiel explains that he is a prophet, protected by an archangel, and he will rank with the biblical prophets. Pulp fiction becomes prophecy, a drunk hack the chosen of God, as mass-culture is traced back to a divine origin, the postmodern world of role-playing imaginary heroes revealed to be the ancient world of gods and their chosen agents. And, as the later episodes often stress, God is father, an echo of the human father who, in the early seasons, is himself a figure "in the dark part of the hut."

The series opens in the dark: Sam has abandoned hunting for university, and, in an early scene of the first episode, Dean breaks into his university apartment in the middle of the night to test his skill as a fighter and ask for his help finding their father. They struggle in the dark, until Dean reveals who he is: the obscure threat becomes the embarrassing brother (he makes a sexual remark about Sam's girlfriend and leers at her), and team Winchester goes back on the road. The first season focuses on one narrative thread within a larger arc narrative that covers the first two seasons: the father cannot be found, the sons search for their father, the father is found and the family is reunited in the old family car, the closest thing the Winchesters have to a home. This is no simple paternal figure, however. Throughout the season, the brothers carry around his journal, turning to it for explanations of the supernatural beings they discover and for hunting strategies. They also look for clues, traces, of where he has been and what he wants them to do; he has not been kidnapped, but is intentionally concealing himself from them, even hiding when the brothers unknowingly visit the house where he is staying. There is a pathetic undertone to all of this: boys who grew up on the road with their father suddenly being denied all access to him, the adult equivalent of 5-year-olds who have been separated from a parent in a grocery store, and even the hyper-masculine older brother, Dean, weeps while leaving a voicemail message pleading with his father to return to them ("Home" 1.9). John Winchester insists that he can only succeed in his hunt for the

Yellow-Eyed Demon if he remains hidden and separated from his sons. His power is overtly tied to his ability to remain concealed, in Burke's "dark part of the hut," even as that concealment has quite Burkean effects on his sons in terrifying, if not terrorizing, them. Moreover, as the series progresses, the parallel between the father and God-the-Father is increasingly explicit, retroactively relating the father's journal to the Bible – the word of the Father, used to guide and explain. In the first half of the first season, this insistently absent father is defined by the trace: the first contact the brothers get from him after his disappearance is coordinates for a hunting job, just two numbers on a slip of paper. He later sends them coordinates by cellphone, and directs jobs to them by adding a voicemail message to his cell telling callers to contact Dean. He phones once, and they trace his phone number but still cannot reach him. The brothers even have debates that echo religious debates about whether obedience to the father is either beyond question (avoiding the word "faith") or needs explanation and justification.

John Winchester is thus insistently constructed as an all-powerful hunter not through direct representation on-screen but through the simulacrum of the sons' representations of him. Even his more skeptical son, Sam, is incredulous when Dean tells him their father once failed to catch a demon ("Something Wicked" 1.18). When John Winchester does appear on-screen, briefly, he is surrounded by objects which suggest his hypermasculinity, from the marine T-shirt he wears in the flashbacks of the first episode to a rather comical scene, with echoes of a famous scene in *Crocodile Dundee* (1986), in which Dean offers him a knife to use as a weapon: John says "I'm OK, thanks," and pulls out a knife more than twice the size of Dean's ("Dead Man's Blood" 1.20). John is also the authority on all things supernatural; his journal is an encyclopedia of supernatural creatures, and the brothers repeatedly express admiration for his research skills in linking apparently trivial facts into patterns meaningful as indications of supernatural activity. In "When the Levee Breaks" (4.21), Dean is asked to show the same obedience to God that he showed to his father, revisiting the first two seasons' many arguments between the brothers about Dean's unquestioned obedience to his father and Sam's rebelliousness (paving the way for Lucifer's interest in him as a vessel, in the Miltonic tradition of Lucifer as rebel):

> CASTIEL: Do you give yourself over wholly to the service of God and his angels?
> DEAN: Yeah, exactly.
> CASTIEL: Say it.
> DEAN: I give myself over wholly to serve God, and you guys.
> CASTIEL: Do you swear to follow his will and his word as swiftly and obediently as you did your own father's?
> DEAN: Yes, I swear.

But, in the first season, family bickering exposes cracks in John's mythic façade, and the absent father becomes the apologetic father who recognizes his obsession has hurt his sons. John Winchester does not, however, simply become "real" instead of "mythic." He is transformed from the self-hidden authority who is only discernible in traces into a very visible and victimized body: in the run up to the first-season finale, John walks into an obvious trap, is seized, beaten, and held prisoner by demons who keep him tied to a bed. As the brothers rescue him, he is possessed by the very demon he has been hunting for over twenty years.

The first season as a whole, then, develops the mythos of an unstoppable demon hunter and then takes it apart as he bodily enters the space of the screen, violating him physically and psychically, while the second season blurs the distinction between father and demon. The series' return to the authentic and the pre-technological is not part of a nostalgic return to the hero of romance, nor is it a naive reversal of the postmodern narrative of declining referentiality. It peeks into the "dark part of the hut": myths are exposed as sources of horror, including the sight of the vulnerable body of the father, tied to a bed or invaded by a demon. The resolution of the second season relies on the tension between the patrilineal transfer of family and the patriarchal transfer of control that governs *Carnivàle*. John makes a deal with the Yellow-Eyed Demon to sacrifice his life so that Dean may live – and, in his dying words, he tells the newly recovered Dean to kill his brother if Sam submits to the evil put in him by the Yellow-Eyed Demon. Much of the series stresses Dean's responsibility to take care of Sam, a substitute father in the absence of John. In the scene that would become the central mystery of the next season, Dean is asked to replace his father as Father – as judge, jury, and executioner rather than caregiver, a secret command that makes him the man "in the dark part of the hut."

Angels and demons: looking for fathers at the end of the *Millennium*

Chris Carter's *Millennium* centers on Frank Black as he works first for the Millennium Group, a consulting firm that advises law enforcement, and then in the third season returns to the FBI. The series draws on both Christian millenarianism and more secular concerns about the end of the millennium, from the now-forgotten Y2K panic that there would be widespread computer systems failures because of software that could not accommodate the year "00," to a more general malaise about social decline, particularly as evident in growing rates of violent crime. This double frame, the sacred and the secular, is kept in view through Frank Black, an FBI-trained profiler with a "gift": as he puts it, "I see what the killer sees," a gothic device that also appears, for instance, in John Carpenter's *Eyes of Laura Mars* (1978), and echoes the visionary abilities of Gail and Sheriff Buck in *American Gothic*. Frank Black is both psychologist and psychic, both man of science and part of a female-dominated group in the series that have supernatural visions – Frank's mother, Frank's daughter, and Frank's profiling partner in the second season, Lara Means, all have visions as well, though they generally see angels whereas Frank sees devils or looks through the eyes of serial killers.

Scholarship on the series to date has largely built on Richard Dyer's early identification of *Millennium* as a "serial-killer fiction," and the ways in which the serial killer encodes the power of white masculinity.[15] Scholars have also noted the significance in the series of that which the serial killer threatens, namely the nuclear family in a suburban home. Wheatley thus suggests that in "episode after episode, victims are attacked within the confines of their own home, thus building up a kind of 'domestic victimology' whereby an image of the North American home as a safe space is no longer valid," Michael Valdez Moses suggests that in both *Millennium* and *The X-Files* "family relations and partnerships are routinely threatened by external forces and institutions," and Samira Kawash points to the visual force of its alternation between brightly lit images of the Blacks' yellow house and "the perpetual night and fog of threatening scenes of mayhem and violence," where the former is always at risk from the latter, launching a suggestive exploration of the image of the "safe house" in the context of US racial politics and concomitant flight to the suburbs.[16] Such discussions of *Millennium* intersect significantly with gothic studies' more traditional concerns: the social commentary implied by the monster or villain, and what Kate Ferguson Ellis dubbed "the contested castle,"[17] the gothic naming, as it has since 1764, the failure of the domestic space to be either as ideal or secure as it is imagined to be in other genres and modes. But the yellow house virtually disappears from the second and third seasons, and the "safe space" of the home is regularly threatened (as in much traditional gothic) from within, not by "external forces." The problem of the home is shifted in key episodes to the problem of the father, and specifically fathers who are surrounded by angels in one form or another.

Frank is, from the outset, characterized by what Malin terms the "sensitive, nontraditional masculinity" which emerged in popular culture in the post-Clinton era: soft-spoken and supportive of his wife's work, he is a caring family man who rarely raises his voice to his preschool daughter, Jordan.[18] In an early episode, Frank tells Catherine (Megan Gallagher) that Jordan was upset that Frank had not "protected" Catherine during an argument she had with a family friend and colleague. Catherine asks, "What did you tell her?" and Frank replies, "I told her that you didn't need protecting. That you knew how to protect yourself," and Catherine approvingly says "Thank you" ("The Well-Worn Lock" 1.8), the dialogue recalling Crower's advice to Healy in *American Gothic* and Ben's condescending excuse for drugging and institutionalizing his wife in *Point Pleasant*: in contemporary gothic television, women can take care of themselves and men who try to "protect" them are acting improperly. Frank, as in so many episodes of season 1, operates as a direct contrast to the kinds of dangerous masculinity on which the series ostensibly focuses as a "serial-killer fiction." This extends beyond the domestic sphere to Frank's working life. He repeatedly argues for the inclusion of women experts that policemen wish kept out of an investigation,[19] and frequently works, always comfortably, with such women, including physicians, forensic scientists, his wife as a clinical psychologist, and a veterinarian. He has women partners in both the second and third seasons. This pattern is all the more remarkable by contrast with the nearly all-male police departments with which Frank regularly works, and even more so in comparison to the crew that worked on the series. Season 1 was entirely written, edited, cast and produced by men; Kathy

Gilroy-Sereda as production manager was arguably the most senior woman that season. She did not become a producer until the second season when they also added one team of women writers for three episodes. I am not interested here in the series production per se, but note this to highlight the ways in which the representation of Frank functioning well in a gender-integrated workplace operates at the level of fantasy, and the series itself foregrounds that fantasy through the juxtaposition of Frank's working practices with those of nearly all-male police forces. In the entire first season, only one female police officer is depicted on-screen, a remarkable statistic given the general televisual convention of handing women and child victims over to the care of women police officers and the predominance of such victims in the series.

Writing just a decade before *Millennium*, Fiske argues that *The A-Team*, "Like most masculine texts," "writ[es] out of its world ... women, work, and marriage."[20] *Millennium* persistently writes them in, dealing in various episodes with men's emotional investments in their marriages as well as women professionals in the workplace. In the first episode of *Millennium*, "Pilot," the traditional gender paradigm of the strong man who protects the home and its occupants is exposed as myth:

> CATHERINE: You think you're protecting me but you make it worse, Frank. You can't shut the world out for me. You can't ask me to pretend that I don't know what you do.
>
> FRANK: Everyone pretends. We all make believe. These men I help catch make us.
>
> CATHERINE: The real world starts to seep in. You can't stop it.
>
> FRANK: I want you to make believe that I can.

Frank's use of the childish phrase, "make believe," calls attention to the series' interest, from its inception, with its own status as fantasy. The series operates at the crux of two paradoxical gender formations: on the one hand, the traditional gothic and its extension in serial-killer narratives in which men are violent and women are victims, and the law is enforced by men who "sacrifice" themselves for the protection of others;[21] on the other, Frank is *also* caught up in what Malin terms a "crisis of masculinity" in his title in which men discard traditional gender models and "seek new identities," including more equitable relationships at home and work.[22] The series pursues both without resolving them, particularly in a series of episodes that deal with angels and demons as symbols of the failure to form an operative, and cooperative, gender identity.

For instance, the first-season episode "Covenant" (1.16) takes as its subject a mainstream, suburban household; the husband, Bill Garry (John Finn), is a sheriff and a conservative Christian, like the prosecutor and other officials depicted in the episode; his wife, Dolores Garry, appears in the episode carrying groceries and shepherding the children into the house so that she can make dinner, and there is no indication that she has any employment outside of the home. The episode opens on Garry in his garage wood-working shop, under a sign that will later be revealed to read, "If a man fails at home / he fails in life." After his family arrives, the camera pans through the interior of the home, dwelling on some of his wife's angel-themed knick-knacks before turning to the violence on which the rest of the episode will focus: the deaths of Garry's wife and children. Garry calls the police and confesses to the murders even though he did not commit them, and seeks his own execution. His lawyer, thinking him guilty of the crimes, explains, "Man wants to die, needs to die. See, according to Garry's religious beliefs, for a murderer, shedder of blood, to be forgiven by God at the time of his death, his blood must also be shed," an argument also presented by the prosecutor. For Garry it is less a matter of his actions than his failure: he failed at home, so he failed at life and so must die. At the end of the episode, the truth is revealed. He had an affair, so his wife killed their children and then herself: "She told Bill it was his fault. She said he made her kill the children and then she stabbed herself one last time"; "He said she couldn't bear the thought of living in a world of adulterers, men like him." So, the perfect conservative household of devoutly religious sheriff, stay-at-home mom, and three children implodes, as do many others in the series, rather than being threatened by a serial killer who lurks in the alley.

In "Covenant," moreover, the camera dwells repeatedly on angel images throughout the house – fridge magnets, a cookie jar, pictures, figurines – and Frank contends that, at the moment of murdering her children, Dolores Garry saw them as angels. This echoes a number of other first-season episodes in which angels, figurative and literal, are juxtaposed with violent homes. In one episode, the child who was left alive after the murder of her parents in their own home is called an "angel" as she leaves the hospital for foster care ("Wide Open" 1.8). In "The Wild and the Innocent" (1.10), a plot of domestic violence and spree killing is punctuated, even punctured, extra-diegetically by a woman's loving letters to her infant son, who she addresses as "Angel." By the final episodes of season 1, angels are appearing on-screen. In "Powers, Principalities, Thrones, and Dominions" (1.18),[23] Peter Watts (Terry O'Quinn) investigates satanic-style murders, going over a murder scene in the victim's home. As a detective tells him the current victim was a promise keeper – a fairly new movement, when the episode first aired, to reinstate traditional masculinity under the aegis of Christian faith – Peter sees an angel outside the house. While early episodes of *Millennium* focus on the abuse of scripture by murderers, using the Bible for extra-diegetic epigraphs or as clues to a murder's psychopathology, the scriptural dimensions of the series become increasingly literal – no longer merely textual, but evident in the plot and on-screen visuals. "Covenant" thus introduces a recurring topos in *Millennium*, of the angel who marks but stands apart from a conservative domestic regime that has spiraled into violence.

Season 2 builds on the implications of season 1 in general and "Covenant" in particular as it addresses the failure of traditional domestic gender divisions. Season 2 is the gothic season, largely overseen by the writing team of Glen Morgan and James Wong. In seasons 1 and 3, almost all of the violence is scientifically explainable; religious texts and supernatural images are the lexicon of the criminally insane, not registers of the otherworldly that disrupts a modern worldview, as it is after "Powers" in season 1 and for most of season 2. In season 2, moreover, the gothic machinery of ghosts and demons are used to police the boundaries of properly effective masculinity, beginning with "Beware of the Dog" (2.2) in which a man who "runs away" from urban crime causes dangerous disorder in the natural world, disturbing the "equilibrium." Living alone, afraid of urban violence, and preferring to sit in his isolated home singing along to musicals, he is a salutary reminder that, as much as the series works to redefine masculinity, it does so within a relentlessly heteronormative framework. At the same time that the season gothically marks the limits of domestic masculinity, it also uses Christian imagery to idealize women, particularly through significant women characters connected to Frank who see angels: first Frank's daughter, who sees angels in her room during her mother's abduction ("The Beginning and the End" 2.1), then

Frank's new investigative partner Lara Means, then Frank's mother in a flashback episode, a woman who, like Dolores Garry, filled her home with images of angels.

In the second season, Frank and his wife are separated; he only gets to visit with his daughter periodically, and he becomes increasingly disillusioned with the Millennium Group; he lives in a small bungalow, marked as much by shadow and low lighting as his yellow house in the first season was by intense light and bright colors. "The Curse of Frank Black" (2.6) includes gothic machinery of the most obvious sort: its setting is Halloween, electronic equipment malfunctions in apparently meaningful ways, the statement, "There's no such thing as ghosts," is repeated three times, and in a key scene teenagers in the basement of Frank's yellow house tell each other a scary story of "The Curse of Frank Black," of a house haunted by Frank's dead friend and of Frank being mysteriously missing. Frank chases them out and then, using the supplies the teenagers brought, eggs his own house. Also marking its affiliation with the gothic, this is the first episode to depict Frank's 1950s childhood through flashbacks, as nostalgia, memory, and ghosts become symbolically intertwined in the narrative. Frank is visited by the ghost of a World War II veteran, Crocell (Dean Winters), whom he met as a child one Halloween night. That night, Crocell asked young Frank if the dead really would visit the living on Halloween, a profound desire contextualized by pictures of his friends from the war and a newspaper with the headline, "Hermann Goering Commits Suicide Hours Before Execution." In a second flashback, years later, a teenage Frank watches as Crocell's body is taken away in an ambulance; his friends think that Crocell was a "Commie" who "liked men, that's why he killed women," while Frank, already a bit of a profiler, says that is not what happened – that Crocell committed suicide. Crocell clearly resists 1950s, traditional masculinity: he is a World War II hero but instead of building 1950s America he is traumatized by grief, so much so that he remains completely isolated from society and the neighborhood boys consider him the antithesis of proper American masculinity (acronymically we might term it PAM – nothing sticks to it, because it is idealized and naturalized). Moreover, as in "Beware of the Dog," the man who lives alone, isolated from society, is homophobically marked as both disruptive and queer in a range of senses, including as serial killer in the minds of the neighborhood boys.

In the narrative present, Crocell appears in Frank's attic smoking a cigarette, and delivers a long monologue that is in some senses Faustian and in others a revision of Charles Dickens's *A Christmas Carol* (1843). He offers Frank a deal, a vision of Halloween future. He says, "I've been sent here because you've become me. The way people look at you, what they say about you. Making stuff up. Pretty soon you come to believe it's true and then it's really all over," connecting the stories told about him by Frank's friends with the ghost story told about Frank. Crocell continues, noting their shared alienation from the domestic:

> I threw things at my house, too. Not eggs though. I think I threw dog crap. Yeah, I threw dog crap from my back yard at my kitchen window. I never cleaned it off. Imagine that. ... Here's the deal, kid. Give up the fight. Sit it out. Forget about this Millennium Group. Go back to your wife and to your daughter and to your puppy and to your yellow house and just live out a nice, happy, normal life and there's going to be a place for all three of you afterwards. A place, believe me, where a lot of souls wish they could be.

Heaven lies in domesticity, and will follow from it; Frank's failure to work within that paradigm is signaled by his violence against his own home, egging it just as Crocell had thrown "dog crap," and Garry had refused to enter his even for dinner. Crocell concludes,

> But you pass on this, and you're going so much farther than I have ever been. Hell, the way you gutted that guy who took your wife, the anger inside of you. Whew. I don't know why you're not being offered a sweeter deal. You got the heat inside of you to fight for this side. So what I'm asking of you is really simple. Sit back and do nothing. Anyone can do it. Hell, most people do. Take this deal, kid. Secure you and your family's future.

So, here is Frank's choice: domesticity or the dark side. His move to the latter is stressed when one of the eggs he throws at his house lands on a window and smears in the shape of a devil's head, recalling the opening scene in which, as he takes his daughter trick-or-treating, he sees a devil watching him from a house window. The devil in this episode lies in the interface between public and private, between policing and fatherhood. The man who is alone – Crocell, Frank apart from his wife and child, Garry in his garage – and violates his own home is in danger of slipping into a realm of lies, "make believe," anger, and violence, the domain of the devil, who "will win. There's no way he can lose."

In "Covenant," Dolores Garry uses the blood of her murdered children to write a biblical reference, Isaiah 28:15, on the kitchen window: the verse reads, "We have made a covenant with death. We have made lies our refuge. And under falsehood we have hid ourselves." Masculinity in the series is shored up by a web of lies, of the myth of a strong father figure who protects and polices the household, of the fantasies of serial killers in which their own powerlessness is remedied, and even of stable gender difference (most strikingly in the alternately male and female, human and demon, Lucy Butler, who I shall discuss below). The contestation between the "safe house" and the invaded house is the symbolic backdrop of a larger exploration of masculinity as the old gender codes are pushed into gothic travesties and horror – the serial killer, the mother who kills her children, and the man who fouls his own house. The images of angels not only ironically mark that gothic horror but also call attention to the hollowness of modernity. While Eden, and the first heteronormative pair, were guarded by warrior-archangels, Dolores Garry has only delusion and cheap figurines.

In all of these series, the writers juxtapose an older mythic world with a more skeptical present. Following the origins of the gothic in Shakespeare's *Hamlet*, they ask viewers to admit the possibility that "There are more things in heaven and earth ... Than are dreamt of in [modern] philosophy"[24] and put at the center of that revelation the shadowy figure of the father. In *Hamlet*, these lines follow the first appearance of the ghost of Hamlet's father – also named Hamlet. "A hero's search for a father," in Vonnegut's phrase, is about revelation: fathers are the "idol in the dark part of the hut," and the power lies elsewhere. In *Millennium*, fathers are exposed as having "made lies [their] refuge": Frank wants his wife to "make believe" he is an old-fashioned father figure as well as a modern man who believes in gender equity, and Garry maintains the façade of the responsible patriarch even to confessing to the murders his wife committed. As in *Carnivàle*, the world is full of "wonder" and unexplainable phenomena, but fathers are all compromised in some way – in Knauf's series, usually physically. *Supernatural* offers a much more streamlined narrative: no mother, no home, no domestic sphere of any sort, and just a Father with a Book demanding obedience from his sons in a war between good and evil. In all three series, these supernatural phenomena, explicitly represented for the viewers, remain hidden from the view of the public depicted in the series: Ben swears those he has healed to secrecy, Frank refers obliquely to his "gift" but overtly relies on his scientific credentials as a profiler, and the Winchesters' codewords (including "hunting" itself) are part of a general practice in which the supernatural is concealed from the general public. In these three series, then, the "idol in the dark part of the hut" is misdirection as well as a fake. "A hero's search for a father" is the wrong quest, because the father is really more like the great and powerful Oz – a projection designed to awe rather than illuminate.

Notes

1 Edmund Burke, *Enquiry Concerning the Origin of our Ideas of the Sublime and Beautiful* (1757), ed. Adam Phillips (Oxford: Oxford University Press, 1998), pp. 54–55.

2 Jean Baudrillard, *Simulacra and Simulation*, trans. Sheila Faria Glaser (Ann Arbor: University of Michigan Press, 1995), pp. 25–26.

3 Lorna Jowett and Stacey Abbott, *TV Horror: Investigating the Dark Side of the Small Screen* (London: I.B. Tauris, 2013), pp. 173–74.

4 Daniel Knauf, "Series concept & background" (known as "The Pitch Document"), available at http://c.ymcdn.com/sites/www.harvardwood.org/resource/resmgr/hwp-pdfs/carnivale_pitch_document.pdf and myriad other locations.

5 Jerrold Hogle, "'Frankenstein' as neo-gothic: from the ghost of the counterfeit to the monster of abjection," *Romanticism, History, and the Possibilities of Genre: Re-forming Literature, 1789–1837*, ed. Tilottama Rajan and Julia M. Wright (Cambridge: Cambridge University Press, 1998), p. 191.

6 The women of the carnival are overtly sexual, but their fertility is compromised in some way, literally by age (the snake charmer, Ruthie) and the likelihood of sexually transmitted disease (the prostitute-dancers), and more metaphorically by ambiguous gender (the boyish Sofie and the bearded lady). For a brief discussion of the depiction of the bodies of the women in the carnival, see Alena Amato Ruggerio, "Sexuality, size, and sin in HBO's *Carnivàle*," *Feminist Media Studies*, 5 (2005), 87–90.

7 Jonesy was a major league baseball player until criminals shattered his

knee as punishment for not throwing a game; the Black Sox scandal centered on eight players for the Chicago White Sox who were accused of accepting bribes to lose games in the 1919 World Series.

8 The anti-Catholic strain in gothic writing has long been a significant issue in gothic studies, and its prevalence has been disputed from Montague Summers in the 1930s to Robert Miles in this century; see, e.g., Montague Summers, *The Gothic Quest: A History of the Gothic Novel* (London: Fortune Press, 1938), widely understood as a foundational if quirky study (for a useful recent discussion of Summers, see Chris Baldick and Robert Mighall, "Gothic criticism," *A New Companion to the Gothic*, ed. David Punter [Oxford: Wiley-Blackwell, 2012], pp. 269–75); Robert Miles, "Europhobia: the Catholic other in Horace Walpole and Charles Maturin," in *European Gothic: A Spirited Exchange 1760–1960*, ed. Avril Horner (Manchester: Manchester University Press, 2002), pp. 84–103; Patrick O'Malley, *Catholicism, Sexual Deviance, and Victorian Gothic Culture* (Cambridge: Cambridge University Press, 2006).

9 John Winthrop, "A model of Christian charity" (1630), http://religiousfreedom.lib.virginia.edu/sacred/charity.html <last date of access: May 10, 2013>.

10 Eric Bronson suggests that Justin is a "noir priest," locating the series in a tradition of religious *film noir* through, for instance, its "use of drab and dreary landscapes" (pp. 142, 132) and religious elements, in "*Carnivàle* knowledge: give me that old-time noir religion," *The Philosophy of TV Noir*, ed. Steven M. Sanders and Aeon J. Skoble (Lexington: University Press of Kentucky, 2008), pp. 131–42, but this reading is complicated by the increasingly lush and pastoral settings for the scenes involving Justin (not to mention his transformation from preacher to anti-Christ).

11 US Pledge of Allegiance.

12 See Kripke's contributions to the "Commentary" for "Pilot" (*Supernatural: Season 1*, DVD), and myriad press articles about the series, including an article in the *Daily Telegraph* (March 8, 2007) (www.news.com.au/dailytelegraph/story/0,22049,21346126–5006014,00.html).

13 Theodor W. Adorno and Max Horkheimer, *Dialectic of Enlightenment: Philosophical Fragments*, ed. Gunzelin Schmid Noerr, trans. Edmund Jephcott (Stanford: Stanford University Press, 2002), esp. "The culture industry: the Enlightenment as mass deception" (pp. 94–136); on the Birmingham school, see, e.g., Stuart Hall et al., eds, *Culture, Media, Language: Working Papers in Cultural Studies, 1972–79* (New York: Routledge, 1991); Baudrillard, *Simulacra and Simulation*.

14 Walter Benjamin, "The work of art in the age of mechanical reproduc-

tion," *Illuminations*, ed. Hannah Arendt, trans. Harry Zohn (New York: Schocken, 1986), p. 210.

15 Richard Dyer, "Kill and kill again," *Sight & Sound*, n.s., 7:9 (September 1997), 16. On the general subject of the televisual serial killer, see also Sarah E. Maier (who does not actually discuss *Millennium* in the essay), "John Doe reads: interrogating the postmodern serial killer in *Millennium*, *Seven* and *Profiler*," *Crime Time – Prime Time – Global Time: Intercultural Studies in Crime Serials*, ed. Ute Fendler and Susanne Fendler (Aachen, Germany: Shaker, 2004), pp. 171–86.

16 Helen Wheatley, *Gothic Television* (Manchester: Manchester University Press, 2006), p. 190; Michael Valdez Moses, "Kingdom of darkness: autonomy and conspiracy in *The X-Files* and *Millennium*" (*Philosophy of TV Noir*, p. 206); Samira Kawash, "Safe house? Body, building, and the question of security," *Cultural Critique*, 45 (2000), 185, 186.

17 Kate Ferguson Ellis, *The Contested Castle: Gothic Novels and the Subversion of Domestic Ideology* (Chicago: University of Illinois Press, 1989).

18 Brenton J. Malin, *American Masculinity under Clinton: Popular Media and the Nineties' Crisis of Masculinity* (New York: Peter Lang, 2005), p. 7.

19 See, for instance, "Loin Like a Hunting Flame" (1.11) and "Monster" (1.4).

20 John Fiske, *Television Culture* (1987) (New York: Routledge, 2006), p. 202. Oddly, Fiske ignores a key recurring female character in the series: the journalist Amy Allen (Melinda Culea) appeared in about a quarter of the episodes, beginning with the "Pilot."

21 The term "sacrifice" is repeatedly used in this context, especially late in season 1 and early in season 2.

22 Malin, *American Masculinity*.

23 The episode's title names four ranks of angels in early Christian thought, terms which appear in Colossians 1:16: "For by him were all things created, that are in heaven, and that are in earth, visible and invisible, whether *they be* thrones, or dominions, or principalities, or powers."

24 William Shakespeare, *Hamlet*, *The Norton Shakespeare*, 2nd edn, ed. Stephen Greenblatt et al. (New York: Norton, 2008), 1.5.168–69; Horace Walpole is explicit about his Shakespearean debts in the first gothic novel, *The Castle of Otranto*, and a number of recent scholars have discussed the significance of *Hamlet* in particular to the gothic (see, e.g., Hogle, "Frankenstein' as neo-gothic").

3

Latchkey hero: the horrors of class in Eric Kripke's *Supernatural*

> "Redneck Aliens Take Over Trailer Park"
>
> *Weekly World News* (2006)

> TOBY: You know, eventually, you may have to resort to manhood.
> JOSH: I'm the victim here – how am I supposed to be a man?
>
> "Faith-Based Initiative" (*West Wing* 6.10)

The first two seasons of *Supernatural*, along with Kripke's slightly earlier work, the film *Boogeyman* (2005),[1] like the series discussed in the previous chapter, participate in a post-Clinton interest in masculinity and an alienated white underclass.[2] For instance, while they do not seem to have been much discussed (if at all) in connection with each other, the similarities between the early seasons of *Supernatural* and the comedy series *My Name Is Earl* (2005–2009) are striking: both aired on Thursday nights, premiered just one week apart in 2005, and are recognized for their retro-music choices.[3] Moreover, both focus on the relationship between two brothers who habitually sleep in a shared motel room, stress the brothers' longstanding use of petty crime to support themselves, and centrally rely on non-Christian, even non-Western, belief systems. In *My Name Is Earl*, the Buddhist concept of karma is the mechanism through which Earl Hickey imagines turning his life around, away from crime and toward communal harmony. In *Supernatural*, the entities fought by the brothers are taken from a globalized mythology, explicitly traced to belief systems from Europe, the Middle East, and pre-colonial America, representations often evocative of Neil Gaiman's *American Gods*: "When the people came to America they brought us with them. They brought me, and Loki and Thor, Anansi and the Lion-God, Leprechauns and Kobolds and Banshees, Kubera and Frau Holle and Ashtaroth, and they brought you. We rode here in their minds, and we took root. We travelled with the settlers to the new lands across the ocean."[4] While the comic impetus (in the Aristotelian sense) of *My Name Is Earl* allows karma to take Earl step by step closer to being "normal" – that is, middle-class, particularly toward the end of the second season when Earl finally gets a (literally) white-collar job – there is no such progressive narrative in *Supernatural*. With a "supernatural" twist, class emerges in Kripke's series as the "beast in the closet"[5] that is haunting America, using the supernatural to gothically tie downward class mobility to the heightened vulnerability of children.

"Class" is, of course, a suspect cultural category. As Gwendolyn Audrey Foster notes,

> The defining terms we have traditionally used to discuss *class* and *class mobility* are outdated and outmoded. Terms such as *blue-collar* and *white-collar* are as dated as the concepts of neat, distinctive categories such as "high culture," "middle culture," and "low culture." Fantasies of cultural mobility are so pernicious throughout popular culture that the realities of classed experience are frequently masked and perhaps even, arguably, surpassed in importance by postmodern ideas about the self and performed identity.[6]

Foster's phrasing itself marks a blindness about class: mobility is, by tacit definition, upward. But if the "realities of classed experience are frequently masked," including the fact of downward mobility in the wake of the erosion of the manufacturing sector and the employer-driven shift to part-time labor, the *fictions* of working-class experience remain and largely on terms that stabilize class hierarchy: the blue-collar work ethic and its attendant construction of stoic masculinity that will accept hardship; lack of access to education and more generally to cultural capital; and the comic type of the lower-class buffoon, a tradition that can be traced back to Shakespeare's plays. For instance, the official website for *My Name Is Earl* remarked on Earl's "seemingly limited intelligence" and his "dim-witted friends,"[7] tacitly assuming a viewership that enjoys feeling superior to the show's characters rather than questions the socioeconomic conditions that limit their options, even though Earl must win a lottery to finance his turn away from crime, his successful attempt to get his GED (equivalent to a high school education), and so forth.[8] *Supernatural*, engaging questions of educational differences, cultural mores, and even conflicting religious perspectives, while also confronting the ways in which the Winchesters appear to conform to the profile of members of dangerous rural militia groups, offers a particularly complex depiction of working-class masculinities that does not always take as its framing perspective that of the higher social strata.

"Just a kid": working-class origins and male vulnerability

While *Supernatural* has done well enough to run for more than ten seasons, despite some difficult timeslots in the early years, Kripke's film *Boogeyman* (2005), produced by powerhouse Sam Raimi, had some early box-office success but was largely panned as clichéd and slow-paced by reviewers who focused on the disappointing monster and the movie's stylistic debts to Japanese horror movies and their Hollywood imitations.[9] Conventionality can be deceiving, however. In both *Boogeyman* and *Supernatural* – setting aside the gothic apparatus, CGI, and horror set pieces – the failure of a father to protect his son from a violent world is represented as disabling the son's access to the American Dream and confining him to a class position lower than the one he enjoyed in early childhood. This new class position is defined in multiple ways: the lack of a stable home, a single-parent family, retro cars and work clothes (though with fashionable flourishes for the Hollywood aesthetic). Both the movie and the series, moreover, deal with the traumatized boy's failed attempts at class-passing.

Boogeyman opens with an 8-year-old boy, Tim, afraid of the title monster because of the stories his father has told him. He asks his father to search his room for hidden threats so that he can sleep but, as the father checks the closet, the Boogeyman abruptly drags him in. The next scenes, focusing on Tim as an adult (Barry Watson), establish first his professional success and then his ongoing trauma: we see him at a party in a luxurious office space for a magazine where he works as an associate editor alongside his rich, blonde girlfriend, Jessica (Tory Mussett), then at his home where there are no closets and his refrigerator has a glass door. While the opening scene places Tim within a working-class, rural, likely Midwest environment, the next scenes situate him as a young, urban professional who can afford good housing and high-end consumer goods that accommodate his fear of closets. The visual reminder of his fear is contextualized by a phone call from his uncle, pressuring him to spend Thanksgiving at home so that his mother can see him. Tim's separation from his family and access to urban success are thus linked, but they are then undercut when Tim arrives in his retro car at the palatial home of Jessica's parents and sits down to Thanksgiving dinner with them. In seconds, another dimension of the closet trauma is revealed. The father's abduction by the Boogeyman has officially become a stereotypical narrative of lower-class dysfunction in which Tim and his mother were abandoned by a ne'er-do-well father and then fell into a spiral of poverty and mental illness:

> JESSICA: Tim's had kind of a strained relationship with his parents. Tim's father ran out when he was eight.
> JESSICA'S SISTER: Oh, that's sad.
> JESSICA: Then he had to go live with his uncle, in a tiny room in the back of his bar.
> JESSICA'S FATHER: Well, what about your mother?
> TIM: She sort of had a tough time after my dad left. It was pretty hard on both of us.[10]

Any of Tim's illusions about fitting into Jessica's world are brought to an abrupt end and he asks Jessica when they are alone, "Is that why you wanted me here, to freak out your family?"

While the film draws on conventions that suggest child abuse, including an overtly Oedipal scene between Tim and his mother's specter, the Boogeyman is strongly tied to Jessica's father: in the first scene with Tim as an adult, a friend, on finding out that Tim is spending Thanksgiving with Jessica's family, scoffs, "if he can survive the weekend with Jessica's father!" and then reminds Jessica that her father terrorized her as a child by throwing her into the water to teach her how to swim. Since the film centers on Tim surviving a weekend with the Boogeyman, the parallel is in plain sight along with the broader message that fathers terrorize their children, one we have already seen in some gothic TV series. But class is not simply articulated through the rich-as-Boogeyman. In nearly every conversation Jessica has with Tim, she ignores his feelings and family attachments while berating him for not behaving as she thinks fit: at the office party, she asks, "You're not getting weird on me again, are you?"; at her house, she complains, as he talks on the phone to his uncle about the urgent need for him to return home (his mother has just died), "What is *wrong* with you? Gawd ...!" Later, she tries to seduce him as he sits nearly catatonic on a motel-room bed, still in shock after being surrounded by the specters of dozens of children abducted by the Boogeyman:

> How're you doing? [*silence*] Tim, come on. I drove four and a half hours to see you here. [*silence*] I can't do this anymore, okay? It's too much, and I'm too tired. Look, can't we just forget about all the bad stuff for one night? Try to have some fun? Pretend that nothing else is out there? [*kisses him*]

Tim is, as Sam and Dean frequently describe themselves in *Supernatural*, a "freak," at least from Jessica's perspective. His family history and his failure to react as Jessica expects, whether at the office party or after he flees his family's haunted house, alienate him from the very upward mobility he seems to have in the early scenes. The logic of the film is straightforward: knowledge of what "is out there" is denied by Jessica but must be faced by Tim. That Jessica goes missing almost immediately after this scene and is never found, despite the film's positive conclusion, furthers the suggestion that the appearance of the Boogeyman is tied to the shock of class difference, and specifically the gap between Tim's family's class position before his father's disappearance and that after his loss, and the gap between Tim's newfound professional status and that of Jessica's very wealthy family. Jessica, secure in her bubble of wealth and privilege, can ignore such horror; Tim, moving in the chasm between classes, cannot.

In *Supernatural*, the trauma also begins with a variation on the Oedipal myth in a large non-urban family home, here in small-town Kansas. But instead of a father leaving the boy alone with his mother, Kripke offers a more gothically rendered violation of the mother. It is a scene repeated in many episodes' opening sequence: supernaturally held to the nursery's ceiling, on fire, with a cut across her torso (somewhat suggestive of an incision for a Caesarian section), Mary Winchester drips blood onto her infant son Sam's head until her husband, ex-marine and garage co-owner John Winchester, enters the room, picks up Sam and flees the nursery to give the baby to a 4-year-old Dean who is ordered to take his brother to safety (and, rather incredibly for a preschooler, implicitly carry him down a flight of stairs). This is the origin of the arc narrative that shapes the first two seasons of the series which are my concern here: in the first episode of the series, Sam's girlfriend dies the same way as his mother, and so the two brothers join their father's hunt for the demon that killed both women; in the finale of the second season, the demon is destroyed with the participation of all three Winchester men.

Sam as an adult follows Tim's upwardly mobile trajectory: in the first episode, he is pre-law at Stanford and living with an ideal girlfriend who is also blonde and named Jessica. His friends at Stanford include Rebecca, whose family home is as palatial as that of Jessica's parents in *Boogeyman*, and he retains from this life a smartphone through which he accesses e-mails from his Stanford friends and a notebook computer that he uses in nearly every episode (see "Skin" 1.6). Completely out of contact with his family while at Stanford, Sam, like Tim, cut off all familial ties in order to make a differently classed life of his own. In *Supernatural*, however, there is also a brother who, like Tim at Jessica's dinner table, inhabits stereotypical narratives of lower-class dysfunction.

For most of season 1, the circumstances of the Winchesters' childhood after their mother's death are vague: they moved around with their father but somehow got a formal education, were sometimes left with other hunters while their father was away, and were trained as hunters by their father. In "Something Wicked" (1.18), however, where the demon-of-the-week is a Shtriga, known for feeding on children, a bleaker picture is drawn: their father would also leave them alone for days while he went "hunting." Through flashbacks, the episode depicts Dean, about 11 years old, solely responsible for taking care of his younger brother in a motel room with a kitchenette. In a flashback triggered by a Shtriga's footprint, Dean and John Winchester rehearse the instructions for staying safe alone. The rehearsal is on one level quite mundane: how many rings indicate that John is calling, who to phone if there is a problem, and other common protocols for underage children left alone. But as they discuss phone security John readies a shotgun and props it up against the wall, and later asks Dean what he is supposed to do if "something tries to bust in": "shoot first," the child answers, "ask questions later." The disorienting effects of these details are compounded by having the actors stand during the conversation, John Winchester (played by 6'2" actor Jeffrey Dean Morgan) physically towering over his slight, pre-teen son (Ridge Canipe). In another flashback, Dean makes his brother dinner but, when Sam demands "Lucky Charms" instead, throws out the hot meal and gives him the cereal, even though it is all they have left and Dean wanted it for his breakfast. Otherwise, Sam is left within a few feet of the television or asleep in bed – passive, even infantilized. After three days alone with Sam, Dean gets bored and leaves his brother asleep in the motel room to play video games, but returns to find the Shtriga feeding on his brother. He picks up a shotgun and aims, but hesitates, as his father bursts through the door, firing his gun, and then rushes to comfort Sam before berating Dean for failing to fulfill his orders. Dean finishes telling the story to Sam:

> DEAN: Dad grabbed us and booked, dropped us off at Pastor Jim's about three hours away. By the time he got back to Fort Douglas the Shtriga had disappeared – just gone. Never resurfaced until now. You know, Dad never spoke about it again. I didn't ask. But he uh he looked at me different, you know, which was worse. Not that I blame him. He gave me an order and I didn't listen and I almost got you killed.
> SAM: You were just a kid.
> DEAN: Don't. Don't…

Dean is represented on pathetic terms as he tries to deal as a child with adult responsibilities and as an adult with his guilt over his failure to protect his brother from the Shtriga – and, like Wesley and Angel, suffers the psychological wound of a father's disappointment. This crisis is echoed by another child, Michael, who inhabits the same position in the present as Dean in the past: his mother runs the motel where the Winchester brothers stay, and Michael is not only shown staffing the motel's reception desk but also pouring milk for his brother's dinner, triggering Dean's memory of doing the same for Sam.[11] And, with narrative compactness, the Shtriga attacks Michael's brother and the Winchesters help him to defeat it, keeping both younger brothers safe and both older brothers effective surrogate parents.

At the critical moment when the pre-teen Dean leaves the motel room, the camera lingers on him locking the door and then putting the key in his pocket, visually reinforcing the episode's identification of him as a latchkey kid, a near-euphemism in post-World War II popular culture for lower-class children at risk.[12] That he leaves the room at night and is only sent back when the arcade closes adds to the sense of threat: about 11 years old, he is out for hours after dark, and he has left his brother, about 7 years old, alone in a motel room with a loaded shotgun. The Shtriga emerges as a gothic symbol of a series of economically produced threats in plain sight: two young children left alone for days in a cheap motel, their food running out, the sole parent absent because of work, and a loaded shotgun leaning against the wall.

The gothic rendering of lower-class children's vulnerability is repeated in a series of conversations about childhood innocence. When Michael confesses to seeing the Shtriga, he tells Dean, "I thought I was having a nightmare," and Dean replies, "I'd give anything not to tell you this, but sometimes nightmares are real." The theme of protecting childhood innocence reappears in "All Hell Breaks Loose 2" (2.22), as Dean soliloquizes before Sam's (temporarily) dead body:

> You know, when we were little, and you couldn't have been more than 5, you just started asking questions. "How come we didn't have a mom? Why do we always have to move around? Where'd Dad go?" He'd take off for days at a time. I remember I begged you, "Quit asking, Sammy, man, you don't want to know." I just wanted you to be a kid. Just for a little while longer.

Such slippages between two forms of innocence – innocence of the supernatural, and innocence of a life of absent parents and itinerant living – is central to the series' tying of class to the gothic. All of "little" Sammy's questions could be asked within any narrative in which a child recognizes the difference between his life and that middle-to-upper-class existence which the media tells him is normal, but the answers to all of these questions lie in the gothic: their mother was killed by a demon, their father's pursuit of the supernatural after their mother's death drew the attention of child services so they had to flee Kansas ("Home" 1.9), and Dad is away hunting ghosts and demons. That Sam's age marks Dean as 9 or 10 years old when Sam was asking these questions only reinforces Dean's childhood loss; as his brother's primary caregiver and protector "for days at a time," he already knows at the age of ten all that Sam would lose by knowing the truth. This representation of the Winchesters' childhood continues in later seasons. In "After School Special" (4.13), for instance, Dean, now in Grade 12, tells his girlfriend that he has no curfew because his father has left him and Sam alone for two weeks: she is horrified, and asks him if he misses having his father around, his teenage bravado colliding with her assumptions about domesticity and childhood security.

In "The Uncanny," Sigmund Freud famously argues that the nineteenth-century gothic tale, "The Sandman" by E. T. A. Hoffman, metaphorically depicts castration anxiety through the boy's fear that the Sandman will steal his eyes. In *Supernatural* and *Boogeyman*, class rather than sex is the ground of the boys' vulnerability. Tim spends his childhood in a psychiatric center, while Dean spends his parenting his brother or helping his father fight demons, and both find themselves tied to that same world as adults. In both instances, the supernatural marks the moment of shifting class position as one of horror. Before his father's disappearance, Tim lived in a comfortable rural home with two parents and lots of toys, and afterwards he had to live with his uncle (though not in the back of a bar, as Jessica claims while she is trying to shock her parents). Before the death of their mother, the Winchesters lived in a comfortable home in Lawrence, Kansas, their father the part-owner of a business; after Mary Winchester's death, they move from motel to motel, living on credit card fraud because their father is always hunting. Downward mobility is narratively triggered not by economic crisis but by a gothic displacement of it – a supernatural event that propels young boys into an unsafe world where nightmares, and poverty, are real.

"Kind of butch": rejecting Middle America

The Winchester brothers, as their popularity on CW and fansites suggest, broadly fill the popular type of hunky heroes who fight the bad and protect the good. They drink beer out of the bottle, win fistfights, outsmart nearly everyone, can (if they want) get the girl in each episode, interact easily with children, often making them feel safer, and engage in witty banter. But despite their shared background and status as "tough guys," the brothers are classed and gendered differently, precisely because of their different relationship to the originary supernatural trauma. Sam does not remember his mother or her death or much of what Dean associates with a difficult childhood; he is depicted as the more sensitive and soft-spoken brother, and is capable of, as well as invested in, upward mobility. Dean does remember their mother, having to carry his brother out of their burning home the night she died, and much more of their childhoods; in short, he remembers the downward turn, from the big house where his mother tucked him in to the rundown motels where he had to care for his brother. He neither pursues upward mobility nor accepts middle-class values; he is "the rugged bad boy" as an early CW site for the series puts it,[13] with significant debts to the "strong and silent" type of *film noir* and Westerns. While fan response has tended to see Sam as the series' protagonist, Kripke has another view:

> I've heard this comment before, and I just don't get it. Not even a little. It's never been a show about Sam. ... A big brother watching out for a little brother, wondering if you have to kill the person you love most, family loyalty versus the greater good, family obligation versus personal happiness. ... These are all issues that Dean faces, and in my opinion, they are just as rich, if not richer, than psychic children and demonic plans. ... It's never going to be a show about just Sam, or just Dean for that matter.[14]

Sam is the hero of a mythic quest; Dean is the center of the series' exploration of competing ideologies and values, including the fractures in popular depictions of working-class life. As the first two seasons unfold, the stoic blue-collar hero unravels.

Dean's "bad boy" masculinity is repeatedly marked as a mask or performance by Sam and implicitly by Dean's frequent references to movie tough guys and rock drummers. After they are mistaken (again) for a couple, Dean asks Sam why: Sam replies, "Well, you are kind of butch – probably think you're overcompensating" ("Playthings" 2.11).[15] But this constructed masculinity is significantly conditioned by class. As Foster argues, in much mainstream US culture, "Class mobility is marked by the contradictory impulses implicit in the capitalist American Dream. On the one hand, the consumer is taught to work hard, the idea being that with pep and determination she can be upwardly mobile. On the other hand, the consumer is taught that, above all, he must be a hedonist, he must be wildly acquisitional."[16] In the early seasons, Sam's ties to his Stanford life follow this pattern. Sam is so successful as a student that he is awarded full funding for his undergraduate work, allowing him to acquire a nice apartment, cellphone, computer, and so forth, and he is about to be interviewed for a full scholarship to law school when the series opens. When Sam leaves his brother briefly in

"Scarecrow" (1.11), he is weighed down by a backpack, a satchel, and a duffle bag. But Dean, who has experienced downward mobility (and not as mere downward class-passing, briefly discussed by Foster), is strikingly unconsumerist: he has a simpler cellphone than his brother and drives his father's old car, and both are essential for his job. He has had the same music cassettes for years ("Pilot" 1.1), possibly his father's originally, does not seem to have a CD or mp3 player until he gets a music-capable cellphone in a later season, and borrows Sam's computer. The difference between the brothers' consumerist ethics is used to comic effect in "Phantom Traveler" (1.4) when Sam laughs at Dean's homemade EMF meter for detecting ghost traces.[17] Dean fails to see the problem or the joke; it works, and the fact that he did not buy it is irrelevant to him. As hunters, the brothers follow Dean's lead. Although they have access to money through credit card fraud, the money is directed entirely at basic living expenses and the work; they stay at cheap motels, eat take-out food, and only buy new clothes when needed for hunting as in, for instance, "Phantom Traveler," so that the same shirts, jeans, and jackets often reappear in different episodes. If, as Susan Jeffords suggests, "identities are defined increasingly in relation to patterns of consumption and shared product references rather than to historic affiliations with concepts of region,"[18] then a series that takes as its founding premise local legends – "every town's got its stories, right?" ("Asylum" 1.10) – logically allies itself with characters who function aslant this trend. To hunt in *Supernatural* is to be immersed in the local, not the multinational-driven culture of brand recognition and globalized consumerism, and this is understood in the series as an insistently classed move.

Dean's separation from middle-class mores goes beyond consumerism and socioeconomic circumstances. For instance, until he is actually "touched by an angel" in season 4, Dean is represented as skeptical of Christianity and, more generally, he does "not believe good's out there" ("Faith" 1.12). As the series develops, this skepticism is connected explicitly to the trauma of their mother's death. In the middle of season 2, Dean tells Sam, for the first time, of a childhood memory. Throughout the first half of the episode, the brothers argue about the existence of angels, with Dean insisting with uncharacteristic vehemence that "there's no such thing" and referring to "those angel yarns" and "this angel crap":

SAM: Maybe we're hunting an angel here and we should stop. Maybe this is God's will.

DEAN: OK, alright, you know what, I get it, you've got faith. That's, hey, good for you – I'm sure it makes things easier. I'll tell you who else had faith like that: Mom. She used to tell me when she tucked me in that angels were watching over us, in fact that was the last thing she ever said to me.

SAM: You never told me that.

DEAN: What's to tell? She was wrong. There was nothing protecting her. There's no higher power, there's no god. I mean, there's just chaos and violence and random unpredictable evil that comes out of nowhere and rips you to shreds.

("Houses of the Holy" 2.13)

Sam, however, with no memory of his mother or her death, does have Christian faith: he not only takes Dean to a Christian faith healer in "Faith," but also tells him in "Houses of the Holy" that he prays every day. Both "Faith" and "Houses of the Holy" end with Dean's skepticism slightly shaken, but in both Dean is placed firmly outside of normative Christianity and, in "Houses of the Holy," specifically because of the loss of his mother. The childhood vulnerability stressed in "Something Wicked" is sustained in the adult's atheism as his belief that the world, in which he was propelled from middle-class security, with his mother and angels guarding him, to a latchkey kid armed with a shotgun, is "just chaos and violence and random unpredictable evil."

Dean's resistance to middle-class TV-defined norms is established through other avenues as well. Bricolage and the self-referentiality of the horror genre are used in the early seasons to class the brothers' knowledge: Sam knows the law, US history (from art history to the history of serial killers in the USA), and computers; Dean knows movies, popular music, and how to repair, even rebuild, his '67 Impala. An exchange in "Croatoan" (2.9) is typical:

SAM: Roanoke? Lost colony? Ring a bell? Dean, did you pay any attention in history class?

DEAN: Yeah. The shot heard around the world, how bills become laws.

SAM: That's not school – that's *Schoolhouse Rock*.

DEAN: Whatever.

More suggestive, however, is Dean's reaction to middle-class homes. Early in the series, Dean walks through a new suburb and tells Sam, "Growing up in a place like this would freak me out. … The manicured lawns, 'How was your day, honey?' I'd blow my brains out" ("Bugs" 1.8). The ideal suburban domestic does not conceal or repress, or even exhibit vulnerability, as in much horror film and television.[19] It is, in its ideal form, a site of terrible strangeness to Dean. And perhaps with good cause: one of the early expositions of Dean's complexity as a character occurs in the next episode, "Home" (1.9), when Dean sneaks away from Sam to call their father. With trembling voice and choking back tears, entirely at odds with his "tough guy" persona to date, Dean leaves a message that he has returned to the suburban house where their mother died and he needs his father desperately. This is not, then, simply the cliché of the hypermasculine man who fears suburban conformity as a threat to US individualism or the longstanding gothic threat of domestication-as-emasculation – although there is at least one joke in this vein in "Bugs" – not least because it is imagined from the space of boyhood ("Growing up in a place like this"). As Kawash notes, "Throughout the postwar period, the house has held a signal place in the US cultural imaginary, providing an affective and symbolic locus for the virtues and desires through which the national subject is interpellated and normalized," including the "American Dream" as Foster defines it.[20] The early seasons of *Supernatural* are a radical intervention in this imaginary. They are less concerned with threats to the middle-class normativity that defines the US subject or with a critique of that normativity, though certainly a number of episodes do work through these established gothic themes in relation to single-episode characters. Rather, the series views class in relation to masculinity from an innovative perspective in which the experience of downward mobility gothically shadows the dominance of the fantasy of upward mobility, a dominance echoed by fans' early perception that Stanford Sam is the real hero of the series. Dean does not desire the suburbs, as a return to his preschool childhood or as the effect of adult economic security or social privilege: his notion of "family," of the ideal he seeks to restore in the first season as the ground of the terms on which he has been "interpellated and normalized," is grasped as the three Winchester men on the road hunting together ("Shadow" 1.16), "blue-collar" and "greasy" as Kripke puts it.[21] The suburban house remains a site of loss, of a childhood terror that voids all desire for it.

At the same time, the series avoids conventional critiques of middle-class homogeneity which would depict Dean as simply freed of middle-class constraints through his lower-class position. The negative effects of class on Dean are instead as sustained as the effects of the childhood traumas that haunt the character and shape his obsession with protecting his brother. While Dean is aesthetically and narratively valued in terms of blue-collar masculinity – that "rugged bad boy" on the CW website – the dialogue often undercuts his masculinity by challenging his authority on the basis of precisely his classed gender performance: Dean, like Tim in *Boogeyman*, is frequently instructed on proper conduct. The preteen Dean of "Something Wicked" defends himself when his father complains that he is not paying enough attention to his instructions: "It's just we've gone over it like a million times, and you know I'm not stupid." But the adult Dean is simply silent when he is corrected, taking his chastisement like a man, and directions like an inferior. Sam, with significant time invested in the world of Stanford University, lectures him on middle-class morality and corrects his behavior when they attempt to masquerade in more mainstream roles, by telling him to "tone it down" when they are impersonating priests in "Nightmare" (1.14), for instance. In "Home" (1.9), Missouri (Loretta Devine), John Winchester's friend, snaps at Dean, "Boy, you put your foot on my coffee table I'm going to whack you with a spoon," smacks him on the back of the head and calls him stupid when she thinks he has been impolite, and orders him to clean up a kitchen that has been destroyed by a poltergeist, while speaking softly to Sam, calling him "honey," and telling him how sorry she is about the way his life is veering away from normalcy. Even when he is behaving properly for the context he is marked as deviant. While they are undercover in prison, Sam asks Dean, incredulously, "Does it bother you at all how easily you seem to fit in here?" ("Fulsom Prison Blues" 2.19). While *Die Hard* famously batters the body of the hypermasculine hero, *Supernatural* also batters that hero's ego through a discourse of class that aligns Dean with the immoral, even criminal, and represents him as subject to the orders of others and less valuable than his upwardly mobile brother, a battering that comes to fruition in the final episodes of season 2.

Alluded to in the first season and explored for much of the second season through Dean's apparent death-wish, self-abjection gradually emerges as the keynote of Dean's characterization. In "Skin" (1.6), a shapeshifter masquerading as Dean exposes his secret: "Me, I know I'm a freak and sooner or later everybody's going to leave me." In the early episodes of season 2, he is weighed down by guilt that he lives because his father, a tacitly more worthy person in his view, has died in his place. At the end of the second season, Dean's problem is fully revealed when family friend Bobby (Jim Beaver), a surrogate father to the Winchester brothers throughout most of the series, discovers that Dean has made a deal with a demon to resurrect Sam in exchange for Dean's soul after just one more year of life. Dean tells Bobby that the deal will make him worthwhile at last: "my life can mean something." Standing in the middle of his junkyard, uncharacteristically verging on tears, Bobby asks Dean, "What? And it didn't before? Have you got that low an opinion of yourself? Are you that screwed in the head?" ("All Hell Breaks Loose 2" 2.22). In the same episode, the demon that the brothers have pursued through two seasons also comments on Dean's self-esteem problem, mocking Dean, as he lies prone on the ground, "I couldn't have done it without your pathetic self-loathing, self-destructive desire to sacrifice yourself for your family." That Dean's "self-loathing" is recognized and condemned by two powerful male figures who are, like Dean, well outside of "mainstream" America, stresses the pathologization of Dean's internalization of class abjection rather than identification of it as an inevitable feature of blue-collar masculinity.

Dean's masculinity is thus consistently classed but within a contradictory framing of his "blue-collar" status that recalls Malin's understanding of President Clinton's popular image as "simultaneously *hyper* and *hypo*masculine":[22] in one frame, Dean operates outside of the consumerist, homogenizing aesthetic of suburbia, freed of property, legality, and other middle-class constraints in a Route 66 ideal of "butch" power, and in the other he internalizes his class position as self-abjection, incapable of moving anywhere but downward to self-annihilation. Both are overtly tied to the loss of innocence from which he tries to protect Sam and others, and as such are inextricable from each other. As in *Boogeyman*, the problem is not a particular class position or even the so-called "crisis of masculinity" in which men compare themselves to unachievable masculine ideals.[23] Rather, Dean and Tim are caught up in a "crisis of class" through the juxtaposition of different classes –

a juxtaposition pursued in *Supernatural* through the Stanford-educated Sam and AC/DC fan Dean, though not as a neatly opposed pair. Even as Sam operates as a normative gaze, judging Dean's behavior according to middle-class notions of propriety and ethics, his upward mobility is marked as performance. Sam never talked to Jessica about his family or told her about "the family business," for instance, though they were together for over a year, but Dean told his girlfriend Cassie after just a few weeks ("Pilot" 1.1; "Route 666" 1.13). Sam, in short, while widely accepted at Stanford through a circle of wealthy friends, had to remain deeply closeted about his background in order to class-pass, while Dean, refusing to class-pass, remained more authentic. When Dean tells Sam he wishes Sam could be "Joe College" again, while Free's "All Right Now" plays in the background, Sam replies, "That's OK. You know, truth is, even at Stanford I never really fit in" ("Skin"1.6). The first two seasons of *Supernatural* thus keep class clearly in view without falling into simple stereotypes or determinisms, not least by firmly identifying Dean as a blue-collar hero while decoupling him from any secure or stable sense of self.

Black and blue: racing the latchkey hero

While the first season of *Supernatural* focuses on the brothers' search for their father, the second follows their integration into a larger world of "hunters," almost universally depicted as male, white, rural, working class, and un-suburban, inhabiting junkyards, roadhouses, and remote rural cabins. But in the series' depiction of demon hunters, the series risks veering into the idealization of rural militia, a connection that is explicitly addressed in "Nightshifter" (2.12) as Dean is on the phone with an FBI agent:

HENRICKSEN: I know about your dad.

DEAN: You don't know crap about my dad.

HENRICKSEN: Ex-marine, raised his kids on the road, cheap motels, backwood cabins, real paramilitary-survivalist type. I just can't get a handle on what type of wacko he was. White supremacist, Timmy McVeigh? Tomato, tomahto.

DEAN: You got no right talking about my dad like that. He was a hero.

Here, the series "hangs a lantern" on an easy allegorical reading of the hunters in *Supernatural* as a rural militia group, protecting post-9/11 America from evil with their secret caches of heavy-duty guns and other weaponry, ex-military personnel, and low-tech concealment of their activities. The military-like rearing of the Winchester brothers is clear from their interactions with their father: he gives them "orders," texts them map coordinates to send them on a hunting job, and when they are reunited after months apart (years apart for Sam), the brothers answer "yes, sir!" in martial unison ("Shadow" 1.16). In the first two seasons' handling of race in America, the "white supremacist" threat is assuaged somewhat through Dean though not always on particularly reflexive terms. Overall, Dean is depicted as having greater access to a multiracial America than his upwardly mobile brother but is still insistently separated from blackness through the one hunter in the early seasons who is not marked as white. Moreover, he is most emotionally and physically battered in the only episode of the first two seasons to address a demon associated with Islam.

Dean is central in two episodes that deal with black history in the south: "Route 666" (1.13) in which the brothers help Dean's ex-girlfriend, Cassie, deal with the ghost of a racist white man who, when alive, assaulted local African-Americans out of rage that his white ex-girlfriend was dating a black man (a couple that would become Cassie's parents); "Crossroad Blues" (2.8), a tale of Faustian deals with the devil. In "Crossroad Blues," a man buries some artifacts at a crossroads to raise a demon and make a deal with his soul as the price – a price due in ten years. In the narrative present, it is an African-American painter, George Darrow; in the narrative past, provided through a series of flashbacks that frame the episode, it is Robert Johnson (1911–1938), the African-American blues artist rumored to have made such a deal. But, in the narrative present, the closed economy of the deal has gone awry: instead of leaving after making the deal with the painter, the demon has stayed and made more deals at a nearby roadhouse. These deals are all with white characters who are, in the episode's present, extremely wealthy: a woman who wished to be chief surgeon at a hospital, a man who asked to become a successful architect, and a rich man who, in an ethical complication of the brothers' position that the deal-makers are getting what they deserve, asked for his dying wife's health to be restored. Now, ten years later, the hellhounds are coming to collect the demon's fee; the architect dies first, then the surgeon. Darrow is still alive because he has used hoodoo to protect himself in his apartment, an apartment full of compelling paintings but unknown because he asked for talent rather than socioeconomic success – the implication, too, of the framing narrative of Johnson. The racialization of both the deal-makers and class position is obvious, particularly in an episode produced after Hurricane Katrina in which the intersections of class and race were widely discussed,[24] and is compounded by the different appearances of the demon – apparently a black woman when making deals with the painter and the blues singer, but apparently a white woman during deals with the rest of the male characters, including the final confrontation with Dean. The episode does not depict the one woman's deal being made, avoiding the complication it would cause in the gendering of the devil and the sexualization of the pact as a seduction, particularly through the use of a kiss between the demon and the deal-maker to mark the agreement. (Late seasons allow male–male kisses to seal deals with the demon, but the deal-makers are represented as uncomfortable with the homosexual implications – the first such kiss is prefaced by the demon's remark, "You can cling to six decades of deep-seated homophobia, or give it up and get a complete bailout for your bank's ridiculous incompetence" ["Abandon All Hope" 5.10]).

While the Winchesters typically rely on research – town records, the father's journal, locals talking about folklore, or calling on their father's friends – to identify supernatural threats, in this episode Dean already has the expertise to solve the mystery, beginning with his recognition that a plant used in spells is growing on all four corners of a crossroad near the bar they are investigating. Sam contributes significantly, but it is Dean who sees the full implications. For instance, Sam recognizes the features of a spell "to summon a demon," and Dean clarifies, "Not just summon one. Crossroads are where pacts are made. These people are actually making deals with the damn thing." Later in the same scene, Sam makes the connection to Johnson and is again corrected:

SAM: So it's just like the Robert Johnson legend, right? I mean, selling your soul at the crossroads kind of deal.

DEAN: Except that wasn't a legend. You know his music. [*no reply*] You don't know Robert Johnson's songs? Sam, there's occult references all over his lyrics. I mean, "Crossroad Blues," "Mean Devil Blues," "Hell Hound on my Trail."

In all of *Supernatural*, this is the only expansion of Dean's musical interests beyond classic rock and it is explicitly distinguished from Sam's knowledge of music. Moreover, in the next episode, "Croatoan" (2.9), Dean verbally echoes Darrow, indicating he is weary of fighting the supernatural and prepared for death. Despite the firm color lines used in the episode, then, Dean is represented as being at the crossroads, so to speak, of those lines: he knows some hoodoo though not as much as Darrow, knows the blues better than Sam, is like Darrow in his weary waiting for death, and is lower-class like Darrow and Johnson but white like the surgeon and architect.

More significantly, "Crossroad Blues" (2.8) is tacitly bracketed by two episodes, "Bloodlust" (2.3) and "Hunted" (2.10), in which Dean confronts another "hunter," Gordon Walker (Sterling K. Brown). "Bloodlust" extends the moral complications of the second season by forcing the brothers to address the conundrum of vampires who choose not to kill.[25] Gordon is introduced as a hunter like John Winchester: he is a model of masculine determination, confidence and power. Dean and Gordon bond over beer, telling hunting stories, while Sam rejects the glorification of killing and sulkily returns to the motel room where he is kidnapped by one of the ethical vampires who brings him to their leader Lenore so that she can explain their situation; he is then safely returned to the motel and argues the vampires' case with Dean. Dean instead goes to help Gordon kill the vampires with some macho swagger about killing evil, an extension of the repeated characterization of Dean as a hunter who enjoys the kill as well as a response to Sam's concern earlier in the episode that Dean is taking unwarranted risks with his own life. But Dean arrives at the vampires' house to find Gordon torturing Lenore, and his horror at the scene causes him to quickly reverse his position and his loyalties. Dean and Gordon fight, in a protracted and particularly violent exchange that ends with Dean tying up Gordon and releasing Lenore. Dean defines new ethical boundaries for himself when he sees Gordon's pleasure in hunting turn from homosocial bonding through the hunt and storytelling to the perverted heterosexuality of torturing a female vampire for pleasure.

Casting, however, adds another layer to the narrative by depicting Gordon as African-American. This defines Dean's new ethical position in opposition to blackness, strongly recalling Toni Morrison's argument in *Playing in the Dark* and especially her call for "studies that analyze the strategic use of black characters to define the goals and enhance the qualities of white characters" in light of "the image of a reined-in, bound, suppressed, and repressed darkness [that] became objectified in American literature as an Africanist persona. ... [T]he duties of that persona – duties of exorcism and reification and mirroring – are on demand and display."[26] Visually, the episode takes as its moment of horror, the moment that triggers Dean's ethical revelation, the image of a black man standing over a bound white woman and taking pleasure in hurting her, an image with a long genealogy in racist discourse. Morrison's account precisely defines Gordon's function in the narrative: his body beaten and bound at the end of the episode ("reined-in, bound, suppressed"), his character reduced to a capacity for rampant violence that Dean has now purged from himself, his role is simply to reframe (and so "enhance," in Morrison's term) Dean's ethics. The second episode with Gordon, "Hunted," uses him the same way. Dean's father, just before dying, issued a new order to Dean: kill Sam if he becomes a danger to others, part of an arc narrative about Sam having some supernatural powers granted, through a drop of demon blood, by the demon that killed his mother. Dean is, in effect, caught between two longstanding moral principles propounded by his father – namely, protect Sam and kill the supernatural – that are suddenly contradictory. In their next meeting, "Hunted," Gordon has discovered Sam's secret and again is free of moral ambiguity: Sam is tainted by the supernatural and therefore must be killed. The brothers, of course, defeat Gordon again. This time, Sam, who Gordon aims to execute, tips the police to Gordon's weapons cache so that the object of vigilante justice puts the vigilante into the hands of official law enforcement, restoring the middle-class order that Sam frequently represents. In both episodes, Gordon embodies the hunting principles laid down by John Winchester as Dean has to establish his own ethical judgment, and so establish both his adulthood (as a separation from his father's law) and his superiority to the only black hunter in the first two seasons of the series. Dean is classed and abjected but still "white," with all of whiteness's assurances about sovereignty and ethical capacity, while Gordon states the racist position that Dean as an ethical, color-blind white man who listens to the blues must reject: vampires as a race must be annihilated ("Bloodlust") and, in a strong echo of discourses of miscegenation and racial purity, one drop of blood is enough to racially Other Sam ("Hunted").

In the last season 2 episode written by Raelle Tucker (also the writer for "Hunted"), Dean, the blue-collar hero, faces a Djinn, a blue-tinted orientalized demon. Chasing down the Djinn in an abandoned building in "What Is and What Never Should Be" (2.20), Dean is grabbed by the Djinn and suddenly finds himself asleep in an apartment, a woman by his side. Within a few minutes of episode time, he realizes that he is living a life in which his mother was not killed, the surviving Winchesters did not become itinerant hunters, Sam's girlfriend is still alive, and he is married to an attractive nurse. Dean relishes all of the suburban details of life with his mother, from getting her to repeat that angels watch over them to eating her sandwiches and mowing the lawn. He has also fully replaced his father in somewhat Oedipal terms: the father was co-owner of a garage before the tragedy, but in this alternate life John is dead and Dean is working as a mechanic at a garage. As with the series as a whole, the dominant narrative is not neatly sustained: this is supposed to be Dean's fantasy based on his unspoken wish when attacked by the Djinn, namely, "Mom never died; we never went hunting." But Dean is alienated from his brother in this fantasy life, and Dean also finds himself generally at odds with this middle-class world: he is uncomfortable at the nice restaurant that his mother and brother like, and the pattern of correcting Dean in the series is stressed in this episode through various comments on his behavior, including drinking, gambling, stealing, not being at work or at home with his wife (like a good suburbanite), and so forth. He accepts these critiques, as he has throughout the series, and only wishes to leave the fantasy because not hunting means that that the people the Winchester men have saved were left to die. Like a good hero, Dean rejects middle-class security and success in order to pursue self-sacrifice in hunting. More suggestively, the episode ends by closely recalling "Bugs," thirty-four episodes earlier in the series. In "Bugs" (1.8), Dean claims, "Growing up in a place like this would freak me out. … The manicured lawns, 'How was your day, honey?' I'd blow my brains out." In "What Is," he realizes that he can only escape the middle-class fantasy created for him the same way. Stabbing himself through the heart, he wakes up in the real world to discover that the illusion was created to keep him passive while he was hanged from a ceiling and his blood drained to feed the Djinn. In both episodes, suicide is the only way out of the nightmare of middle-class privilege – a self-annihilation that, like Dean's general ethic of self-sacrifice and concomitant problem of self-abjection, counters the American Dream's emphasis on consumption and being "wildly acquisitional," as Foster puts it.[27]

On one level, the episode is an elaboration of Dean's discomfort with Middle America, and Middle America's discomfort with him. The allegorical reading is straightforward: well-to-do suburbia, and the possibility of a blue-collar, latchkey kid having access to it, is simply a remote fantasy through which men such as Dean are kept passive while their bodies are used and their egos bruised. But, as with casting in "Bloodlust," the selection of the Djinn significantly compounds the episode's implications. Post-9/11, the representation of the lower classes is rendered more contemporaneously than general socioeconomic conditions and cultural practices (as in, say, *Roseanne* [1988–1997] and *Malcolm in the Middle* [2000–2006]) to suggest the war in Iraq. In the West, the military offers the lower classes access to education and the possibility of upward mobility. That Dean is offered a fantasy of middle-class privilege and security – a well-to-do family home, a professional wife, a successful brother (though, of course, Dean himself remains "blue-collar" and "greasy" as a garage mechanic) – to acquiesce to his body's violation by an Islamic demon thus extends the series' exploration of the position of the lower classes in the American imaginary in new directions. That he rejects that fantasy in order to defend the lives of others further allies him with a foundational military ethic in which self-sacrifice, rather than upward mobility, is supposed to be the central motivation. Legible as both a foreign threat to lower-class men's bodies and as a symbol of the impact of the war in Iraq itself on those bodies, the Djinn, on-screen for only a few seconds, functions as a device, like so many of the series' supernatural beings, through which to explore America's haunting by class after having safely disposed of the racist resonance of the hunter's persona through Gordon Walker. Dean, in short, is a "good soldier," not a "white supremacist, Timmy McVeigh," in a gothic depiction of the disproportionate effects of war on the lower classes.

While *My Name Is Earl* finds comedy in the lives of its characters and sentimental reassurance for Middle America in Earl Hickey's determination to make amends to all of those who he has wronged (though through karma rather than Alcoholics Anonymous),

Supernatural renders class difference and working-class alienation in gothic terms. "Overcompensating" through masculine performance for a childhood trauma tied to downward class mobility, a gun-toting hero who is chastised by powerful male figures for his pathologically low self-esteem, Dean Winchester is the site at which popular depictions of class and masculinity unravel, including those embodied, though occasionally complicated, by his more conventional brother. That this unravelling is propelled by gothic machinery keeps the focus of the series on the unravelling itself rather than any actual socioeconomic and cultural crises perpetuated by the dominance of the myths of suburbia, white masculine autonomy, and the American Dream. But the series nevertheless undercuts those myths, using the gothic to explore and challenge depictions of class and masculinity in twenty-first-century US popular culture from the perspective of a latchkey hero who has lost, rather than seeks to secure or escape, middle-class privilege and its assurances of bodily security and a well-ordered, knowable world.

Coda

The previous sections of this chapter are a slightly revised version of an essay I submitted to *Genders* in the late summer of 2007, as the third season of *Supernatural* was about to begin. It was published in early 2008, and has since been linked and discussed on a few fansites, including the Supernatural Wiki's list of academic articles; one response on *Sequential Tart* even suggests that a *Supernatural* character named "Julia Wright" is part of a larger reference to my 2008 essay in the episode, "I Believe the Children Are Our Future" (5.6).[28] In subsequent seasons of *Supernatural*, Dean's status has shifted somewhat as his brother has spiraled over to the dark side by consorting (in multiple senses of the term) with a demon, but the series has continued to address his sense of low self-worth. When first dealing with an angel's decision to rescue him from hell, Dean identifies various of his moral failings, including "stealing and ditching chicks," and suggests his self-sacrifices as a hunter only help him to break even, morally speaking ("Are You There, God? It's Me, Dean Winchester" 4.2). The series has also continued to call attention to the Winchesters' childhood status as essentially latchkey kids. In "A Very Supernatural Christmas," Dean has to steal presents for his brother Sam because their father, once again, has left them alone in a motel for longer than intended and will not be there for Christmas. In "I Believe the Children Are Our Future," the Winchesters discover another latchkey kid, Jesse, making his own dinner, and Sam remarks, "I used to make my own dinner too, when I was a kid." Even though the series veered in season 4 from a polyreligious framework in which folk belief, established religion, monsters and deities, all jostle for screen time, to a predominantly Christian one (with occasional appearances by gods from other world religions), it continues to understand the Winchesters on classed as well as gendered terms.

Notes

1 Kripke is the creator and, for the early seasons, the executive producer of *Supernatural*, and is credited as writer on a number of individual episodes; for *Boogeyman*, he was the author of the story and co-wrote the screenplay with Juliet Snowdon and Stiles White. *Boogeyman* was released in the USA in February 2005, while *Supernatural* premiered on the WB on September 13, 2005.

2 On the challenge that President Clinton, and Hillary Rodham Clinton, posed to classed and gendered norms during the Clinton presidency, see, e.g., Brenton J. Malin, *American Masculinity under Clinton: Popular Media and the Nineties' Crisis of Masculinity* (New York: Peter Lang, 2005); Stephen J. Ducat, *The Wimp Factor: Gender Gaps, Holy Wars, and the Politics of Anxious Masculinity* (Boston: Beacon Press, 2004); Loren Glass, "Publicizing the president's privates," *Postmodern Culture*, 9:3 (1999).

3 There is also significant overlap between the two series' soundtracks, from Bachman-Turner Overdrive to Blue Öyster Cult.

4 Neil Gaiman, *American Gods* (New York: HarperCollins, 2001), p. 137.

5 I take this influential phrase from Eve Kosofsky Sedgwick, *Epistemology of the Closet* (Berkeley: University of California Press, 1990).

6 Gwendolyn Audrey Foster, *Class-Passing: Social Mobility in Film and Popular Culture* (Carbondale: Southern Illinois University Press, 2005), p. 79.

7 "About." *My Name Is Earl*. NBC website. www.nbc.com/My_Name_Is_Earl/about <date of access: July 14, 2007> (no longer available).

8 The series certainly depicts its characters more complexly than the marketing blurb suggests, and directly addresses myriad biases and stereotypes such as these.

9 See, e.g., Stephen Cole, "Bogus horror flick belongs in the closet,"

Globe and Mail, February 5, 2005; Matthew Leyland, rev. of *Boogeyman*, *Sight & Sound*, 15:4 (April 2005), 47; Frank Scheck, rev. of *Boogeyman*, *Hollywood Reporter*, February 7, 2005.

10 The mother's mental illness is repeatedly suggested but not explicitly addressed, as here when it is indicated that she was unable to care for Tim; Tim's mental health is however the subject of a lengthy scene in which he visits a children's psychiatric center and the psychiatrist that cared for him as a boy.

11 It is also fifteen years between the first and second scenes of *Boogeyman* – the appearance of the monster and its defeat.

12 For a survey, and critique, of popular assumptions about "latchkey kids," see Dave Riley and Jill Steinberg, "Four popular stereotypes about children in self-care: implications for family life educators," *Family Relations: Interdisciplinary Journal of Applied Family Studies*, 53 (2004), 95–101. "Something Wicked" stresses the aspects of "self-care" that Riley and Steinberg suggest are being addressed through educational programs, namely "how to avoid being victimized by strangers" and "coping with fear, boredom, and loneliness" (p. 97).

13 "Cast," *Supernatural*, CW website, www.cwtv.com/shows/supernatural/cast/jensen-ackles <date of access: July 12, 2007>.

14 Eric Kripke, "Eric Kripke fields your questions about *Supernatural*," *TV Guide*, February 15, 2007. www.tvguide.com/News/eric-kripke-fields/070215–04 <date of access: June 28, 2007>; second ellipsis in original. Some fan response to an earlier version of this chapter, published in *Genders* in early 2008, objects to the de-centering of Sam. I am not suggesting, however, that Sam is not the hero – but that he is one kind of hero, and Dean is another. Sam, in the early seasons, exemplifies the possibility of upward mobility; Dean, at the same time, persistently marks the threat of downward mobility.

15 They face the same confusion in "Bugs" (1.8) and "Something Wicked" (1.18), for instance.

16 Foster, *Class-Passing*, p. 22.

17 This is a common variation on Matheson's EMR meter (see Richard Matheson's *Hell House* [1971]).

18 Susan Jeffords, "Breakdown: white masculinity, class and US action-adventure films," *Action and Adventure Cinema*, ed. Yvonne Tasker (New York: Routledge, 2004), p. 219.

19 For a particularly generative discussion of depictions of "the suburban landscape," see Robert Beuka, *SuburbiaNation: Reading Suburban Landscape in Twentieth-Century American Fiction and Film* (New York: Palgrave Macmillan, 2004); on the "suburban gothic," see, e.g., Kim Michasiw, "Some stations of suburban gothic," *American Gothic: New Interventions in a National Narrative*, ed. Robert K.

Martin and Eric Savoy (Iowa City: University of Iowa Press, 1998), pp. 236–57.

20 Samira Kawash, "Safe house? Body, building, and the question of security," *Cultural Critique*, 45 (2000), 185; Foster, *Class-Passing*, p. 22.

21 Kripke, "Commentary." This ideal fades with the father's death as well as the development of the character in new directions because of various moral crises, and is reversed in "What Is and What Never Should Be" (2.20), discussed below.

22 Malin, *American Masculinity*, p. 18.

23 Malin provides a useful historical overview in *American Masculinity*, pp. 11–15.

24 CNN anchor Wolf Blitzer, while speaking over footage of the Hurricane's aftermath, notoriously said, "so many of these people, almost all of them that we see, are so poor, and they are so black" (CNN, September 1, 2005) (available at www.youtube.com/watch?v=1Sfo32rlkiE).

25 This is the same conundrum central to Joss Whedon's *Buffy the Vampire Slayer* and *Angel*. Gordon also has the same trauma as *Angel*'s Gunn, the first regular in either Whedon series to be cast as African-American: a sister who was turned into a vampire. To add to the allusions to Whedon in "Bloodlust," Lenore is played by Amber Benson, a cast regular in *Buffy*.

26 Toni Morrison, *Playing in the Dark* (New York: Vintage, 1993), pp. 52–53, 38–39.

27 Foster, *Class-Passing*, p. 22.

28 See Suzette Chan, "Tarts talk about SPN 5.06: I Believe the Children Are Our Future," *Sequential Tart*, December 14, 2009, www.sequentialtart.com/article.php?id=1572. (The series' writers often incorporate references to the show's wider reception.)

4

Gothic foundations: "The Pest House," "Hell House," and "The Murder House"

> Shadow inserted his coin. The drunk in the graveyard raised his bottle to his lips. One of the gravestones flipped over, revealing a grasping corpse: a headstone turned around, flowers replaced by a grinning skull. ... The clockwork story was deeply unsettling.
>
> "You know why I show that to you? ... That is the world as it is. That is the real world. It is there, in that box."
>
> Neil Gaiman, *American Gods* (2001)

> Our Father which art in heaven, Hollywood be thy name.
>
> Richard Matheson, *Hell House* (1971)

In Gothic studies, there is considerable critical consensus for a deep connection between the gothic mode and the suspicion of modernity, especially as nostalgia for the pre-modern as the site of a lost authenticity. In this argument, the gothic emerges in the late eighteenth century as a response to the transformations of modernity, resurrecting the materials of the past – castles, folk belief, feudalism – to critique contemporary claims to rationality, progress, and civility, the benchmarks of modernity in Enlightenment thought. Robert Miles thus suggests that "the Gothic aesthetic sets up, as one of its poles, contemporary decadence, a 'modernity'" defined by "fashion" and "effeminate culture,"[1] while Dale Townshend and Fred Botting characterize recent trends in Gothic studies as "allied to the postmodern challenge to norms and hierarchies that arises from a disillusion toward the grand narratives sustaining modernity."[2] Enlightenment thinkers developed the idea of modernity as cultural and scientific progress, as well as marked its limits through sometimes gothic depictions of the "primitive."[3] Against the Enlightenment's idealized vision of modernity as cultural and civic advancement (through rationality and science, equality and political reform) the gothic was consistent with an emerging nostalgia for the pre-modern as more authentic, unmuddied by artificial cultural codes and the technology that alienated humanity from the organic world. *Point Pleasant*'s critique of patriarchy in the figure of the medical doctor who insists on reason and empiricism is a case in point: Ben exemplifies a kind of Enlightenment modernity that is doomed to fail before the pre-modern truth of the supernatural and the Catholic Church.

While Enlightenment historiography imagines, like its later manifestation in Darwin's theory of evolution, steady progress and improvement across time, this optimistic view of history was shadowed by a fear that there is instead a growing separation from the site of truth, completeness, and integrity: voice degrades to writing, writing degrades to electronic media, as we move from pure presence to pure fiction, a "simulacrum" in Baudrillard's terms. Jeffrey Sconce describes this view of history in relation to television: "In this postmodern vision of the media occult, the post-war period has represented the supernatural dissolution of TV into life, the dissolution of life into TV.' From this perspective, the ubiquitous circulation and constant mediation of television imagery have contributed to an accelerated evaporation of reality into 'hyperreality' ...[,] the increased dissolution of all referentiality," while more recent media critics "frequently embrace[] these phantom landscapes and synthetic identities."[4] Sconce is concerned here with the different valuations of the "media occult," but my concern is rather with the narrativization of its arrival, in which Baudrillard's hyperreal is, I would suggest, the gothic shadow of the technological progress celebrated by the Enlightenment.

As Hogle has noted, Baudrillard's larger argument about simulation understands the process as originating in the Renaissance. For Hogle, the gothic, arising in the eighteenth century, is the second step away from authenticity: "The counterfeit, or more precisely the Renaissance counterfeit of the medieval, has now become the 'signified' of the Gothic signifier, so the Gothic is haunted by the ghost of that already spectral past – and thus by its refaking of what is already fake and already an emblem of the nearly empty and dead."[5] Hogle suggests that this mediation by the "mirage" lies at the origin of the gothic, as the central anxiety that the gothic seeks to engage. Discussing "the most basic presuppositions underlying the Gothic" via Baudrillard's discussion of simulation, Hogle thus writes of the Gothic's "re-presentation of antiquated symbols largely emptied of their older meanings" – or, as Baudrillard writes, "the era of simulation is inaugurated by a liquidation of all referentials."[6] Sconce's title, *Haunted Media*, alludes to the gothic inflection of simulation in Western culture, while a 1994 article by Botting locates Baudrillard as the gothic center of a debate about the nature of postmodern culture and poststructuralist theory.[7] In other words, the gothic mode repeatedly intersects with the larger history of theorizations of the loss of referentiality as the sign of modernity and then postmodernity – a concern that takes as its starting point the priority and stability of the signified.

At the risk of over-generalizing, I am even tempted to suggest that the gothic is a central mode through which Western culture has investigated the ways in which the world of signs supplants the world of the "real," from early gothic literature to recent theory and cultural criticism.[8] As Baudrillard notes, simulation is threatening precisely because it blurs the line between the real and the not-real; Baudrillard, quoting Littré, contends that someone who "simulates an illness produces in himself some of the symptoms,"[9] turning dissimulation, fakery, into simulation, the production of effects that correspond to a cause that is present only through fakery. This also recalls Michel Foucault's point about the Panopticon: "A real subjection is born mechanically from a fictitious relation."[10] Prison, aristocratic tyrants, conjurors, victims made helpless by their own fear – the gothic returns again and again to the ways in which fiction can become *effectively* if not ontologically "real." This confluence of postmodern theories of digital simulation and of the gothic arises precisely from their shared interest in the loss of a stable ground of meaning as the "mirage" "replac[es] the real world"[11] or, perhaps more properly, the real world is revealed to be a mirage – a "myth," to be "debunk[ed]," as Kolchak contends, or a "French Mistake," as in *Blazing Saddles* and *Supernatural*. Here, I examine three series' engagement with this loss: first, the critique of Enlightenment science in *Millennium*; second, the argument that the mirage creates the material world in *Supernatural*; and, finally, in the first season of *American Horror Story*, the durable effects of Hollywood's flickering images via the persistence of the industry's history. All of the episodes at the center of my discussion here are named for houses, but not private houses – they are public institutions and media constructs, and thus offer a suggestive complication of the formulation of "domestic" gothic television.[12]

"Mine, not me": the failures of the Enlightenment in Millennium

While *Carnivàle* is nostalgic for a time before the "false sun/son" of the atom-bomb test at Trinity, *Millennium* is relentlessly concerned, especially in its second season, with the limits of science, particularly psychology, on terms that anticipate the critique of the physician Ben in *Point Pleasant* and the psychologist Ben in the first season of *American Horror Story*. In much traditional literary gothic, psychology governs that which an Enlightenment worldview cannot accommodate – haunting is the Freudian "return of the repressed," doppelgängers the manifestation of subconscious desires, and so forth. In *Millennium*, however, psychology is a science that claims to have fully described and theorized even the most idiosyncratic and unsavory of psyches. In other words, psychology no longer names that which exceeds Enlightenment reason but instead that which has been thoroughly codified within that rational framework. While early gothic texts such as Walpole's *Castle of Otranto* apologize for the supernatural elements by indicating that they are interested in having their characters "think, speak and act, as it might be supposed mere men and women would do in extraordinary positions,"[13] *Millennium* focuses on extreme situations to break down assumptions about what is "real," extreme situations that include mundane violence as well as supernatural events. Thematizing the paranoid over-interpretation associated with Catholic conspiracy narratives,[14] the second season of *Millennium* develops a series of meditations on faith – in science and in religion – in opposition to unmediated perception. Positively established in "Beware of the Dog" through Frank's argument for visceral response to sensation, this position is negatively established through the unwinding of profiling's mystic hold on the magical containment of the largely phantasmatic threat to domestic security, the serial killer – a ritualized exorcism for a secular society. I say "phantasmatic" for this reason: count the number of actual serial killers in the United States over the last thirty years, and then count the number of serial-killer characters in US film and television over the same period. The profiling series *Criminal Minds* alone, which formally riffs off of

Millennium in its use of literary epigraphs and other elements, has dealt with dozens. The serial killer has become, as Dyer implied in 1997,[15] a plot device, a boogeyman for the modern age, but in the second season of *Millennium* that device is examined through a critique of profiling and the fantasy of control that it offers.

In seasons 1 and 3, profiling is relentlessly effective: it catches killer after killer in the first season and continues to work in the third. The only time profiling fails in these two seasons it is done for comic effect: in a parodic episode of the final season, Frank is told by his FBI partner that he has to study horror films to understand a serial killer who is modelling his murders on movie plots. Frank begins by applying profiling to the serial killers on-screen, a hermeneutic approach that is comically represented and fails. By the end of his classic horror-film marathon, however, he has a new profiling rubric he dubs "the movie model": "if you try to protect yourself ... then you die," for instance, and "The leading lady dies last" ("...Thirteen Years Later" 3.5), easily recognizable as a variation on *Scream*'s three rules. With this new profiling "methodology," he figures out who the killer is, and the case is taught at the FBI Academy, demonstrating the capacity of modern profiling to refine itself as evidence emerges, even through the analysis of film plots. Nevertheless, the case is treated as a particularly horrifying one: Frank tells the students, "the case I'm about to describe is so horrific it should never be discussed outside this room. It challenged every preconception. It followed no rules. If it has a moral, I do not know what that moral is." Particularly disturbing, according to Frank, is the breakdown of individuality and the boundary between fiction and psychological fact: "Even during the commission of a heinous crime, he was still in character. It was Bianco's uncanny ability to completely immerse himself in a role, a talent never seen before or since. Some of the crime scene reflected his native personality and some the character he was playing. Either he was the greatest actor the world had ever known, or, he was completely deranged" (3.5). Recalling Hogle's argument, the case takes them into the realm of simulation, where serial killers are method actors looking for their break-out role, cinema is "uncanny," and detectives have to be film historians. And, to highlight the episode's interest in gothic masquerade, the final sequence is played out at a KISS concert.

While "...Thirteen Years Later" formally parodies horror-film conventions and extends profiling to include "the movie model," episodes in the second season go further to challenge the epistemological framework represented by profiling. In the first episode of the season, Frank is trying to find the "polaroid man" who has kidnapped his wife Catherine. As Frank works on-screen through the evidence, researching the suspect's background and biography, the polaroid man comments through an extensive voice-over:

> I don't fit into the serial-killer profile he's come to understand. Now, I am so far beyond. I wasn't from a broken home; he'll find no homicidal triad in my childhood, no setting of fires, no bed wetting, no cruelty to animals. I've had a formal education, responsibility, money. Until recently, not a loner. He'll work on the principle that behavior reflects personality. He'll evaluate the criminal act itself, then the specifics of the crime scene, analyze the victim (which, of course, he knows well) before attempting the development of a profile with critical offender characteristics. This will lead him nowhere, absolutely nowhere, because until now I've committed no crime. This is something he's never experienced before. ... He'll consider complex theories regarding grandiose subtypes of delusional disorder or even photographic paraphilia, blah, blah, blah.
>
> ("The Beginning and the End" 2.1)

In pointed contrast, this episode opens with Frank's voice-over to scientific and religious representations of a comet. But now, instead of competing artistic representations of a comet's progress from beyond the solar system to crash into the sun, a narrative with a clear beginning and end, we have Frank looking for narrative – poring through evidence using scientific protocols to try to find a familiar narrative that will transform the polaroid man into a recognizable serial killer. Instead, the evidence he finds contradicts the conventional narrative: pictures of a happy child, university records indicating academic success. The kind of methodology which undergirds popular representations of profiling is revealed as a kind of genre analysis rooted in conventions of character and plot; the detective looks for the threads of narrative that led to the crime, the lives of the criminal and the victim, expecting them to move his own narrative of detection forward. But the narrative of detection is stalled – "this will lead him nowhere" – when the protagonist does not fit into one of these conventional types, because his life story does not conform to narrative conventions. And they are so conventional and familiar that they do not even need articulation: "blah, blah, blah."

The episode as a whole turns to story-telling at key moments. About halfway through the episode, Peter Watts, the father of three daughters, tells Frank an almost biblical story of his pact with God, that he would find the killer of a baby boy and in return would finally have a son, explaining to Frank, "I wanted a boy, for reasons that I don't have to explain to another guy." At the end a policeman tells Catherine a story of what happened in the house so that Frank will not be charged with brutally stabbing her kidnapper, a story in which Frank only applied the necessary force to protect his family. She assents sarcastically, "Yes sir!" – and then moments later kicks Frank out of their happy yellow house. Both of these narratives are conservatively patriarchal: all men want sons and all men understand this; and a man has the right to kill if he is protecting what is his, including those in his domestic circle. In both cases, Frank is the silent interlocutor who allows these claims to stand without explicitly agreeing. In the latter case, Catherine's actions overlay an overt critique of such narratives, especially when she explicitly signals her rejection of the policeman's rationalization of Frank's actions as he gets ready to move out of the house, telling Frank, "I don't know yet if it was wrong, what you did."

But the polaroid man's voice-over challenges such dominant narratives. The polaroid man's assertion of his normality calls attention to the familiar first rule of profiling: serial killers are almost exclusively white men and, as Dyer points out, men who have more power than their victims.[16] There is a paradox here: the serial killer is both an exemplar of white male privilege, as Dyer notes, and, through profiling, defined as failed masculinity, a pathology rather than normalcy. But the polaroid man is no such failure. The polaroid man is not "from a broken home" and so grew up in a heteronormative household; he has "formal education, responsibility, money," in other words, the power attached to middle-class white masculinity; "no setting of fires, no bed wetting[,] … no crime," and hence he has demonstrated the self-control necessitated by Enlightenment masculinity, too. The polaroid man voids the paradox of the serial killer by simply highlighting white male power. But this makes him invisible to profiling, which understands the serial killer as a sick individual rather than as a symptom of social inequity – a hyperbolizing of white male privilege. As a figure of normative white masculinity, the polaroid man can understand, but cannot be made understandable through, a branch of psychology that is exclusively interested in the abnormal – hence, as he notes, Frank will only find him when he drops profiling methodologies and turns to his "gift," to sensation rather than interpretation. In other words, the first episode of season 2 disrupts the serial killer mythos on two levels: first, by critiquing the psychiatric profile as the master narrative through which killers can be subjected, made known and captured, and, second, by exposing the serial killer as a boogeyman who is not a monster or a pathology, but simply figures white male dominance – like other villains of the series, such as the upstanding civic leader and businessman who sexually molests his daughter and has another daughter by her who he also threatens when she gets older.

"The Pest House" (2.4), written by Morgan and Wong, is arguably their most sustained critique of profiling in particular and modern psychology in general as a model through which to understand identity and behavior, a critique that continues the series' interest in textuality. It foregrounds story-telling, opening with a young man (an English major, of course) telling his girlfriend a scary story about a serial killer, just before he is killed in accordance with the hookman urban legend he was recounting (recalling the narrative device of *Scream*, released a little over a year before "Pest House" aired). The episode as a whole pivots on this blurring of lines between fiction and fact on terms that anticipate the movie-parody episode of the third season: someone is killing people in accordance with urban legends. Frank dismisses as absurd the idea of actual murders conforming to urban legends, but then seems to blithely accept the information that the urban-legend killers' methods are consistent with those of actual serial killers being held at a high-security mental institution near the locations of the new murders. The paradox of the correspondence between urban legend, explicitly tied to tale-telling in the opening scene of the episode, and the documented facts of the men's medical histories is never dealt with, but remains one of the unresolvable conundrums of an episode in which such moments foreground the failure of scientific models precisely because they attempt to interpret what is at least partly aesthetic – the episode implies that the incarcerated serial killers are themselves copycat killers who mimicked urban legends. But this becomes even more complicated, and more gothic, when it is revealed that the new murders Frank and Peter Watts are sent to investigate are actually being committed by a medical worker, Edward. Edward is stealing the incarcerated serial killers' dreams, and then commits the murders they would commit if they were free, making him less a copycat killer than, in Hogle's terms, a counterfeit killer – "a refaking of what is already fake."[17] The stealing of dreams itself is explicitly linked to psychiatry: Edward leads group therapy sessions in which inmates are pressured to talk about their dreams. Focusing on the textuality of psychiatry, the Freudian "interpretation of dreams," the episode throws viewers into a *mise en abyme* of fakery and tale-telling: serial killers whose methods echo urban legends have dreams which are interpreted and assimilated by a psychiatric worker who then becomes, and acts, just like the serial killers of urban legend.

At the same time, the episode stages various debates between Dr. Stoller (Melinda McGray), the psychiatrist who runs the asylum, and Frank Black and Peter Watts, both FBI-trained profilers. Their debates explode any illusion that psychology is a monolithic paradigm. All trained in psychology, they fundamentally disagree on the value of treatment for the "criminally insane." Frank and Peter Watts insist that there is no cure for violent offenders while Stoller is a committed reformer, not only convinced by, but also a keen advocate of, the position "that counseling, intensive therapy, even medication, can rehabilitate the sick." The dispute represents psychology not as the magical method that will solve crimes, as it does in the first and third seasons, but as a set of sometimes competing interpretive models that are still being developed. And psychology is further challenged by a series of supernatural events that undermine the very possibility of a nameable, describable, individual identity.

The first investigative scene opens with a superficial, conservative critique of overly sympathetic psychiatrists who fail to control patients who are simply evil: in the asylum, patients and doctors are dressed alike in order to void institutional elitism, but with the effect of making it possible for a patient to impersonate a doctor when Frank and Peter Watts arrive. This apparent critique becomes, as the episode unfolds, a resonant symbol that is explored in a more sustained way throughout the episode. For instance, in the opening scenes, the patient impersonating a doctor, then a "real" doctor, and then Frank, all offer precisely the same diagnosis of Jacob Woodcock, a lead suspect in the first killing. Another early scene depicts the serial-killer patient, Purdue (Michael Massee), play on his knowledge of another patient's psychological problems to trigger a violent incident. The lack of uniforms, then, is only an outward symbol of a central conundrum: if both patients and doctors understand the same psychological methodologies and terms, then what does distinguish them? This of course is also a conundrum posed by "The Beginning and the End": the polaroid man's understanding of profiling is expressed verbally through a voice-over to a series of images that visually validate his ability to predict precisely what steps Frank will take as he works on his case, trying to predict what the polaroid man will do next. The profiled becomes a profiler, the psychiatric patient becomes a psychiatrist, and the psychiatric nurse becomes a serial killer.

"The Pest-House" challenges, in broad terms, the difference between knowledge and identity. The murderer takes not only serial-killers' dreams but also their technical knowledge. A sailor's knot, a precise cut that takes experience to perfect, and so forth are details of the first crime scene, details that make the incarcerated killer Jacob Woodcock declare, "I didn't do it. But it's mine. It's all mine." His declaration that he "didn't do it" is credible; he needs a wheelchair to move around and is locked in the asylum. But he takes ownership of it as something that he, in a very "real" if not material sense, created. The next serial killer whose dreams are taken also refers to the crimes as "mine." The patient known as "Bear" keeps repeating, "mine, not me," his first words for some time, in a variation on Kristevan abjection: "what is *abject* …, the jettisoned object, is radically excluded and draws me towards the place where meaning collapses. … A massive and sudden emergence of uncanniness, which, familiar as it might have been in an opaque and forgotten life, now harries me as radically separate, loathsome. Not me."[18] The crimes are theirs, but it is not them committing the crimes: "mine not me," their intent but not their crime, their creation but not their act. And yet they are all uncannily familiar as longstanding urban legends.

At key moments, psychology fails dramatically. At the second crime scene, Frank delivers his profile of a new murderer, leaving the local police detective incredulous, asking, "Mr. Black, you said the other murder was scripted and this one is disorganized. Are you suggesting two different maniacs out there?" Frank replies confidently, "Yes I am," and Peter Watts delivers an expert profile of both murderers to highlight the differences between them. From a profiling perspective, the series of murders and an attempted murder appear to be the work of very different pathologies and hence different perpetrators, and therefore statistically improbable in one small rural area; from a supernatural perspective, validated at the end of the episode, there is one murderer. The profilers Frank and Peter are absolutely confident in their assessment that there are multiple murderers and stick to that assessment throughout, even though the murderers they are identifying are physically incapable of committing the crimes. Another branch of psychology is abruptly challenged again in the next scene. Over lunch in the asylum cafeteria, Dr. Stoller debates, again, criminal psychology with Frank and Peter Watts, and insists, "there is absolutely no sliver of proof that anyone from this hospital had anything to do with the recent murders" – at which point she discovers a kind of "sliver of proof," finding a victim's finger in her lunch. These back-to-back scenes, like the debates between the three psychiatric experts, do not support one psychological perspective over another but represent both clinical psychiatry and profiling as alike unable to manage the evidence before them.

And then psychology is thrown out the window for a medieval narrative of evil and the soul. The real murderer, Edward, having seen the failure of psychology because of violent incidents in the hospital, has attempted to go beyond "counseling … therapy … [and] medication" to simple excision. He tells Frank how he wants to cure his patients: "I would take it out of them by any means possible or impossible, every violent thought, every sick impulse." There is some consensus among the inmates that "tak[ing] it out of them" means absorbing it himself: at the end of the episode, Frank agrees, "I think he figured out a way to take it out of them, but he couldn't take it out of himself." He also remarks, "We who hunt monsters, who touch evil, run the risk that evil will touch us." Evil becomes a substance, a tangible "it," that can be transferred rather than a behavior that develops across time, can be understood through therapy, and perhaps modified. Evil is not an effect of a particular *Bildungsroman* but a thing that contaminates the self – it is "not me," "the danger to identity that comes from without," as Kristeva puts it.

But before accepting Edward's responsibility, Frank concludes that the patient Purdue, by narrow profiling logic, will be the next serial killer to strike:

FRANK: I think he's attempting to find you. The lights are out, the phones are dead. He's making a real attempt to complete his fantasy.
STOLLER: And that would culminate in killing me?
FRANK: That's my interpretation.

Frank's suddenly hesitant language – "I think," "that's my interpretation" – belies his invocation of the term "real." And he is flatly wrong. It is Purdue that saves the day, both correctly evaluating the situation and stopping the serial killer by killing him:

FRANK: Why did you come back?
PURDUE: I never left. It was Edward all the time. He used Woodcock, then Bear, then me. He ate our sins but couldn't digest them.
STOLLER: That's a load of crap, Purdue. You're just trying to build another insanity defense.
PURDUE: No, doctor. Killing Edward was the sanest thing I ever did.

Stoller's colloquialism seems pointed: Purdue offers a supernatural explanation rooted in the metaphor of digestion, in which Edward "ate [their] sins," while Stoller suggests that Purdue has successfully digested psychology and so can produce an "insanity defense" that will be "crap," bringing us back to the recurring trope of abjection in the episode – on that which is "mine," but "not me." Kristeva asks, "Why does *corporeal waste*, menstrual blood and excrement … represent – like a metaphor that would have become incarnate – the objective frailty of the symbolic order? … Excrement and its equivalents … stand for the danger to identity that comes from without: the ego threatened by the non-ego, society threatened by its outside."[19] Stoller cannot tolerate a mystical view of events, any more than the medically trained Bens in *Point Pleasant* and *American Horror Story*.

Purdue, however, is vindicated by the end of the episode, all of his suggestions validated by what happens on-screen. Purdue has consistently described Edward in the language of the supernatural, telling Stoller early on, "Edward – he's the devil," and insisting to Edward, "I don't believe your lies about life everlasting." Purdue warns Frank and Dr. Stoller over the facility's PA system, in yet another key scene in the series in which a disembodied voice explains events while the viewers watch them unfold:

When the devil comes to call, he will tempt you, then threaten every sacred thing and take the rest. Fight like hell. He wants the only thing

> that's ever been worth a damn. The only thing that he doesn't have. The fuel in your head. Don't listen to his lies. What you get isn't life, it's nothing. ... My soul was taken. But something lives on. It's too powerful to die an anonymous death. So I will kill again. But out of self-defense. No lies, no excuses. This one will come from a clear, clean conscience.

And this is where the psychological interpretations of both Frank and Stoller meet the crisis of their own failures: Purdue, the patient in an insane asylum, will kill the devil "from a clear, clean conscience," "the sanest thing [he] ever did." Moreover, the episode returns in this lecture by Purdue to the problem of identity. Purdue is the patient who triggers a violent incident by deftly manipulating the mental illnesses of other patients; he is represented as understanding both supernatural and scientific paradigms. If Purdue is right, then neither psychology nor religion can account for what is happening: "My soul was taken. But something lives on." This "dangerous supplement" – that which is not "lost," or "perdu" in French, suggesting a pun in the character's name – undoes both totalizing models, both the religious and the scientific.[20]

Despite Purdue's assertion of this supplement's non-anonymity, however, much of the final sequence only extends the episode's blurring of the boundaries between identities, as Edward, on-screen, takes on the appearance of all three serial killers – Jacob Woodcock, Bear, and Purdue – and Stoller mistakes Frank for Purdue in the darkness. Profiler, medical worker, patient – all become difficult to distinguish, as in the first scene in the asylum when Frank and Peter cannot distinguish a patient from a doctor. The repeated stagings of the debate between Stoller, Frank and Peter, as well as the play of doppelgängers, contributes to the gothic narrative's decentering of psychology from its role in the first season (and again in the third season) as a reliable, indisputable, and even naturalized "science." This episode offers, against profiling and therapeutic psychology, a gothic challenge to the Enlightenment ideal of the autonomous individual in the doppelgänger, the double who undoes the singularity of the individual, the counterfeit who reveals "the uncertainly grounded self," in Hogle's phrase – "mine," but emphatically "not me."

While early anglophone gothic literature resurrected Catholic and non-Christian elements of the supernatural to suggest, with Hamlet, that "There are more things in heaven and earth" "Than are dreamt of in our philosophy," the second season of *Millennium* imagines a world in which the "castle" is not as "contested" as philosophy itself.[21] Over and over again, the season represents modes of interpretation as dangerous because they are blind to possibilities that are available to perception, while privileging those who, through sensation, transcend such worldviews: Lara Means responds to the Owls and Roosters schism in the Millennium Group by invoking her visions of angels as the only thing she can trust, and Purdue declares that there is something of himself that survives the loss of his soul and enables him to save the day. As an extension of the gothic, the season turns the mode back in on itself, returning it to its Burkean roots in sensation and abiding mystery by pulling apart the psychological rubrics that have been used to systematize and rationalize it.

Rewriting history: *Supernatural* and the popular

While *Millennium* challenges modern science through an episode rooted in urban legend and quasi-medieval notions of the "soul," *Supernatural* resists the Enlightenment narrative of progress through increasing commercial sophistication, especially through digital technology. In their gothic exploration of the relationship between signification and "reality," the early seasons of *Supernatural* sustain an interest in multiple modes of signification as productive not only of meaning but also of different networks of community. Specifically, by making oral culture the focus of most of the early episodes, the series dislocates the conventional postmodern trajectory, putting a new twist on Eric Savoy's point that "nostalgic representations of 'America' veer toward the gothic."[22] Folklore is not nostalgically sought but is alive and well in Kripke's America, and more socially rooted than in urban-legend horror films – living everywhere in high schools, websites, small-town gossip, city records, and the music that the brothers play in their retro car. An episode discussed earlier, for instance, delves into the legend around the life and death of 1930s bluesman Robert Johnson, and the DVD set of that season includes 1930s archival footage of blues performances as well as blues historians and folklorists discussing the ways in which the legend draws on various African and Western religious beliefs and 1930s competition between different blues musicians ("Crossroad Blues" 2.8). The episode, like a number of others in the series, frames the gothic as comprehensible and hence manageable – at least in the brothers' ability to end the supernatural threat – through a re-engagement with an oral culture that has never gone away although it has fallen from view in mainstream Hollywood-centered culture. The socially isolated brothers' quest in the early seasons of *Supernatural* can be grasped as a series of attempts to temporarily recover community through oral traditions – forging connections with regional groups as well as the pan-regional world of hunting. But this does not negate the value of popular electronic media, which itself provides a language for community-building across localized regions. Instead of working sequentially through the standard developmental narrative, from the oral to the written to the electronic, different forms of communication are depicted as operating simultaneously across different scales of community networks. In the early seasons, the Winchesters are only effective insofar as they can tap into those oral traditions. In "Crossroad Blues," for instance, they have to encounter an entirely oral folk tradition, as a character who learned hoodoo from his grandmother mocks them, "you boys think you know somethin' about somethin' but not Goofer dust?" (2.8). Goofer dust in hand, they save the day (and again use the same material in season 7).

In the first-season episode, "Hell House" (1.17), set in Texas, there is an illustrative weaving of electronic, print and oral media that exemplifies the trends of the early seasons as a whole. The allusions to popular culture are particularly dense in this episode, with references to *Ghostbusters*, *Buffy the Vampire Slayer*, *Lord of the Rings*, and various horror films. Even the title of the episode, "Hell House," is densely allusive, invoking a novel by Richard Matheson (1971) and a movie based on it, *The Legend of Hell House* (1973), as well as *The Haunting of Hell House* (1999) and *Hell House* (2001), the last a documentary on the "Hell House" set up by a Texas church group to edify wayward teenagers. For a show known for its use of music from the 1970s and 1980s and an episode partly set in a used record store, it is important to note as well that Lynyrd Skynyrd worked on an early album in 1970 at a farm in Alabama called "Hell House."

In the episode, some teenagers, one of whom works at the used-record store, decide to invent a story that a local house is haunted and supplement the narrative with some elaboration of the setting according to contemporary popular culture: they scrawl occult symbols culled from a comparative religion textbooks and album covers onto the walls of the house, and one of them poses as a hanged victim in the basement, recalling Hogle's point about the gothic's "re-presentation of antiquated symbols largely emptied of their older meanings":[23] staging bricolage, they fake various icons that once had meaning but to them only evoke a style, the images of horror. Then one of the pranksters takes a group of teenagers to the house, beginning the proliferation of the story through the community and ultimately onto a website, www.hellhoundslair.com (the show's producers set up a webpage with this address, and it subsequently spawned a webseries) – at time of writing, the website was still available with postings of local legends, many of which begin, "I heard." Then a second group goes to the house on another night, where a ghost attacks and hangs a teenager, in the same part of the basement as the staged hanging before. Now the ghost is "real" as dissimulation becomes simulation, in Baudrillard's sense. But, as different groups approach the house, the ghost keeps changing: in the Winchesters' first contact with the ghost, it is not trying to hang anyone but swings an axe. The brothers' usual method for "putting ghosts to rest" – a shotgun blast of rock salt – also fails to work. Town archives yield no answers. Interviews with various townspeople about the legend and events at the house reveal contradictions instead of some core of oral tradition, as is usually the case. Gradually they realize that the answer lies not at the house, but in oral culture and its internet extension, a relationship that leapfrogs over writing and print. The ghost keeps changing as different rumors from the region are posted on the hellhoundslair website and then recirculate through a larger population, as the belief of the site's readers make each variant of the basic ur-haunted-house story manifest, "like a game of telephone." Instead of what Hogle terms "the ghost of the counterfeit" we have "the counterfeit of a ghost," made possible in part by the pranksters' use of an eastern symbol that makes thoughts real if enough people think the same thing at the same time.

But the Winchesters do not solve the crime only by recognizing this meaningful symbol. Instead, this supernatural conundrum is solved when Dean recognizes one of the symbols in the haunted house as being from a Blue Öyster Cult album while Sam recognizes the Eastern mystical symbol that makes thoughts real, mixing popular culture and world religion more directly than in most episodes (their linked discoveries continue the early representation of Dean as blue-collar and uneducated, and Sam as a former university student). The pop-culture reference cues the constructedness of the scene, but it still simulates a haunted house: there is a ghost, faked or not, and it is killing people. But because it is founded on false premises, it cannot be understood and stopped. So the Winchester brothers plant a new, false version on the website which encodes a method for destroying the ghost: they forge an archival document, show it to the website's writers, to authenticate their "BS story" that the ghost will be destroyed if shot by a .45. The website crashes, however, so it cannot circulate, overturning the Winchesters' plans. But the brothers "improvise" based on part of the story that has not changed in all of its various forms, namely that the ghost cannot leave the house. They burn the house down as Sam asks, "Kind of makes you wonder. Of all the things we hunted, how many existed just because people believed in them?" Electronic media works in conjunction with oral culture, just as the Blue Öyster Cult symbol inhabits the same faked space as the mystic Eastern symbol, and the point is less the Baudrillardian "precession of simulacra" than the ways in which a small town in Texas is multiply connected to different cultural networks symbolized through different "real" and digital locations: hellhoundslair.com, the used record store, the fast-food hangout for the area's teenagers, the town archives, the old house, and so forth.

The early seasons of the series *Supernatural* thus deny the "empty[ing]" of "antiquated symbols" by insisting on the survival of oral tradition and its ongoing power, while also maintaining the simulacrum of popular culture as another vehicle of communication and of misdirection. If US gothic is affiliated with nostalgia, as Savoy suggests and as we saw in *Carnivàle*, it is easy to see the nostalgia in the series for tale-telling, 1970s film and television, retro muscle cars and classic rock. But in its engagement with media the series overturns the conventional narrative of regression in which we fall from voice to writing to digital media, each step moving us further away from "presence." In the tradition of the gothic, simulation is a tool of sociopolitical power as well as an effect of technology; both are magical, making the fictional real, like a father's power over his sons – the man in the "dark part of the hut." Voice in *Supernatural* is neither lost nor restored, but rather recognized and explored as an ongoing source of knowledge and community building despite its low-tech flavor in what we are told is an increasingly digitized world. The two forms of the popular – one commercial and electronic, the other oral, even oracular, and outside of capitalist modernity – interweave in a present that is represented through a synchronic, rather than diachronic, interplay of various media and media technologies. *Supernatural* suggests, in short, that we never leave a medium behind, not even a medium of communication as "primitive" as speech. This goes to the heart of the series' challenge to the norms of televisual realism: yes, the horror is often gruesomely represented in visual detail, but in most episodes the consumer objects on-screen do not give viewers clear cues as to the temporal setting of an episode and the blending of analog and digital in "Hell House" (symbolized by the record store on one side, and the web team on the other), as well as through the two brothers in the early seasons, goes to the heart of the understanding of the contemporary moment as one of digitization and desire for new electronics.[24] Televisual realism markets this vision, and these products, by representing them as nearly ubiquitous among US television's generally well-heeled teenagers and young adults – its network's main target audience. *Supernatural* has two guys in an old car who wear the same clothes, week in, week out, and one of them rigs a working ghost detector out of an old cassette player ("Phantom Traveler" 1.4). The series not only questions the accessibility of this digital universe but, in "Hell House," also challenges the very possibility of moving cleanly from the old to the new, from the analog to the digital, from the cassette player to the iPod.

Gothic Hollywood: the first season of *American Horror Story*

While *Millennium* takes aim at an idealized vision of contemporary science and its regulation of crime dramas and *Supernatural* challenges the Enlightenment myth of progress that is now less scientific than technological and advertising-driven (if you want to look up to date, you had better have the right electronic toys), *American Horror Story* sets its sights on Hollywood itself as an industry. This is not an anxiety about the simulacra of the flickering images on our screen, but a long, hard look at what happens off-screen. There is a substantial tradition of this. At the center of Billy Wilder's tale of early Hollywood, *Sunset Blvd.* (1950), is Norma Desmond's mansion on that street: "It was a great big elephant of a place, the kind of place crazy movie people built in the crazy twenties."[25] Focusing on Desmond (Gloria Swanson), a silent-film star who draws into her orbit a would-be screenwriter, Joe Gillis (William Holden), and makes him her gigolo, the movie's various tragedies involve various characters who want to make it "big" in Hollywood, from Desmond, who tries revive her stardom, to Gillis and his other love interest, Betty Schaefer (Nancy Olson), who, despite plastic surgery, does not have the right look for an actress and so aspires to make it as a screenwriter. The film is heavy-handed about the ways in which Hollywood builds up egos and tears them down: as Cecil B. De Mille (playing himself) complains, in response to the remark that Desmond during her heyday "was a terror to work with," "a dozen press agents working overtime can do terrible things to the human spirit." Desmond murders Gillis, and, at the start of the famous final scene in which she treats the police, reporters, and news cameras as the accoutrements of a movie set, a gossip columnist dubs her mansion, "the murder house."

"Murder House" is also the title of the third episode of *American Horror Story* and, after the series was renewed, retroactively of the entire first season. The first season of *American Horror Story* also centers on a "place crazy movie people built in the crazy twenties": the house, its architecture often central in the episodes, was purportedly built in 1922 by Nora and Charles Montgomery (Lily Rabe and Matt Ross; "The Murder House" 1.3); Charles descends from a physician who caters to the movie industry, to an obsessed madman who commits the first murders in the house.[26] As in *Sunset Blvd.*, the mansion first appears abandoned (children enter through bent, open gates covered in ivy in the opening seconds of the season), and various details are, one by one, tied to its history: Desmond's home has tile floors because Valentino liked them, but no locks because of Desmond's suicide attempts, for instance; in *American Horror Story*, the Tiffany stained glass was meant to reflect the color of Nora's eyes (1.3), and the walls bear the traces of different owners' tastes. Constance (Jessica Lange) repeatedly echoes scenes from Wilder's film, and her larger narrative echoes the basic plot: in "Spooky Little Girl" (1.9), she talks at length to her boyfriend, Travis, about her failed acting career and the inevitability of his failure as well. He, like Gillis in the film, is much younger, and takes money and orders from his lover. Specific scenes echo the movie. For instance, establishing his role as gigolo, one key scene in the movie has Desmond hold up a bill between her forefingers for Gillis, so that he can go buy her cigarettes; in "Halloween Part 1" (1.4), Constance does the same with Travis, who keeps the change for himself. In both scenes, the women avert their eyes from the men they are giving money, implying embarrassment at their humiliating dependency. In the penultimate scene of the season, Constance sits at a table in front of a mirror in a hair salon and speaks of her dream of being "a star of the silver screen" ("Afterbirth" 1.12), while the hairdresser behind her reacts, visually echoing Desmond's penultimate scene in *Sunset Blvd.* where she sits in her bedroom at her dressing table in front of a mirror, with police behind her, as she primps her hair and tells them she has to "get ready for [her] scene." *American Horror Story*, like much gothic, is riddled with references to literature, film, and other cultural materials, and *Sunset Blvd.* is arguably not even the most prominent, but I start with these echoes of Wilder's film because, while critical focus to date has been on the series' depiction of sexuality, a key part of this first season's overall narrative (and particularly its gothic dimensions) is the history of Hollywood and the "terrible things" it can do "to the human spirit."

Overall, the series offers a suggestive revision on the 1960s anthology format (see my discussion of this in the Introduction to this book): each season is a different standalone narrative of 12–13 episodes, but the same actors reappear from season to season. Season 1, *Murder House*, centers on the Harmons, an upper-middle-class family trying to get a fresh start in an old house in Los Angeles; as the season unfolds, it becomes clear that anyone who dies in the house (and they all die violently) is trapped in the house as a ghost, and one of the more wrenching scenes depicts Constance desperately trying to drag her daughter Addie (Jamie Brewer), the victim of a hit and run, from the street and onto the Harmons' property so that she can survive at least as a spirit (1.4). Season 2, *Asylum*, is set in a Catholic-run institution for the criminally insane, Jessica Lange's new character anticipated by Constance's first-season aside, "why is it always the old whore who acts the part of a moralistic prude?" ("Pilot" 1.1),[27] and draws on a wide array of popular US narratives, from serial killers to alien abduction to Nellie Bly's *Ten Days in a Mad-house* (1887), an exposé based on Bly's time as an undercover journalist in a mental institution. Season 3, *Coven*, interweaves a narrative in present-day New Orleans, focusing on a refuge for teenage girls with supernatural powers, with a narrative about slave-owning New Orleans and a woman who violently abused and tortured her slaves and also had ties to witchcraft – in this season, mothers are monsters, parasites seeking to feed on the young because youth is power.

The first season of *American Horror Story* overlays, interweaves, and otherwise drenches its narratives in cultural, social, and domestic histories. Opening with the Harmon family about to embark on a fresh start in a newly purchased house in a different part of the country (like *Millennium* and so many other gothic narratives), the season is one long refusal of such a possibility, most gothically through the premise that everyone who dies in the house remains there forever as a ghost and most mundanely in the futility of the family's attempt to forget the trauma of both a miscarriage and the father's subsequent affair with one of his university students. This refusal is reinforced through the season's narrative structure, with repeated switches in timeframe having the same temporal effect as the ghosts themselves: the past is always on the verge of erupting into, and refiguring, the present. This theme is also pursued through relentless bricolage, most obviously with the founding references to the film *Twisted Nerve* (1968), about a family seeking to maintain its gentility, with a remarried mother, a child with Down's syndrome, and a murderous son – the precise configuration of Constance's family. To stress the reference, the theme that is whistled by the murderer in *Twisted Nerve* as he stalks the heroine also plays in the background as Constance's son, Tate (Evan Peters), arrives at his high school to shoot some of his fellow students (the whistled tune is also used in Quentin Tarantino's *Kill Bill: Volume 1* [2003]). A central concern of *Twisted Nerve*, and the source of the title, is the premise that there might be a biological predisposition to violence – that murder might be an effect of heredity rather than a decision taken by a rational subject with free will. This is played out across the season, ending with the theme to *Twisted Nerve* playing after Tate's toddler son is discovered covered in blood from a murder he has just committed (the same theory of inheritable murderousness appears again in *Asylum*). The twisted nerve determines violence; there is no choice; and there are no fresh starts, because we are not born blank slates as John Locke would have it, and the world is not a blank slate either. In a nutshell, for this first season of *American Horror Story*, biology is destiny, and death is no escape.

At the center of this relentless absence of free will is the inability of the father, Ben Harmon (Dylan McDermott), a psychiatrist, to control his house, both his workspace and his domestic space. Like Darrin in *Bewitched*, he has a home office that emblematizes the breakdown of the boundaries between home and work, starting with Constance's son Tate (perhaps coincidentally also the surname of Darrin's boss). Tate, while still apparently a patient of Ben's, roams around the domestic portions of the house and pursues a relationship with Ben's teenaged daughter, constantly frustrating Ben's efforts to control his behavior. Ben even rejects him as a patient. But, of course, Tate is a ghost: he has been roaming around the house for decades and knows its spaces and its secrets better than anyone, and it used to be his house when he was alive. Just as Tate's precursor in *Twisted Nerve*, Hamlet-like, constantly challenges his stepfather as a usurper, Tate provokes and, Oedipus-like, replaces Ben, most literally when he dons a black rubber suit so that Ben's wife mistakes him for Ben in a sexual encounter. As in *Point Pleasant*, Ben's scientific worldview is unable to accommodate the supernatural; as in *Millennium*, psychiatry is unraveled as a viable methodology, and Ben declares it a "con" in the final moments of the last episode.

The season as a whole juxtaposes two rationales for the dysfunctional relationships on which it focuses: first, the domestic narrative, in which the house is figured as a body and functions as the site on which women's bodies are used as if they are objects, along with the usual gothic tropes for such misogynist violence (demonic pregnancy, rape, abortion, various murders of nonconforming women);[28] second, the historical narrative, in which the house is a record of the past, biology is destiny, and trauma an inescapable prison for which there is no talking cure, as Freudian psychiatry would have it. While the former is openly addressed through dialogue from the first episode, the latter is repeatedly silenced – speeches are broken off, children with disabilities are hidden away, characters refuse to talk to each other, and, in one telling episode, Ben falls asleep while meeting with a depressed patient. But the narratives are two sides of the same patriarchal coin: in broad terms, the historical narrative insists on the spiritual that the reductively materialist domestic narrative denies. That most of the ghosts are children, women, or gay men reinforces the implication that patriarchal violence, both physical and epistemological, is the guiding concern of the season.

The two narratives are most clearly linked in "The Rubber Man" (1.8), as the maid, Moira (Frances Conroy), asks Vivien Harmon (Connie Britton) if she "know[s] 'The Yellow Wallpaper' by Charlotte Perkins Gilman," an 1892 tale influential for its gothic account of a woman's attempt to deal with patriarchal oppression and specifically the discourse of hysteria. When Vivien replies that she does not know it, Moira gives a summary of the tale, and then explains the etymology of "hysteria" in a larger history of women and medicine that leads to the assertion, "men are still inventing ways to drive women over the edge" – and then Moira explains that "this house is possessed. … There are spirits here," leaving out the point that one of them is Moira herself. This short scene begins and ends with the gothic, moving from literature, to history, to the diegesis of the episode, and from the protagonist of "The Yellow Wallpaper" trapped in her room to Vivien's unsuccessful attempt to leave the Murder House after this conversation (ghosts prevent her). Moira is the nub of the season's contradictions on the question of biological determinism, a point reinforced by her two distinct appearances: she appears old and dowdily dressed to women and young and less than fully clothed to (straight) men (or, put in other terms, she alternates between looking like Aunt Esmeralda [Alice Ghostley] dressed as a maid in *Bewitched*, and more like Magenta [Patricia Quinn] from *The Rocky Horror Picture Show* [1975]). Moira repeatedly argues, as she does in her lecture on hysteria, that women are oppressed by patriarchal fictions but also that men are universally determined to behave in patriarchal ways. Women are constructed, men are determined; women are spiritual, men are physical. Hence, Moira remarks, "I'm not naive to the ways of men – their need to objectify, conquer. They see what they want to see. Women, however, see into the soul of a person" (1.3); "You're a man. Isn't this what all men want? The freedom to satiate their needs guilt-free?" (1.9). According to Moira, men live in a material world, stripped of others' interiority, and only women can see "the soul."

Moira is not the only source of such examinations of patriarchy. The second-last episode opens in 1984, as a young Tate plays with a bright yellow truck, while his mother Constance is passed out in the living room. The television – a very rare sight in the series – is playing an episode of *Newhart* (1982–1990), as Newhart explains to his wife, "You always give a guy a second chance; that's, like, the golden rule of guys. … The problem is I can't let him know. … Look, Joanna, you can go ahead and make fun of this, but this is real important. I mean, I'm telling you what guys think, and if you want to be one of the guys, you don't break the code" ("Birth" 1.11). Tate then has his first encounter with the ghosts in the basement, one that tacitly precipitates both his homophobia and compulsion to protect young women – another part of "the golden rule of guys." Between biology and patriarchal culture, the season seems to suggest, men do not stand a chance. Tate's violence might arise from an inheritable "twisted nerve," but television, toys, and experience all shape that violence: he is obsessed with and emotionally overwrought in response to Violet (Taissa Farmigia) and rapes her mother; he commits two homophobic murders; and, when he cannot be "one of the guys," he turns school shooter and targets athletes.

If Tate demonstrates the violent extremes of heteronormative masculinity (confusing sexuality and control) and "the code," then his counsellor Ben represents the more mundane ways in which those same imperatives shape more ordinary lives. Like Ben in *Point Pleasant*, as noted earlier, the Ben in *American Horror Story* has medical training and resists the idea of the supernatural, to the point of committing his wife to a mental institution; they are alike bound by the physical world and an empiricism that acknowledges only the material, and alike insistent on directing those in their domestic sphere toward their vision of order. The confrontation with this father's blindness happens in the first half of the season rather than the final episode, as it does in *Point Pleasant*:

> BEN: I won't be the victim of your sick extortion. You're in it together!
> LARRY: Oh, wow! You really don't get it do you? Your narrow clinical worldview doesn't let you! Buddy you are so screwed. You know what the thing about the dead is? They've got nothing left to lose.
> BEN: Enough of this bullshit! I want some goddamn answers.
> LARRY: Oh, baby, you don't even know what the goddamn question is.
>
> ("Halloween Part 2" 1.5)

In the next episode, Constance tells Ben's daughter, Violet, who has just started to realize that Tate is a ghost, "You're a smart girl. How can you be so arrogant as to think there is only one reality?" ("Piggy, Piggy" 1.6). Here, though, that "reality" is not part of some transhistorical struggle between Good and Evil, as it is in *Point Pleasant*, but about the survival of the past in the present. Ghosts are only the most obvious vehicle of this point.

The inability to recognize or deal with the durability of the past, especially through the trope of spirits, is a problem for many of the powerful men in the series. In "Open House" (1.7), the wealthy developer Joe Escandarian considers buying the "Murder House" to level it for low-income housing:

> CONSTANCE: Used to be no one was from here. People came here to escape their pasts, find a plot of land that not even a red indian had set foot on and make a new life for yourself.
>
> JOE: Gimme a number [a price for her house]. If I want history, I'll go talk to Gene Autry.
>
> CONSTANCE: But now there are no more virgin plots. We live on top of each other. That's California now, and that's the world. There is no more space, and yet it's human nature to want to claim your own turf. So build away we do. Every time you put up one of these monstrous temples to the gods of travertine, you're building on top of someone else's life.
>
> JOE: I'm a developer. I improved on the past. I build a new future.
>
> CONSTANCE: You should show some respect. You're not an archaeologist. You should stop unearthing while you're ahead. It only brings a haunting. We have a responsibility as caretakers to the old lands – to show some respect.
>
> JOE: Cemeteries are for the past. This is my time.

A few seconds later, in the next scene, Tate tells Ben, in his home office for meeting with patients, "I don't have any more visions. I think it might have just been, like, a screwy chemical imbalance, and of course, the parenting." Joe Escandarian, Tate, Ben – they all imagine themselves launched into a future freed of the past by sheer force of will, a will that the "twisted nerve" and "the code" say they do not have. But the details are rich here. Gene Autry died in 1998, and Joe's allusion suggests something else: Autry founded a museum devoted to representing not only the myth of the "West" but also its historical diversity, including the perspectives of indigenous peoples, women, and other traditionally silenced groups.[29] The reference is a canny one to the very history that Constance is urging him to "respect" even as she uses racist epithets herself.

Moreover, Constance links the failure to respect history with "haunting." The full weight of this remark reverberates through the season. Ben, for instance, is trying to escape the consequences of his affair with a university student, Hayden (Kate Mara), but that history keeps asserting itself: Vivien brings it up, Hayden calls, Hayden shows up at the Murder House, Hayden is killed by Larry with a shovel and buried in the backyard, and then Hayden becomes one of the more malevolent ghosts in the house. The "return of the repressed" is not Freudian but quite literal here, and it is the past that keeps coming back. The function of the house as a cover for its own violent past, largely concealed in the basement, is made explicit in "The Murder House" (1.3) as Ben builds a gazebo over the buried body of his murdered girlfriend, and the murdered girlfriend of a previous owner: the episode dramatizes the relentless repetition of the same violent patterns, the burial of the evidence to conceal the violence, and it all still comes back through haunting. The same episode and the one following deals with the entrapment of the living as well, following three couples, including the Harmons, in three different timeframes, who are trapped in a house they cannot afford and cannot sell. In a middle of a fight with his partner, Chad (Zachary Quinto) snaps back, "Then leave! Oh, I forgot, you can't, because all of your money and mine is in this house that we agreed to flip and make a mint on and now we can't because the economy is in the shitter" (1.4).

American Horror Story's first season thus brings on-screen what Catherine Spooner, drawing on Chris Baldick, defines as quintessentially gothic: "In Gothic texts, the past returns with a sickening force: the dead rise from the grave or lay their cold hands upon the shoulders of the living. This fearful scenario is compounded by physical imprisonment."[30] That past, moreover, is centrally a past of violence against women and especially in connection with Hollywood as an industry – a past that is the subject of repetition, both in the "real" and the supernatural world. The second episode of the series, "Home Invasion," is a thinly veiled reference to the murders of eight student nurses in 1966 Chicago, and, more importantly, the media's commemoration of serial killers: the Harmons' LA Home is invaded by killers intent on recreating the murders of two student nurses in the same house in 1968 (to complete the allusion, the surname of the episode's 1968 serial killer is the same as the middle name of the actual 1966 serial killer). Later episodes refer to serial killer Ted Bundy and a number of murders connected to the film and television industry, including the notorious Black

Dahlia murder (1947), the murder of Sal Mineo (1976), and the murders of Nicole Simpson and Ronald Goldman (1994), most mentioned on the Eternal Darkness tour bus that appears a couple of times in the series, including "The Murder House." The tour, also called "the Murder House tour" (1.4), visits various sites of famous Hollywood murders and, after an on-screen dramatization of its account of Sal Mineo's murder, "concludes with one of the most famous houses of horrors in the City of Angels, better known as the Murder House" (1.3), the Harmons' home.

The tour guide tells the story of its first owners, Nora Montgomery, "prominent East-coast socialite," and Dr. Charles Montgomery, "acclaimed surgeon to the stars" (1.3) – Tate calls him "doctor to the stars" (1.4). When Charles fails to make sufficient money to please Nora, she pushes him to become an abortionist to the vulnerable young women the new film industry attracts: Nora encourages their first patient, "Such a pretty girl, but you can't become a legend of the silver screen with an obligation hanging on your skirt" (1.3). In a tale Tate recounts to Violet Harmon in the basement the night before Halloween (1.4), the Montgomerys' infant son, Thaddeus, is kidnapped, killed, dismembered, and returned to his parents. Charles, falling further into his "terrifying Frankenstein complex," stitches his son back together and reanimates the baby's corpse by giving it the heart of a woman that Charles had murdered. Nora, horrified, kills her husband and son and then commits suicide. The Montgomery narrative, stretched across various episodes, is itself a kind of Frankenstein-creation, mixing together the Lindbergh kidnapping, the Manson murders ("Charles Montgomery" was an alias of one of the Manson family),[31] the Thin Man series (centering on the socialite Nora and her detective-husband Nick Charles), and the Black Dahlia murder of Elizabeth Short, since Charles, in this revision of Hollywood history, is the one who dissects the victim, as well as a later victim in the season, Travis. Charles lies at the nexus of the season's various references to the history of Hollywood, from 1920s abortionist to would-be actresses to 1940s accessory to the murder of the would-be actress Elizabeth Short to present-day accessory to the murder of another aspiring actor, Constance's gigolo-boyfriend, Travis. In the same episode that introduces the Montgomerys (1.3), Larry, yet another aspiring actor, begs Ben to "run a scene with [him]" and give him money for "head shots." The history of Hollywood swirls in and around the Murder House, and it is referenced again and again in the episode of that title: it is the "absent cause" in Fredric Jameson's sense, and a McGuffin in Hitchcock's.[32] It drives the action but is never there, "inaccessible to us except in textual form."[33] We see no films and only one brief shot of television; there are no working actors, directors, writers, or billboards. There is only the Murder House tour. To return to Jameson more fully: "History is what hurts, it is what refuses desire and sets inexorable limits to individual as well as collective praxis, which its 'ruses' turn into grisly and ironic reversals of their overt intention. But this History can be apprehended only through its effects, and never directly as some reified force."[34] This is *American Horror Story*'s Hollywood, and perhaps part of what made the season so disturbing for many is the way in which the episodes are effects of this Hollywood history: the season is itself a Hollywood production, re-energizing the career of its key actor, Jessica Lange, in a strange echo of Norma Desmond's desire for a comeback that is further reinforced through the figure of the maid who, in switching between youthful and middle-aged forms, constantly calls attention to Hollywood's appetite for young women and thus the unemployability of both Norma Desmond and Constance – a concern with the rendering of aging women as monstrous that will return with much greater emphasis in the third season of *American Horror Story*, *Coven*.

Moreover, all of these Hollywood narratives are associated with the drive for upward mobility, including the variant of the American Dream in dreams of stardom, from Nora's complaints that her husband is not wealthy enough to Constance's maneuvering, over decades, to get back into the larger, more ornate "Murder House," to the various aspiring actors who want less to ply their trade than to become rich and famous: as Constance sneers to Travis, "What career? What? This dream you have of appearing half-naked in your skivvies sixty feet high above Times Square? … I know that dream. I had that dream. I was going to be a big star!" (1.9). It is this history on which the house is built, and this history which is resurrected, again and again, in the season: the American Dream as an attempted flight from enduring history into transient fame that never succeeds. Constance is the central icon of this history, a failed actress who still reads the trades, her story rife with allusions to Billy Wilder's *Sunset Blvd.*, from keeping a failed Hollywood hopeful as her lover and giving him money to get her cigarettes, to the echoes between her penultimate scene and Norma Desmond's in *Sunset Blvd.* This is not to suggest that *American Horror Story* is rewriting *Sunset Blvd.*, or *Twisted Nerve*, or the history of serial killers in the US, or even the seedier side of Hollywood history, but that it alludes to all of these cultural materials in a larger discussion of the ways in which the film and television industry is representable as a conventional gothic villain in its treatment of women and, at the same time, salaciously gothicizes the serial killer as an extreme form of what Moira describes as quintessentially masculine, the "need to objectify" (1.3) – to turn the (young) female body into a thing to be seen, posed, possessed, discarded. In the first season of *American Horror Story*, it is Hollywood, not the devil or some other supernatural entity, that motivates many of the displacements and exaggerations that have long undergirded the gothic's depictions of patriarchal violence and women's vulnerability.

These three undomestic houses bring me back again to Richard Matheson's *Hell House* (1971), not for their deployment of supernatural devices such as a malevolent controlling spirit, like Matheson's Belasco, and a house filled with trapped and tortured souls, also used in Matheson's novel, but for their concern with media and the construction of narrative. From the "campfire stories" of "Pest-House" to the web postings of "Hell House" and the Hollywood history of *Murder House*, all three series stress the "real" effects of fiction and two (*Supernatural* and *American Horror Story*) comment on the desire to be part of Hollywood in particular. At the end of *Supernatural*'s "Hell House," Sam Winchester plays a prank on the ghostbuster wannabes by claiming to be a Hollywood agent calling them to LA for a movie deal, further layering the episode's wry commentary on the false but effective lure of modern media – particularly since Matheson's novel features an actress who rejected the hollowness of Hollywood. These series, like Matheson's *Hell House*, have a sustained interest in a specifically gothic concern with authenticity, veracity, and verifiability in a post-Enlightenment world. The "refaking of what is already fake," in Hogle's phrase, comes up again and again in gothic television not only as a continuation of gothic literature but also as a deployment of the gothic to comment on the televisual medium itself. *Supernatural*'s "Hell House" spawned not only a website (hellhoundslair.com) and web series but also later episodes featuring the paranormal investigators that "Hell House" introduced; "Ghostfacers" (3.13), for instance, closely echoes the founding plot of Matheson's *Hell House* in which a team, including one couple, investigates a notorious haunted house, and discovers the body of the key ghost in a hidden underground room, while simultaneously parodying the documentary-style TV series, *Ghost Hunters* (2004–).

In a brief exchange in the second-last episode of *Murder House*, the two teenagers born decades apart, Violet and Tate, now both ghosts, discuss their future and Violet remarks, "One of these days this computer will be obsolete. People will have microchips implanted in their brains or something. We won't be able to watch YouTube. We'll be like all the others here, prisoners in a windowless cell" ("Birth"). There seems to be no TV in the Harmon house, and only Violet's laptop computer and music players to connect the Murder House to the Hollywood culture that so many of the house's ghosts aspired, and expired, to join. This is the hell of their own making: not the hyperreal with its "phantom landscapes and synthetic identities"[35] that so many characters yearn to participate in, "sixty feet above Times Square," but the fixity and narrowness of being trapped in a house without any connections to media. There is no ground on which to found some nostalgic return to meaning or a progressive future to happiness – only different degrees of alienation from a world of myriad media. The only possibility for happiness in the series lies in the madness of accepting the lie. The *Murder House* season ends on a deeply ironic note with the Harmons, now all dead, mimicking a Norman Rockwell scene as they happily chat and decorate a Christmas tree, with strange lighting and overacting stressing the irony of this conclusion to twelve episodes of sexist violence. Despite the implication of Harmon harmony at last, the whole family is never within the same frame of any shot. *Supernatural*'s "Hell House" concludes with the elated paranormal investigative team driving off to fame and fortune in Hollywood because of Sam's prank call. *Millennium*'s "Pest House" ends with Dr. Stoller's non-response to Frank's unpsychological explanation about evil touching those who investigate it: "I want to go home now." I want to end this chapter on that phrase – on the desire for the house as home precisely at the moment that the horror of the pest house cannot be comprehended, like the Harmons' Rockwell fantasy after episode after episode of gruesome violence and horror, and like the dream of Hollywood fame after what *Supernatural* depicts as the gritty, painful, and alienating work of "hunting things." The domestic here is not the everyday ground that is subject to gothic inversion or critique – the domestic is, instead, precisely the space of the fantastic where violent reality is denied.

Notes

1 Robert Miles, *Gothic Writing, 1750–1820: A Genealogy*, new edn (Manchester: Manchester University Press, 2002), p. 45.
2 Fred Botting and Dale Townshend, "Introduction," *Gothic: Critical Concepts in Literary and Cultural Studies*, 4 vols (New York: Routledge, 2004), vol. 1, p. 16.
3 Many of the leading philosophers in this eighteenth-century intellectual movement are invoked by characters' names in the sometimes-gothic series, J. J. Abrams' *Lost* (2004–2010): Edmund Burke, Anthony Ashley Cooper (Lord Shaftesbury), David Hume, John Locke, and Jean-Jacques Rousseau are invoked in the series by Edmund Burke (and Juliet Burke), Anthony Cooper, Desmond David Hume, John Locke (for a time with the pseudonym Jeremy Bentham), and Alexandra and Danielle Rousseau. The characters do not exemplify their namesakes' philosophies, leaving the references largely at the level of bricolage.
4 Jeffrey Sconce, *Haunted Media: Electronic Presence from Telegraphy to Television* (Durham, NC: Duke University Press, 2000), p. 5.
5 Jerrold Hogle, "'Frankenstein' as neo-gothic: from the ghost of the counterfeit to the monster of abjection," *Romanticism, History, and the Possibilities of Genre: Re-forming Literature, 1789–1837*, ed. Tilottama Rajan and Julia M. Wright (Cambridge: Cambridge University Press, 1998), p. 189.
6 Hogle, "'Frankenstein' as neo-gothic," p. 178; Jean Baudrillard, *Simulacra and Simulation*, trans. Sheila Faria Glaser (Ann Arbor: University of Michigan Press, 1995), p. 2.
7 Fred Botting, "Signs of evil: Bataille, Baudrillard and postmodern gothic," *Southern Review*, 27 (1994), 493–510.
8 Sconce suggests "that postmodern theory is in itself simply another in a long series of *occult fantasies* inspired by electronic media" (*Haunted Media*, p. 170; emphasis added).
9 Baudrillard, *Simulacra and Simulation*, p. 3.
10 Michel Foucault, *Discipline and Punish: The Birth of the Prison* (1975), trans. Alan Sheridan (New York: Vintage, 1979), p. 202.
11 Sconce, *Haunted Media*, p. 169.
12 See, e.g., Lenora Ledwon, "*Twin Peaks* and the television gothic,"

Literature/Film Quarterly, 21:4 (1993), 260–70, but especially Helen Wheatley, *Gothic Television* (Manchester: Manchester University Press, 2006).

13 Horace Walpole, "Preface to the Second Edition," *The Castle of Otranto*, ed. W. S. Lewis, Intro. E. J. Clery (Oxford: Oxford University Press, 1998), p. 10. See also S. T. Coleridge's account of "The Rime of the Ancient Mariner" and his other contributions to *Lyrical Ballads*: "incidents and agents were to be, in part at least, supernatural; and the excellence aimed at was to consist in the interesting of the affections by the dramatic truth of such emotions, as would naturally accompany such situations, supposing them real" (*Biographia Literaria*, in *Selected Poetry and Prose of Coleridge*, ed. Donald A. Stauffer [New York: Modern Library, 1951], p. 264).

14 See, e.g., Svetlana Boym, "Conspiracy theories and literary ethics: Umberto Eco, Danilo Kis and *The Protocols of Zion*," *Comparative Literature*, 51 (1999), 97–122; Umberto Eco, *Six Walks in the Fictional Woods* (Cambridge, MA: Harvard University Press, 1998); Victoria Nelson, "Faux Catholic: a gothic subgenre from Monk Lewis to Dan Brown," *boundary* 2, 34 (2007), 87–107.

15 Richard Dyer, "Kill and kill again," *Sight & Sound*, n.s., 7.9 (September 1997), 14–17.

16 Dyer, "Kill and kill again."

17 Hogle, "'Frankenstein' as neo-gothic," p. 189.

18 Julia Kristeva, *Powers of Horror: An Essay*, trans. Leon S. Roudiez (New York: Columbia University Press, 1982), p. 2. In his work on the gothic, Hogle draws extensively on Kristeva's notion of the abject, a concept particularly amenable to discussions of the gothic because of the field's longstanding interest in the Freudian uncanny.

19 Kristeva, *Powers of Horror*, pp. 70, 71.

20 Jacques Derrida takes this phrase from Jean-Jacques Rousseau's *Confessions* (1782) where it is "use[d] ... in order to explain, precisely, a 'condition almost unintelligible and inconceivable [to reason]'" (*Of Grammatology*, trans. Gayatri Chakravorty Spivak [Baltimore: Johns Hopkins University Press, 1976], p. 149 [square brackets in original]).

21 William Shakespeare, *Hamlet*, *The Norton Shakespeare*, 2nd edn, ed. Stephen Greenblatt et al. (New York: Norton, 2008), 1.5.168–69; Kate Ferguson Ellis, *The Contested Castle: Gothic Novels and the Subversion of Domestic Ideology* (Chicago: University of Illinois Press, 1989).

22 Eric Savoy, "The face of the tenant: a theory of American gothic," *American Gothic: New Interventions in a National Narrative*, ed. Robert K. Martin and Eric Savoy (Iowa City: University of Iowa Press, 1998), p. 8.

23 Hogle, "'Frankenstein' as neo-gothic," p. 178.
24 For a recent overview of the series' treatment of time as fluid, see Michael Fuchs, "'Play it again, Sam … and Dean': temporality and meta-textuality in *Supernatural*," *Time in Television Narrative: Exploring Temporality in Twenty-first Century Programming*, ed. Melissa Ames (Jackson: University of Mississippi Press, 2012), pp. 82–94.
25 *Sunset Blvd.*, dir. Billy Wilder, wr. Billy Wilder, Charles Brackett, and D. M. Marshman Jr. (Paramount, 1950).
26 The narrative's dating of the house is not consistent with the house used as the set: the house used for the exterior shots was built in 1902 by and for architect Alfred F. Rosenheim, and various details noted in the season are more consistent with that date than 1922. Tiffany stained glass, for instance, a feature of the house, was popular at the turn of the century.
27 Lange's *Asylum* character is, literally, an "old whore" who runs the mental institution in the guise of a sexually repressive nun. The line about the "old whore" appears soon after a gothic depiction of "a state mental institution" that also anticipates *Asylum*: "trust me, those places make prison look like Club Med" ("Pilot" 1.1).
28 For a discussion of the season's discussion of sexuality, primarily as a response to US sexual conservatism but also as deeply rooted in the larger gothic literary tradition, see Tosha Taylor, "Who's afraid of the Rubber Man? Perversions and subversions of sex and class in *American Horror Story*," *Networked Knowledge*, 5:2 (September 2012), 135–53.
29 According to its website, "The Autry is the first major American museum to recognize the contributions of the lesbian, gay, bisexual, and transgender (LGBT) community to the American West," Autry National Center, http://theautry.org/whats-here/overview <date of access: May 28, 2013>.
30 Catherine Spooner, *Contemporary Gothic* (London: Reaktion, 2006), p. 18.
31 See http://americanhorrorstory.wikia.com/wiki/Charles_Montgomery <date of access: May 31, 2013>.
32 Fredric Jameson, *The Political Unconscious: Narrative as a Socially Symbolic Act* (Ithaca, NY: Cornell University Press, 1981), p. 35.
33 Jameson, *Political Unconscious*, p. 35.
34 Jameson, *Political Unconscious*, p. 102.
35 Sconce, *Haunted Media*.

Conclusion: gothic conspiracy and the eyes of Lara Means

Something happens to US gothic television as its narratives develop – it folds back in on its cultural origins, turning from contemporary secularism or broad religious inclusiveness to Catholicism and its gothic accoutrements. *Supernatural* in the first three seasons is entirely centered on folk beliefs, exposing a Christian faith healer, for instance, as successful because his wife is using magic to control a Reaper ("Faith" 1.12) and revealing a purported angel to be a simple ghost ("Houses of the Holy" 2.13). In the fourth season, however, an angel becomes a recurring character. Not only are angels in a struggle with the demons that have been the series' focus but they also interact with, and even masquerade as, the other supernatural figures of the first three seasons – the Nordic "Trickster" of the early seasons is thus revealed to be the archangel Gabriel in "Changing Channels" (5.8), and the Winchesters are suddenly pawns in the angels' ongoing power struggle. Instead of an absent father driving his sons to search for him, as in the opening season, God is missing in all of the late seasons of the series and the angels cannot find him – and struggle for power in his absence. In *Millennium*, most of the first season is entirely secular: Frank's visions are often comprehensible as flashes of insight, the Millennium group is a consulting firm, and nothing supernatural happens. Then, in "Sacrament" (1.15), Frank's daughter has a vision of her aunt's suffering during a kidnapping and, in "Powers, Principalities, Thrones, and Dominions" (1.19), an angel appears, and Frank, and the viewers, are suddenly able to see "supernatural" events alongside "natural" ones. In season 2, the most clearly gothic season, Frank sees and interacts with demons, his partner has visions of angels, the Millennium Group is part of a millennium-old Catholic conspiracy, holy relics have supernatural properties, and a recurring character, Lucy Butler, is overtly demonic. *Point Pleasant*, within its short span, becomes more and more religious as the season progresses, finally tying the main narrative of Christina to a Catholic conspiracy to protect the world from the threat she poses through the transformation of the gentle Jesse into the warrior who will kill Christina – a transformation that he resists, to the point that they have to kidnap him, physically restrain him, and generally coerce him into cooperation. In *American Gothic*, the child's struggle to be good with the mentorship of the local doctor, his friend, sister's ghost, and a woman who takes him in utterly collapses, and he becomes as fully dangerous and supernaturally powerful as his demonic father would wish. Even *Angel*, which maintains a non-Christian worldview through the insistently vague and somewhat Hellenic "powers-that-be," draws on the gothic trope of conspiracy in its final two, breakneck-speed episodes by revealing that a secret society of supernatural entities, "The Circle of the Black Thorn," has been controlling commerce, politics, and other social engines. As these series unravel masculinity and patriarchy, their arc narratives turn to the old gothic trope of religious conspiracy and the medieval icons of angels and demons.

Drawing on the work of J. M. Roberts' *Mythology of Secret Societies* (1972), Ronald Paulson argues that conspiracy in early gothic literature was allied to the problem of agency:

> The assumption of individual agency (as opposed to the more popular modern explanation of social and economic determinism) is evident not only in the allegorizations of revolution as the actions of a single man ... but also in the comforting retreat to Satanic responsibility in the Miltonic fictions of rebellion in heaven and in the Garden of Eden – in Rosario-Matilda [in Lewis's *The Monk*], the Devil who in fact determines all the events that Ambrosio seemed responsible for.[1]

Bringing us forward two centuries, Robson suggests that "conspiracy is what makes *The X-Files* truly Gothic," arguing that, through the conspiracy of the "political and economic elite" of the "post-war" era, *X-Files* "takes the conviction of many Generation X-ers that their parents had effectively mortgaged their future for short-term gain and turns it into a specific threat."[2] In both eras, gothic conspiracy explains a lack of agency among its (generally male) characters by positing not a "twisted nerve" but a conspiracy of super-agents: a group of powerful beings (again, generally male) who secretly control events and characters. In gothic television, it manages postmodern crisis: instead of a lack of agency in a random world, it offers a supernaturally controlled world in which masculine agency is compromised because of a more powerful force that supervises world history. Male characters' powerlessness is thus not a failure of their masculinity, in style or substance, but an effect of hidden conspiracies and concealed historical machinations. In this vision, patriarchy in "the dark part of the hut" negates individual masculinity while maintaining the power of masculinity in principle.

This resonates with a crisis in Enlightenment thought that carries through into modern neoliberal thought: as Stefan Andriopoulos has argued, Adam Smith's economic concept of an "invisible hand" that directs individual self-interest toward the collective interest is a gothic device that echoes another "invisible hand" in Walpole's *Castle of Otranto*.[3] It is this "invisible hand" that voids any need for government controls over the market – the market, through this sleight of hand, is automatically corrected. Both Smith and Walpole imagine a higher order that is outside of and manages human actions. As Angel says of "The Circle of the Black Thorn," "We're in a machine – the Black Thorn runs it": "Power endures. We can't bring down the senior partners but, for one bright, shining moment, we can show them that they don't own us" ("Power Play" 5.21). And this ultimately is what many of these series suggest: that "resistance is futile" (in the words of *Star Trek*'s Borg collective), but it is nevertheless the only vehicle through which male sovereignty still acts. In the angel seasons of *Supernatural*, for instance, the hypermasculine and very effective hunters, the Winchester brothers, are suddenly just "meat suits" for angels, bodies to be used as "vessels" through which the angels can fight each other: "team free will" is their nearly hopeless, even ironic, effort to establish some autonomy against it. In *Point Pleasant*, Jesse proves his heroic status by resisting the Catholic conspiracy in his confrontation with Christina. The game cannot be won; the only choice is to refuse to play the game. Resistance may be futile, but it is the only way to assert agency when a small group holds all the power.

It is the second, gothic season of *Millennium*, however, where the conspiratorial order is most widely developed. In the final five episodes of the season, Morgan and Wong present conspiracy after conspiracy in which agency, and especially male agency, is compromised, managed, or simply set aside. Most of the season sets up the Millennium Group as itself a conspiracy – a secret society that, for a thousand years, has tried to manage the West – but this conspiracy only leads to other conspiracies: the Millennium Group battles the Odessa Group, a Nazi secret society; the Millennium Group is fractured by two secret societies within its ranks, the Owls and the Roosters (one group believes the apocalypse will be caused by a far-off astronomical event, and the other that it is religious and imminent); and, in the first of the five-episode grouping at the end of the season, the Millennium Group appears to be watching another conspiracy, one that protects the women who bear the bloodline of Christ. These late-season conspiracies are explicitly gendered: women on one side, allied with angels or demons, and men on the other, thinking that they have power but learning that they are helpless or largely irrelevant.

The first episode in this five-episode conspiracy arc is "Anamnesis" (2.19). The term refers to the recollection of past lives and means literally "loss of forgetfulness," the episode itself building on the alternative Christian myth popularized in *Holy Blood, Holy Grail* (by Michael Baigent, Richard Leigh, and Henry Lincoln) and later Dan Brown's *The Da Vinci Code*: Mary Magdalene and Christ had a child, and a secret order is protecting the bloodline of Christ up to the present: "And thus, from age to age, she passed from body to body, into one female body after the other." The episode focuses on women's visions of angels and Mary Magdalene, and the investigation of those visions' legitimacy, a vision reinforced by the use of Patti Smith's "Dancing Barefoot" in the opening and closing scenes – itself a revision of female divinity in Christianity ("she is benediction …").[4] In "Anamnesis," the teenaged Clare is the descendant of Mary and Jesus, and she is having visions, originally believed to be of the Virgin Mary but later revealed to be of Mary Magdalene. Reaction in the community is divided: the minister and his son see Clare as a wayward troublemaker who is, according to the son, "going to hell." The school secretary, Clare's inner circle of female friends, and Lara Means all believe that Clare has the visions. Lara highlights what is, early in the episode, already obvious: "It's interesting how reactive religious hostility is following predictable gender lines." But these gender lines are enforced through various other means. For instance, Lara complains that she does not see "him," her angel, while she is in proximity to Clare. Referring to Clare's refusal to be baptized by the minister who thinks her visions are satanic, Lara defends her reaction: "How would you feel if you were baptized against your will by a religion who transformed Mary Magdalene of the gnostic texts, the apostle of the apostles, into a mere prostitute?"

The episode not only offers a feminist re-visioning of early Christianity in which Mary Magdalene is "the apostle of the apostles" maligned by two millennia of church patriarchy, but also *performs* that alternative women's history. Frank Black, the series protagonist, does not appear once in the episode. Lara and Frank's wife Catherine investigate Clare and her visions, at the behest of the school's vice-principal – a woman who is an old friend of Catherine's. Scene after scene is all-female, in a series that focuses on a male profiler whose speciality is male serial killers and sadists. There are male characters in the episode: there are bit players, the angrily defensive minister and his son, and Ben Fisher, the guardian-apostle (as his surname suggests) sent to protect Clare. But the investigation that is the central plot of all *Millennium* episodes proceeds on women's orders, by women, and of women. They do not agree – Catherine is skeptical, her friend believing but resistant, Lara a complete believer – but epistemological control is represented as being in their hands. And, at the end, Lara gives the evidence that Clare is the descendant of Christ not to her boss Peter Watts, but to Catherine, recalling Clare's early assertion to Catherine, "We have to finish it and you have to write it down," making Catherine her apostle. Peter Watts appears only in one scene to reinforce his role as a patriarchal figure in the season: in a stairwell, seen from a distance by Catherine, he asks Lara, who has just told him that Clare is "formidable," "And him? What about him?" In other words, the episode both recovers an alternative women's history of Mary Magdalene and her bloodline and suggests that women should investigate and preserve that history, the "loss of forgetfulness" signaled by the episode title. And this women's history completely sidelines men: Ben Fisher, the man who interests Watts, sacrifices himself to save Clare, Frank Black is physically absent and Peter Watts nearly entirely so as well as far off the point.

This positive vision of a women's history of angels and Christ's bloodline is countered by one of the notable exceptions to the apparent realism of the first season and its focus on male serial killers: Lucy Butler (Sarah-Jane Redmond). The horror story told by the teenagers in "The Curse of Frank Black" draws on the narrative "Lamentation" (1.18), specifically Lucy Butler's murder of Frank's friend Bletcher in the basement of the bright yellow house – the event that first drives Catherine out of it, long before her separation from Frank in season 2. Bletcher is killed by Lucy Butler who appears on-screen switching between three forms: male, female, and demonic. About the middle of the episode, and well before this revelation, Peter Watts asks Frank, "They say genius is the ability to hold two contradictory thoughts in your mind at the same time. What do you call a man who holds two contradictory personalities?" Frank replies, "The Devil." The figure of Lucy Butler, one of the creepiest characters in the Chris Carter universe, begins the gothic work of unsettling all of the series' scientific certainties, and she is a woman who repeatedly plays on her sexual desirability to gain control over men. She is a throwback, to the Magdalene as whore, to the seductress, to Lilith of the apocrypha, and to the succubus, explicitly in "Antipas" (3.13), a rare gothic episode in the third season in which she has sex with Frank in what he thinks is a nightmare.

Frank's nemesis across the series, she is a monster of uncertain gender who re-deploys the conventional gender roles that the series largely works to displace or criminalize – or demonize. In "A Room with No View" (2.20), the episode which immediately followed "Anamnesis," she is revealed to be over a century old: she kidnaps promising teenagers, imprisons them, and there subjects them to Paul Mauriat's saccharine "Love Is Blue," played over and over again on a loop, as well as sexual teasing and monotonous food until they become what she wants, that is, as bland as "Love Is Blue." Although she seems to kidnap both girls and boys, and was herself once a promising teenage girl, all of her on-screen victims are male. Her new victim, Landon (Christopher Masterson), is repeatedly depicted trying to help other young men. In an early scene, he argues with the school guidance counsellor, Teresa Roe (Mariangela Pino), about his friend's aspirations:

LANDON: This isn't about me – it's about Howard's life.
ROE: I don't want him to be disappointed.
LANDON: And you're holding him down.

ROE: A setback early in life is hard to overcome for someone like Howard.

LANDON: Leave your own life out of Howard's. ... Are you too incapable of comprehending anything other than your own failure?

("A Room with No View" 2.20)

The counsellor believes in the tyranny of standardized testing over students' future lives: "there's a system in place, gentlemen, one that constantly evaluates our youths and our lives with no application of relativity. A 4.0 will succeed, a 2.5 will not. Below 750 on the SATs and certain doors close. A quality of person, sense of humor, heart, these are not on any applications. It's all about your numbers." But the episode represents this as a matter of class rather than scores: Landon, though "voted most likely to succeed" by his peers, expects to work with "construction guys," the guidance counsellor dismisses him as a future "Quickie Lube" employee, and his divorced father is a blue-collar worker who does not understand what his son reads (Nabokov, Eco, and other postmodern authors) nor why his son chose to live with him rather than his comfortably middle-class and clever mother. Believing in the tyranny of the "system," the counsellor shuttles students like Landon to Lucy Butler, who tells the promising, individual, and helpful Landon,

> You are nothing! Nothing lies ahead for you. You lie awake in the middle of the night, or you look around at others, and you feel inside, in your heart, that maybe, no, definitely, that you are different, that you are special, that you can make a difference? You are nothing. The sooner you realize that mediocrity is all that you are, the sooner your love will be blue.
>
> (2.20)

Or, rather, he will become fully blue-collar. The perpetuation of privilege through the systemic abjection of such "spirited kid[s]" is visually ascribed to a system of women – the guidance counsellor and Lucy Butler – who act violently and demonically to belittle young men and rob them of their agency, while diegetically the script includes female kidnap victims and an ungendered "system," the gap between visual shot and verbal detail exposing an objectively neutral system as gender as well as class biased. While the counsellor claims the "system" of numbers will marginalize such people anyway, the episode uses the gothic device of demonic conspiracy to enforce that system as well as focus it on the disabling of masculine agency.

So, in the closing episodes of season 2, back-to-back episodes offer a secret women's history of Christianity in which women hold privilege as visionaries, heirs and historians, and a secret history of privilege in which "numbers," with the assistance of demonized women, suppress men's potential. Both narratives focus on (feminine) conspiracy that disempowers or marginalizes patriarchal control through objective means – divine bloodlines and test scores. The next episode, "Somehow, Satan Got Behind Me" (2.21) echoes the others on comic terms: four devils meet in a coffee shop, and discuss the ways in which they tempt humanity and push individuals to violent deaths. All but one object of the devils' manipulation is male, and that one female victim, an aging stripper, influences the devil who seduces her – he falls in love with her, drives her to suicide to regain his credibility as a demon, and then grieves terribly, grief witnessed by Frank who remarks, "You must be so sad." Once again, conspiracy derails masculine autonomy, and even the male devils are susceptible to the power of women.

These episodes pave the way for the final two episodes of the season, the first, "The Fourth Horseman" (2.22), setting up the crises of the second, "The Time Is Now" (2.23). "The Time Is Now" follows Frank Black as he learns of the coming plague and the Millennium Group's part in it, but it culminates in an extended sequence in which Lara Means, newly initiated into the Group's mysteries, goes insane. Repeatedly in Lara's scenes, dice hit a table, giving us for the first time a visual correlative to the percussive sound that has punctuated the series as well as marked the series' theme song, while, interleaved, are scenes in which a member of the Millennium Group, Mr. Lott, largely through voice-over, explains the Malthusian principles of the Group's "Plan":

> The Millennium Group is not concerned with any single individual life. … Our responsibility – and remember that word, it will come up again – our responsibility is to the life of the whole of mankind. And so we must proceed in a manner that increases the odds of that survival. Sounds like a paradox, but it is the very nature of our responsibility. If one life appears to interfere with our protection of billions of lives, well, it really becomes a no-brainer. And the courage to be responsible for all those lives – that is the first thing that you must understand and accept. … And for those who are not broken by

> the danger and the responsibility of knowing comes the intensity of living with that responsibility for the rest of their lives and the actions which must be taken to achieve the Millennium Group's success of purpose. This is who we are.
>
> (2.23)

As the voice-over proceeds, viewers are shown the Millennium Group's assassination of another man. The interleaving of scenes implies that Lara has been "broken" by the knowledge, its Malthusian calculations obsessing her as she rolls the dice over and over again, recording the results on a piece of paper. Lara's descent into madness is focused on probability. She asks Frank, "Why were we born now? Do you realize the probability – the probability of even being born at all? The chances of any life being here – let alone you and me? If it ends – when it will end – we'll be amongst the 10 percent of all humans who ever lived. Do you understand the odds of being born at the time it all ends?" The interleaving of the three scenes – Lott's explanation of "this is who we are," a Millennium Group catchphrase that has remained mysterious until this point; the assassination of an operative; and Lara Means alone in a cabin – sets up a series of suggestive juxtapositions in which Lott's mathematical rationalization, and focus on "mankind" rather than "humanity," is undercut by Lara's sense of improbability, and the sacrifice of "one life" is made literal both by the assassination and by Lara's loss of reason.

Confronting numerical randomness by recording the outcomes of dice throws, she is drawn deeper into her visions in a protracted scene set to Patti Smith's "The Land." Smith's lyrics not only provide some of the images for the scene but also formally thematize the episode's central concern: Smith has termed lyrics such as those for "The Land" "babelogues." Simon Reynolds and Joy Press say of such "gushing gibberish" that the "babelogue is the opposite of a monologue or soliloquy, forms that are centred and self-aggrandising," and that "The Land" in particular "has both the rock hero and rock form surrendering to an inundation of chaos"[5] – as here, where the character Lara Means and televisual form are simultaneously fractured through an apocalyptic "inundation of chaos," of randomness. An extended portion of this babelogue deals with "possibilities," picking up on the trope of the landing dice in these scenes in *Millennium*. Smith's song is the backdrop for a nearly ten-minute sequence of visuals which feature the dice, visions of angels, images from Smith's lyrics (horses, for instance), atom-bomb explosions, natural disasters, violence, and the "scientific" representation of a comet's annihilation in the sun from the first episode of the season, mixed in with distorted visuals of Lara's emotional distress as she pulls at her hair, screams in terror at a vision of an angel bleeding (his blood the color of the red dice, which his face suggests), and throws herself against the walls and floors until Frank bursts in and she is (like the mothers of *Point Pleasant* and *American Horror Story*) carried out by paramedics for containment in a mental institution. This stunning scene, an absolute refusal of televisual realism and of conventional television divisions into short scenes, partly cinematic and partly music video, ends with a final shot of the dice on the table.

The season thus does not give us an answer to the Millennium Group's schism, does not privilege science over religion, or Owls over Roosters. The randomness of the scientific view, of the tyranny of numbers, drives Lara Means mad, leaving her (and viewers) awash in images, both visual and verbal, without causal connection – "a sea of possibility," in Smith's phrase. Extra-diegetically, the linking of landing dice with the percussive sound that has punctuated the series offers two possibilities: first, it has always represented landing dice, suggesting the randomness of the critical moments and quotations that it marks; second, the dice serving as a visual correlative to the percussive sound is itself coincidental, an arbitrary connection in a universe without meaning. The gothic anxiety about referentiality is attenuated by the landing dice as the answer to the series' repetition of a sound without a visual. And this set of conspiracy narratives – Christ's bloodline, the "system" run by test scores, the four devils who tempt humanity, and the exposure of the Millennium Group as a secret society (of mostly men) that will kill and of secrets that can drive members insane – is bracketed by Patti Smith, "Dancing Barefoot" being used in the opening and closing scenes of "Anamnesis" and "The Land" as the score for Lara's collapse into insanity. This is all the more suggestive because of another string of musical references in the season: Frank, who reflects on his 1950s childhood in a number of episodes, listens to and discusses Bobby Darin's music throughout the season. Patti Smith's songs are heard extra-diegetically: a soundtrack that is never discussed or explained within the logic of the episode even though her lyrics comment directly on the plot and visual content of those episodes.

Bobby Darin is woven into the scripts directly: Frank struggles to get his Bobby Darin CD to play, and discusses Darin's music with a serial killer. One an icon of feminist rock, the other an icon of 1950s nostalgia, they musically mark the divisions that the conspiracies highlight, between an idealized masculinity of agency, the American Dream, and institutional control, and a disruptive, often incomprehensible, femininity that counters that nostalgic vision.

The final episodes of the gothic second season are relentlessly interested in exploring the inadequacy of religious and scientific truth claims, making manifest, to invoke Baudrillard again, the "hyperreality" of the televisual. Baudrillard suggests that "Cinema plagiarizes itself, recopies itself, remakes its classics, retroactivates its original myths."[6] The second season of *Millennium* repeatedly calls attention to such counterfeiting and textual debts, using the gothic mode to subvert the televisual realism of the detective show. Moreover, in these conspiracy-driven episodes, dominant narratives are exposed as fictions. "Anamnesis" explodes the Millennium Group's narrative of itself as a Catholic conspiracy which harbors the truth by placing it on the margins of another narrative, a women's history of Christ's bloodline. "A Room with No View" explodes the myth of the American Dream, suggesting that class and the "system" will not only trump but squash masculine potential. And "The Time Is Now" offers the "gothic sublimity" (in David Morris's phrase) of another set of numbers: probability and the cold Malthusian equations in which individuals are sacrificed by a secret society in its defense of the collective good.

All of this brings me back to *American Horror Story* and its depiction of Hollywood history as the Jamesonian "absent cause" of the violence and horror of much of the first season. One of the influential trends in popular culture studies, traceable back to the foundational work of Adorno and Horkheimer, has stressed cultural production as marketing, constituting viewers as consumers who buy all that popular media such as television sell – from its vision of the "real" to the hair products, diet aids, clothing, bargain renovation materials, and financial services that offer to move our actual lives closer to that vision. Conspiracy narratives, episodes that "debunk that [realist] myth" (in Kolchak's phrase), the visual unfolding of the layers of artifice that lie behind televisual verisimilitude, the narrative unravelling of stock realist types (such as the strong and practical-minded father figure) and stock realist methodologies (such as the scientific investigation of crime) – all of these features of gothic television complicate this vision of popular media as the vehicle of consumer training. This is not to idealize gothic television as somehow a means by which viewers can resist the multinational corporate machine's manipulations, a meta-conspiracy like "The Circle of the Black Thorn," but to suggest that gothic television in contesting televisual realism and the worldview it presents as "natural" carves out a space in which some aspects of those manipulations are on view – it "debunk[s] that myth."

Masculinity here is not merely ideal, or monstrous, or a reflection of ideological change in US society, but also a provocation to think about the category's representation in culture, like the title of an early episode of *Lost*: "All the Best Cowboys have Daddy Issues" (1.11). There are no cowboys in the series, of course, and this particular episode deals centrally with the kidnapping of a pregnant woman, the murder and then resurrection of her companion, and the realization that one of the survivors is actually an infiltrator from the island's original and still largely mysterious inhabitants, with only a flashback sequence working through a surgeon's difficult relationship with his surgeon father. This resonant title is not representational but allusive, offering a trenchant critique of Westerns' stylized masculinity, a hint at some of the character concerns of the episode, and a comment on the ways in which the series, set on a Pacific island, draws not only on gothic machinery but also on Western tropes: good guys and bad guys, the frontier mentality of surviving in a hostile landscape, and its extension in the threat of the "Others," those who lived on the island before the plane crash's "settlers" arrived. The allusive title operates at the level of cultural analysis, and suggests that characters with the sorts of concerns I have discussed in this book – "daddy issues" in general – is an aesthetic requirement. In formalist terms, all the *best* heroes have daddy issues – a struggle, an insecurity, or an obsession that shapes the character's complexity and compromises his full autonomy on terms vital to dramatic tension and other narrative elements. Philosophically, free will is the fantasy of release from paternal control, anxiety over "how to be a man," and "the golden rule of guys," at the same time that it is a key element in post-Enlightenment notions of male subjectivity. Various gothic series' almost compulsive return to the failure of free will because of a higher level of patriarchal power marks an attention to this contradiction as well as its narrative potential: "Popular folklore would have us believe that ... there are ruthless men who fear nothing – this story should debunk that myth."[7]

Notes

1 Ronald Paulson, "Gothic Fiction and the French Revolution," *ELH*, 48 (1981), 541. This has become a staple of discussions of early gothic literature: see, for instance, Markman Ellis, *The History of Gothic Fiction* (Edinburgh: Edinburgh University Press, 2005), ch. 4; Robert Miles, "The 1790s: the effulgence of the gothic," in *The Cambridge Companion to Gothic Fiction*, ed. Jerrold Hogle (Cambridge: Cambridge University Press, 2002), pp. 57–58; E. J. Clery, *The Rise of Supernatural Fiction, 1762–1800* (Cambridge: Cambridge University Press, 1995), who cites Paulson in this context (p. 162).

2 Eddie Robson, "Gothic television," *The Routledge Companion to Gothic*, ed. Catherine Spooner and Emma McEvoy (New York: Routledge, 2007), pp. 247, 248.

3 Stefan Andriopoulos, "The invisible hand: supernatural agency in political economy and the gothic novel," *ELH*, 66 (1999), 739–40.

4 Patti Smith and Ivan Kral (lyrics), "Dancing Barefoot," performed by Patti Smith, *Wave* (Arista, 1979).

5 Simon Reynolds and Joy Press, *The Sex Revolts: Gender, Rebellion, and Rock 'n' Roll* (Cambridge, MA: Harvard University Press, 1996), pp. 358–59, 358.

6 Jean Baudrillard, *Simulacra and Simulation*, trans. Sheila Faria Glaser (Ann Arbor: University of Michigan Press, 1995), p. 47.

7 "The Zombie," wr. Zekial Marko and David Chase, *Kolchak* (ABC, September 20, 1974).

Episodes discussed in detail

American Gothic. Created by Shaun Cassidy. Perf. Gary Cole, Lucas Black and Paige Turco. CBS, 1995–1996

1.1 "Pilot." Wr. Shaun Cassidy. Dir. Peter O'Fallon. September 22, 1995.

1.2 "A Tree Grows in Trinity." Wr. Shaun Cassidy. Dir. Michael Katleman. September 29, 1995.

1.3 "Eye of the Beholder." Wr. Shaun Cassidy and Judi Ann Mason. Dir. Jim Charleston. October 6, 1995.

1.4 "Damned If You Don't." Wr. Stephen Gaghan and Michael R. Perry. Dir. Lou Antonio. October 10, 1995.

1.5 "Dead to the World." Wr. Robin Green, Mitchell Burgess, Shaun Cassidy, Michael R. Perry and Stephen Gaghan. Dir. James A. Contner. October 13, 1995.

1.10 "Inhumanitas." Wr. Stephen Gaghan and Michael R. Perry. Dir. Bruce Seth Green. January 17, 1996.

1.11 "The Plague Sower." Wr. Robert Palm. Dir. Mel Damski. January 24, 1996.

1.17 "The Buck Stops Here." Wr. Steve De Jarnatt. Dir. Lou Antonio. July 10, 1996.

1.22 "Strangler." Wr. Stephen Gaghan and Michael R. Perry. Dir. Doug Lefler. Unaired.

American Horror Story. Created by Brad Falchuk and Ryan Murphy. Perf. Jessica Lange and Evan Peters. FX, 2011–

1.1 "Pilot." Wr. Brad Falchuk and Ryan Murphy. Dir. Ryan Murphy. October 5, 2011.
1.3 "Murder House." Wr. Jennifer Salt. Dir. Bradley Buecker. October 19, 2011.
1.4 "Halloween Part 1." Wr. James Wong. Dir. David Semel. October 26, 2011.
1.5 "Halloween Part 2." Wr. Tim Minear. Dir. David Semel. November 2, 2011.
1.6 "Piggy, Piggy." Wr. Jessica Sharzer. Dir. Michael Uppendahl. November 9, 2011.
1.7 "Open House." Wr. Brad Falchuk. Dir. Tim Hunter. November 16, 2011.
1.8 "The Rubber Man." Wr. Ryan Murphy. Dir. Miguel Arteta. November 23, 2011.
1.9 "Spooky Little Girl." Wr. Jennifer Salt. Dir. John Scott. November 30, 2011.
1.11 "Birth." Wr. Tim Minear. Dir. Alfonso Gomez-Rejon. December 14, 2011.
1.12 "Afterbirth." Wr. Jessica Sharzer. Dir. Bradley Buecker. December 21, 2011.

Angel. Created by Joss Whedon and David Greenwalt. Perf. David Boreanaz. WB, 1999–2004

1.14 "I've Got You Under My Skin." Wr. Jeannine Renshaw and David Greenwalt. Dir. R. D. Price. February 15, 2000.
1.15 "The Prodigal." Wr. Tim Minear. Dir. Bruce Seth Green. February 22, 2000.
1.20 "War Zone." Wr. Garry Campbell. Dir. David Straiton. May 9, 2000.
2.6 "Guise will be Guise." Wr. Jane Espenson. Dir. Krishna Rao. November 7, 2000.
2.8 "The Shroud of Rahmon." Wr. Jim Kouf. Dir. David Grossman. November 21, 2000.
2.10 "Reunion." Wr. Tim Minear and Shawn Ryan. Dir. James A. Contner. December 19, 2000.
2.19 "Belonging." Wr. Shawn Ryan. Dir. Turi Meyer. May 1, 2001.

2.20 "Over the Rainbow." Wr. Mere Smith. Dir. Fred Keller. May 8, 2001.
2.21 "Through the Looking Glass." Wr. and dir. Tim Minear. May 15, 2001.
3.6 "Billy." Wr. Tim Minear and Jeffrey Bell. Dir. David Grossman. October 29, 2001.
3.20 "A New World." Wr. Jeffrey Bell. Dir. Tim Minear. May 6, 2002.
4.11 "Soulless." Wr. Sarah Fain and Elizabeth Craft. Dir. Sean Astin. February 5, 2003.
4.20 "Sacrifice." Wr. Ben Edlund. Dir. David Straiton. April 23, 2003.
5.5 "Life of the Party." Wr. Ben Edlund. Dir. Bill Norton. October 29, 2003.
5.7 "Lineage." Wr. Drew Goddard. Dir. Jefferson Kibbee. November 12, 2003.

Bewitched. Created by Sol Saks. Perf. Elizabeth Montgomery. ABC, 1964–1972

1.3 "It Shouldn't Happen to a Dog." Wr. Jerry Davis. Dir. William Asher. October 1, 1964.
2.2 "A Very Special Delivery." Wr. Howard Leeds. Dir. William Asher. September 23, 1965.

Buffy the Vampire Slayer. Created by Joss Whedon. Perf. Sara Michelle Gellar. WB and UPN, 1997–2003

5.1 "Buffy vs. Dracula." Wr. Marti Noxon. Dir. David Solomon. Original air date September 26, 2000.

Carnivàle. Created by Daniel Knauf. Perf. Nick Stahl, Michael J. Anderson, and Clea DuVall. HBO, 2003, 2005

1.1 "Milfay." Wr. Daniel Knauf. Dir. Rodrigo García. September 14, 2003.
1.6 "Pick a Number." Wr. Ronald D. Moore. Dir. Rodrigo García. October 19, 2003.
1.11 "Day of the Dead." Wr. Toni Graphia. Dir. John Patterson. November 23, 2003.

1.12 "The Day That Was the Day." Wr. Ronald D. Moore. Dir. Rodrigo García. November 30, 2003.
2.4 "Old Cherry Blossom Road." Wr. Dawn Prestwich and Nicole Yorkin. Dir. Steve Shill. January 30, 2005.
2.7 "Damascus, NE." Wr. John J. McLaughlin and William Schmidt. Dir. Alan Taylor. February 20, 2005.

Kolchak, the Night Stalker. Created by Jeffrey Grant Rice. Perf. Darren McGavin. ABC, 1974–1975

1.2 "The Zombie." Wr. Zekial Marko and David Chase. Dir. Alexander Grasshoff. September 20, 1974.

Millennium. Created by Chris Carter. Perf. Lance Henriksen and Megan Gallagher. Fox, 1996–1999

1.1 "Pilot." Wr. Chris Carter. Dir. David Nutter. October 25, 1996.
1.8 "The Well-Worn Lock." Wr. Chris Carter. Dir. Ralph Hemecker. December 20, 1996.
1.16 "Covenant." Wr. Robert Moresco. Dir. Rod Pridy. March 21, 1997.
1.18 "Lamentation." Wr. Chris Carter. Dir. Winrich Kolbe. April 18, 1997.
2.1 "The Beginning and the End." Wr. Glen Morgan and James Wong. Dir. Thomas J. Wright. September 19, 1997.
2.2 "Beware of the Dog." Wr. Glen Morgan and James Wong. Dir. Allen Coulter. September 26, 1997.
2.6 "The Curse of Frank Black." Wr. Glen Morgan and James Wong. Dir. Ralph Hemecker. October 31, 1997.
2.19 "Anamnesis." Wr. Erin Maher and Kay Reindl. Dir. John Peter Kousakis. April 17, 1998.
2.20 "A Room with No View." Wr. Ken Horton. Dir. Thomas J. Wright. April 24, 1998.
2.21 "Somehow, Satan Got Behind Me." Wr. Darin Morgan. Dir. Darin Morgan. May 1, 1998.
2.22 "The Fourth Horseman." Wr. Glen Morgan and James Wong. Dir. Dwight H. Little. May 8, 1998.
2.23 "The Time Is Now." Wr. Glen Morgan and James Wong. Dir. Thomas J. Wright. May 15, 1998.

3.5 "...Thirteen Years Later." Wr. Michael R. Perry. Dir. Thomas J. Wright. October 30, 1998.
3.13 "Antipas." Wr. Chris Carter and Frank Spotnitz. Dir. Thomas J. Wright. February 12, 1999.

Point Pleasant. Created by Marti Noxon. Perf. Elisabeth Harnois and Grant Show. Fox, 2005–2006

1.3 "Who's Your Daddy?" Wr. Ben Edlund. Dir. Marita Grabiak. January 27, 2005.
1.8 "Swimming with Boyd." Wr. Jenny Lynn and Jeff Diaz. Dir. James Contner. March 17, 2005.
1.9 "Waking the Dead." Wr. Robert Doherty, Ben Edlund, and Zack Estrin. Dir. Marita Grabiak. June 19, 2005.
1.10 "Hell Hath No Fury Like a Woman Choked." Wr. Ron Milbauer, Terri Hughes Burton, and Jeff Diaz. Dir. Mel Damski. June 26, 2005.
1.11 "Missing." Wr. Andrea Newman and P. K. Simonds. Dir. Michael Lange. July 3, 2005.
1.12 "Mother's Day." Wr. Jeff Diaz, Robert Doherty, Zack Estrin, and Diego Gutierrez. Dir. Felix Alcala. September 9, 2006.
1.13 "Let the War Commence." Wr. Jenny Lynn and Marti Noxon. Dir. Chris Long. September 9, 2006.

Supernatural. Created by Eric Kripke. Perf. Jensen Ackles and Jared Padalecki. WB and CW, 2005–

1.6 "Skin." Wr. John Shiban. Dir. Robert Duncan McNeill. October 18, 2005.
1.8 "Bugs." Wr. Rachel Nave and Bill Coakley. Dir. Kim Manners. November 8, 2005.
1.9 "Home." Wr. Eric Kripke. Dir. Ken Girotti. November 15, 2005.
1.10 "Asylum." Wr. Richard Hatem. Dir. Guy Norman Bee. November 22, 2005.
1.11 "Scarecrow." Wr. John Shiban and Patrick Sean Smith. Dir. Kim Manners. January 10, 2006.
1.12 "Faith." Wr. Sera Gamble and Raelle Tucker. Dir. Allan Kroeker. January 17, 2006.

1.14 "Nightmare." Wr. Sera Gamble and Raelle Tucker. Dir. Phil Sgriccia. February 7, 2006.
1.18 "Something Wicked." Wr. Daniel Knauf. Dir. Whitney Ransick. April 6, 2006.
1.20 "Dead Man's Blood." Wr. Cathryn Humphris and John Shiban. Dir. Tony Whamby. April 20, 2006.
2.7 "The Usual Suspects." Wr. Cathryn Humphris. Dir. Mike Rohl. November 9, 2006.
2.9 "Croatoan." Wr. John Shiban. Dir. Robert Singer. December 7, 2006.
2.10 "Hunted." Wr. Raelle Tucker. Dir. Rachel Talalay. January 11, 2007.
2.11 "Playthings." Wr. Matt Witten. Dir. Charles Beeson. January 18, 2007.
2.12 "Nightshifter." Wr. Ben Edlund. Dir. Phil Sgriccia. January 25, 2007.
2.13 "Houses of the Holy." Wr. Sera Gamble. Dir. Kim Manners. February 1, 2007.
2.19 "Fulsom Prison Blues." Wr. John Shiban. Dir. Mike Rohl. April 26, 2007.
2.22 "All Hell Breaks Loose 2." Wr. Eric Kripke and Michael T. Moore. Dir. Robert Singer. May 17, 2007.
4.13 "After School Special." Wr. Andrew Dabb and Daniel Loflin. Dir. Adam Kane. January 29, 2009.
4.14 "Sex and Violence." Wr. Cathryn Humphris. Dir. Charles Beeson. February 5, 2009.
4.18 "The Monster at the End of this Book." Wr. Julie Siege and Nancy Weiner. Dir. Mike Rohl. April 2, 2009.
4.21 "When the Levee Breaks." Wr. Sera Gamble. Dir. Robert Singer. May 7, 2009.
5.13 "The Song Remains the Same." Wr. Sera Gamble and Nancy Weiner. Dir. Steve Boyum. February 4, 2010.
6.15 "The French Mistake." Wr. Ben Edlund. Dir. Charles Beeson. February 25, 2011.

Bibliography

"About." *My Name Is Earl*. NBC website, www.nbc.com/My_Name_Is_Earl/about <date of access: July 14, 2007>.

Adams, James Eli. *Dandies and Desert Saints: Styles of Victorian Masculinity*. Ithaca, NY: Cornell University Press, 1995.

Adorno, Theodor and Max Horkheimer. *The Dialectic of Enlightenment: Philosophical Fragments*. Ed. Gunzelin Schmid Noerr. Trans. Edmund Jephcott. Stanford: Stanford University Press, 2002.

Allard, James. "Spectres, spectators, spectacles: Matthew Lewis's *The Castle Spectre*." *Gothic Studies*, 3 (2001): 246–61.

American Gothic. Created by Shaun Cassidy. CBS, 1995–1996.

American Horror Story. Created by Brad Falchuk and Ryan Murphy. FX, 2011– .

Andriopoulos, Stefan. "The invisible hand: supernatural agency in political economy and the gothic novel." *ELH*, 66 (1999): 739–58.

Angel. Created by Joss Whedon and David Greenwalt. WB, 1999–2004.

Austin, J. L. *How to Do Things with Words*. 2nd edn. Cambridge, MA: Harvard University Press, 1962.

Autry National Center. http://theautry.org/whats-here/overview <date of access: May 28, 2013>.

Baldick, Chris and Robert Mighall. "Gothic criticism." *A New Companion to the Gothic*. Ed. David Punter. Oxford: Wiley-Blackwell, 2012, pp. 267–87.

Baudrillard, Jean. *Simulacra and Simulation*. Trans. Sheila Faria Glaser. Ann Arbor: University of Michigan Press, 1995.

Baudrillard, Jean. "The structural law of value and the order of simulacra." Ed. John Fekete, trans. Charles Leven, *The Structural Allegory: Reconstructive Encounters with the New French Thought*. Minneapolis: University of Minnesota Press, 1984, pp. 54–73.

Beeler, Stan. "Outing Lorne: performance for the performers." *Reading Angel: The TV Spin-off with a Soul.* Ed. Stacey Abbott. London: I.B. Tauris, 2005, pp. 88–100.

Benjamin, Walter. *Illuminations.* Ed. Hannah Arendt, trans. Harry Zohn. New York: Schocken, 1986.

Beuka, Robert. *SuburbiaNation: Reading Suburban Landscape in Twentieth-Century American Fiction and Film.* New York: Palgrave Macmillan, 2004.

Bewitched. Created by Sol Saks. Perf. Elizabeth Montgomery. ABC, 1964–1972.

Blazing Saddles. Dir. Mel Brooks. Wr. Mel Brooks, Norman Steinberg, Andrew Bergman, Richard Pryor, and Alan Uger. Warner, 1974.

Boogeyman. Dir. Stephen Kay. Wr. Eric Kripke, Juliet Snowden, Stiles White. Perf. Barry Watson, Emily Deschanel, and Lucy Lawless. Special edition DVD. Sony Pictures, 2005.

Bordwell, David. *The Films of Carl Theodor Dreyer.* Berkeley: University of California Press, 1981.

Botting, Fred. *Gothic Romanced: Consumption, Gender and Technology in Contemporary Fictions.* London: Routledge, 2008.

Botting, Fred. "Signs of evil: Bataille, Baudrillard and postmodern gothic." *Southern Review*, 27 (1994): 493–510.

Botting, Fred and Dale Townshend. "Introduction." *Gothic: Critical Concepts in Literary and Cultural Studies.* 4 vols. New York: Routledge, 2004, vol. 1, pp. 1–18.

Boym, Svetlana. "Conspiracy theories and literary ethics: Umberto Eco, Danilo Kis and *The Protocols of Zion.*" *Comparative Literature*, 51 (1999): 97–122.

Bradney, Anthony. "Choosing laws, choosing families: images of law, love and authority in 'Buffy the Vampire Slayer.'" *Web Journal of Current Legal Issues*, 2 (2003), http://webjcli.ncl.ac.uk/2003/issue2/bradney2.html

Brantlinger, Patrick. "What is 'sensational' about the 'sensation novel'?" *Nineteenth-Century Fiction*, 37 (1982): 1–28.

Bronson, Eric. "*Carnivàle* knowledge: give me that old-time noir religion." *The Philosophy of TV Noir.* Ed. Steven M. Sanders and Aeon J. Skoble. Lexington: University Press of Kentucky, 2008, pp. 131–42.

Buchbinder, David. "Passing strange: queering whiteness in Joss Whedon's *Angel.*" *White Matters.* Ed. Susan Petrilli. Rome: Athanor, 2007, pp. 229–35.

Buffy the Vampire Slayer. Created by Joss Whedon. WB and UPN, 1997–2003.

Burke, Edmund. *Enquiry Concerning the Origin of our Ideas of the*

Sublime and Beautiful. 1757. Ed. Adam Phillips. Oxford: Oxford University Press, 1998.

Butler, Judith. "Imitation and gender insubordination." *Inside/Out: Lesbian Theories, Gay Theories*. Ed. Diana Fuss. New York: Routledge, 1991, pp. 13–31.

Carnivàle. Created by Daniel Knauf. HBO, 2003, 2005.

Carrie. Dir. Brian De Palma. Wr. Laurence D. Cohen (novel by Stephen King). Perf. Sissy Spacek. MGM, 1976.

"Cast." *Supernatural.* CW website. www.cwtv.com/shows/supernatural/cast/jensen-ackles <date of access: July 12, 2007>.

Cavender, Gray. "Detecting masculinity." *Making Trouble: Cultural Constructions of Crime, Deviance, and Control.* Ed. Jeff Ferrell and Neil Websdale. New Brunswick, NJ: Transaction, 1996; repr. 2009, pp. 157–75.

Chan, Suzette. "Tarts talk about SPN 5.06: I Believe the Children Are Our Future." *Sequential Tart*, December 14, 2009, www.sequentialtart.com/article.php?id=1572

Clery, E. J. *The Rise of Supernatural Fiction, 1762–1800.* Cambridge: Cambridge University Press, 1995.

Cole, Stephen. "Bogus horror flick belongs in the closet." *Globe and Mail*, February 5, 2005.

Coleridge, Samuel Taylor. *Selected Poetry and Prose of Coleridge.* Ed. Donald A. Stauffer. New York: Modern Library, 1951.

"Commentary on 'Pilot' with Eric Kripke, David Nutter, and Peter Johnson." *Supernatural: Season 1.* DVD. Warner Home Video, 2006.

Derrida, Jacques. *Of Grammatology.* Trans. Gayatri Chakravorty Spivak. Baltimore: Johns Hopkins University Press, 1976.

Die Hard. Dir. John McTiernan. Wr. Roderick Thorp, Jeb Stuart, and Steven E. de Souza. Perf. Bruce Willis, Alan Rickman, and Bonnie Bedelia. Twentieth-Century Fox, 1988.

Ducat, Stephen J. *The Wimp Factor: Gender Gaps, Holy Wars, and the Politics of Anxious Masculinity.* Boston: Beacon Press, 2004.

Dyer, Richard, "Kill and kill again." *Sight & Sound*, n.s. 7:9 (September 1997): 14–17.

Eco, Umberto. *Six Walks in the Fictional Woods.* Cambridge, MA: Harvard University Press, 1998.

Eichler, Rolf. "In the Romantic tradition: *Frankenstein* and *The Rocky Horror Picture Show.*" *Beyond the Suburbs of the Mind: Exploring English Romanticism.* Ed. Michael Gassenmeir and Norbert Platz. Essen: Verlag Die Blaue Eule, 1987, pp. 95–114.

Elias, Justine. "Television; 'American Gothic' settles in on the dark side," *New York Times*, October 22, 1995, www.nytimes.com/1995/10/22/arts/television-american-gothic-settles-in-on-the-dark-side.html

Ellis, Kate Ferguson. *The Contested Castle: Gothic Novels and the Subversion of Domestic Ideology*. Chicago: University of Illinois Press, 1989.

Ellis, Markman. *The History of Gothic Fiction*. Edinburgh: Edinburgh University Press, 2005.

Eyes of Laura Mars. Dir. Irvin Kershner. Wr. John Carpenter and David Zelag Goodman. Perf. Faye Dunaway, Tommy Lee Jones, and Brad Dourif. Columbia Pictures, 1978.

Fiske, John. *Television Culture*. 1987. New York: Routledge, 2006.

Foster, Gwendolyn Audrey. *Class-Passing: Social Mobility in Film and Popular Culture*. Carbondale: Southern Illinois University Press, 2005.

Foucault, Michel. *Discipline and Punish: The Birth of the Prison*. 1975. Trans. Alan Sheridan. New York: Vintage, 1979.

Freud, Sigmund. "The Uncanny." Vol. 17, *The Standard Edition of the Complete Psychological Works of Sigmund Freud*. Trans. James Strachey. London: Hogarth Press, 1955, pp. 219–52.

Fuchs, Michael. "'Play it again, Sam ... and Dean': temporality and metatextuality in *Supernatural*." *Time in Television Narrative: Exploring Temporality in Twenty-first Century Programming*. Ed. Melissa Ames. Jackson: University of Mississippi Press, 2012, pp. 82–94.

Gaiman, Neil. *American Gods*. New York: HarperCollins, 2001.

Gamble, Sera. Interview. "Exclusive: Supernatural's Sera gamble on old and new characters, plus dealing with gore!" (posted November 15, 2007; date of access August 7, 2013). CW Source. http://blogs.trb.com/network/cwsource/2007/11/exclusive_supernaturals_sera_g.html

Glass, Loren. "Publicizing the president's privates." *Postmodern Culture*, 9:3 (1999).

Goodlad, Lauren M. E. "Looking for something forever gone: gothic masculinity, androgyny, and ethics at the turn of the millennium." *Cultural Critique*, 66 (2007): 104–26.

Grønstad, Asbjørn. *Transfigurations: Violence, Death, and Masculinity in American Cinema*. Amsterdam: Amsterdam University Press, 2008.

Halfyard, Janet K. "The dark avenger: Angel and the cinematic superhero." *Reading Angel: The TV Spin-off with a Soul*. Ed. Stacey Abbott. London: I.B. Tauris, 2005, pp. 149–62.

Hall, Stuart et al. eds. *Culture, Media, Language: Working Papers in Cultural Studies, 1972–1979*. New York: Routledge, 1991.

Hebdige, Dick. *Subculture: The Meaning of Style*. London: Methuen, 1979.

Hogle, Jerrold. "'Frankenstein' as neo-gothic: from the ghost of the counterfeit to the monster of abjection." *Romanticism, History, and the Possibilities of Genre: Re-forming Literature, 1789–1837*. Ed. Tilottama Rajan and Julia M. Wright. Cambridge: Cambridge University Press, 1998, pp. 176–210.

Hogle, Jerrold. "The ghost of the counterfeit – and the closet – in *The Monk*." *Romanticism on the Net*, 8 (November 1997) http://erudit.org/revue/ron/1997/v/n8/005770ar.html?lang=en

Hogle, Jerrold. "Gothic." *Handbook to Romanticism Studies*. Ed. Joel Faflak and Julia M. Wright. Oxford: Wiley-Blackwell, 2012, pp. 195–212.

Hogle, Jerrold. "Stoker's counterfeit gothic: *Dracula* and theatricality at the dawn of simulation." *Bram Stoker: History, Psychoanalysis and the Gothic*. Ed. William Hughes and Andrew Smith New York: St. Martin's Press, 1998, pp. 205–24.

Hogle, Jerrold. "The struggle for a dichotomy: abjection in Jekyll and his interpreters." *Dr. Jekyll and Mr. Hyde after One Hundred Years*. Ed. William Veeder and Gordon Hirsch. Chicago: Chicago University Press, 1988, pp. 161–207.

Internet Movie Database. www.imdb.com

Jameson, Fredric. *The Political Unconscious: Narrative as a Socially Symbolic Act*. Ithaca, NY: Cornell University Press, 1981.

Jeffords, Susan. "Breakdown: white masculinity, class and US action-adventure films," *Action and Adventure Cinema*. Ed. Yvonne Tasker. New York: Routledge, 2004, pp. 219–34.

Jeffords, Susan. *Hard Bodies: Hollywood Masculinity in the Reagan Era*. Brunswick, NJ: Rutgers University Press, 1994.

Jowett, Lorna. "'Not like other men'?: the vampire body in Joss Whedon's *Angel*." *Studies in Popular Culture*, 32 (2009): 37–51.

Jowett, Lorna and Stacey Abbott. *TV Horror: Investigating the Dark Side of the Small Screen*. London: I.B. Tauris, 2013.

Kawash, Samira. "Safe house? Body, building, and the question of security," *Cultural Critique*, 45 (2000): 185–221.

Knauf, Daniel. "Series concept & background" (known as "The Pitch Document"). Available at http://c.ymcdn.com/sites/www.harvardwood.org/resource/resmgr/hwp-pdfs/carnivale_pitch_document.pdf

Kolchak, the Night Stalker. Created by Jeffrey Grant Rice. ABC, 1974–1975.

Kripke, Eric. "Eric Kripke fields your questions about *Supernatural*." *TV Guide*, 15 February 2007. www.tvguide.com/News/eric-kripke-fields/070215-04 <date of access: June 28, 2007>.

Kristeva, Julia. *Powers of Horror: An Essay*. Trans. Leon S. Roudiez. New York: Columbia University Press, 1982.

Krutnik, Frank. *In a Lonely Street: Film Noir, Genre, Masculinity*. New York: Routledge, 1991.

Law-Abiding Citizen. Dir. F. Gary Gray. Wr. Kurt Wimmer. Perf. Gerard Butler and Jamie Foxx. The Film Department, 2009.

Ledwon, Lenora. "*Twin Peaks* and the television gothic." *Literature/Film Quarterly*, 21:4 (1993), pp. 260–70.

Lehman, Peter. "Introduction." *Masculinity: Bodies, Movies, Culture.* Ed. Peter Lehman New York: Routledge, 2001, pp. 1–6.

Leyland, Matthew. Review of *Boogeyman. Sight & Sound*, 15:4 (April 2005): 47.

Lost. Created by J. J. Abrams, Jeffrey Lieber, and Damon Lindelof. ABC, 2004–2010.

Maier, Sarah E. "John Doe reads: interrogating the postmodern serial killer in *Millennium*, *Seven* and *Profiler*." *Crime Time – Prime Time – Global Time: Intercultural Studies in Crime Serials.* Ed. Ute Fendler and Susanne Fendler. Aachen, Germany: Shaker, 2004, pp. 171–86.

Malin, Brenton J. *American Masculinity under Clinton: Popular Media and the Nineties' Crisis of Masculinity.* New York: Peter Lang, 2005.

Matheson, Richard. *Hell House.* 1971. New York: Tor Books, 1999.

Meyer, Michaela D. E. "From rogue in the 'hood to suave in a suit: black masculinity and the transformation of Charles Gunn." *Reading Angel: The TV Spin-off with a Soul.* Ed. Stacey Abbott. London: I.B. Tauris, 2005, pp. 176–88.

Michasiw, Kim. "Some stations of suburban gothic." *American Gothic: New Interventions in a National Narrative.* Ed. Robert K. Martin and Eric Savoy. Iowa City: University of Iowa Press, 1998, pp. 236–57.

Miles, Robert. "Europhobia: the Catholic other in Horace Walpole and Charles Maturin." *European Gothic: A Spirited Exchange 1760–1960.* Ed. Avril Horner. Manchester: Manchester University Press, 2002, pp. 84–103.

Miles, Robert. *Gothic Writing, 1750–1820: A Genealogy.* New edn. Manchester: Manchester University Press, 2002.

Miles, Robert. "The 1790s: the effulgence of the gothic." *The Cambridge Companion to Gothic Fiction.* Ed. Jerrold Hogle. Cambridge: Cambridge University Press, 2002, pp. 41–62.

Millennium. Created by Chris Carter. Fox, 1996–1999.

Morris, David B. "Gothic sublimity." *New Literary History*, 16 (1985): 299–319.

Morrison, Toni. *Playing in the Dark.* New York: Vintage, 1993.

Moseley, Rachel. "Glamorous witchcraft: gender and magic in teen film and television." *Screen*, 43:4 (2002): 403–22.

Moses, Michael Valdez. "Kingdom of darkness: autonomy and conspiracy in *The X-Files* and *Millennium*." *The Philosophy of TV Noir.* Ed. Steven M. Sanders and Aeon J. Skoble. Lexington: University of Kentucky Press, 2008, pp. 203–27.

My Name Is Earl. Created by Greg Garcia. Perf. Jason Lee, Ethan Suplee, Jaime Pressly, Eddie Steeples and Nadine Velazquez. NBC, 2005–2009.

Nelson, Victoria. "Faux Catholic: a gothic subgenre from Monk Lewis to Dan Brown." *boundary* 2, 34 (2007): 87–107.

Night Stalker (*Kolchak*). Created by Frank Spotnitz, based on characters by Jeffrey Grant Rice. Space, 2005–2006.

The Night Stalker (*Kolchak*). Wr. Richard Matheson and Jeffrey Grant Rice. Dir. John Llewellyn Moxey. ABC, January 11, 1972.

The Night Strangler (*Kolchak*). Wr. Richard Matheson and Jeffrey Grant Rice. Dir. Dan Curtis. ABC, January 16, 1973.

O'Malley, Patrick. *Catholicism, Sexual Deviance, and Victorian Gothic Culture*. Cambridge: Cambridge University Press, 2006.

Palmer, Lorrie. "Ruby red and emerald green: the queer demon diva of my dreams." *Camera Obscura*, 23 (2008): 194–99.

Paulson, Ronald. "Gothic fiction and the French Revolution." *ELH*, 48 (1981): 532–54.

Poe, Edgar Allan. *Selected Writings of Edgar Allan Poe*. Ed. Edward H. Davidson. Boston: Houghton Mifflin, 1956.

Point Pleasant. Created by Marti Noxon. Fox, 2005–2006.

Radcliffe, Ann. "On the supernatural in poetry." *New Monthly Magazine*, 16 (1826): 145–52.

Revolution. Created by Eric Kripke. NBC, 2012– .

Reynolds, Simon and Joy Press. *The Sex Revolts: Gender, Rebellion, and Rock 'n' Roll* Cambridge, MA: Harvard University Press, 1996.

Rice, Anne. *Interview with the Vampire*. 1976. New York: Ballantine, 1997.

Riley, Brendan. "From Sherlock to Angel: the twenty-first century detective." *Journal of Popular Culture*, 42 (2009): 908–22.

Riley, Dave and Jill Steinberg. "Four popular stereotypes about children in self-care: implications for family life educators." *Family Relations: Interdisciplinary Journal of Applied Family Studies*, 53 (2004): 95–101.

Robinson, Sally. *Marked Men: White Masculinity in Crisis*. New York: Columbia University Press, 2000.

Robson, Eddie. "Gothic television." *The Routledge Companion to Gothic*. Ed. Catherine Spooner and Emma McEvoy. New York: Routledge, 2007, pp. 242–50.

Ruggerio, Alena Amato. "Sexuality, size, and sin in HBO's *Carnivàle*." *Feminist Media Studies*, 5 (2005): 87–89.

Savoy, Eric. "The face of the Tenant: a theory of American Gothic." *American Gothic: New Interventions in a National Narrative*. Ed. Robert K. Martin and Eric Savoy. Iowa City: University of Iowa Press, 1998, pp. 3–19.

Scheck, Frank. Review of *Boogeyman*. *Hollywood Reporter*, February 7, 2005.

Scheidt, Dave. "Talking about Itty Bitty Hellboy with Art and Franco: an illustrated interview." *HuffPost*, August 29, 2013. www.huffingtonpost.com/dave-scheidt/itty-bitty-hellboy-comic_b_3819676.html

Sconce, Jeffrey. *Haunted Media: Electronic Presence from Telegraphy to Television*. Durham, NC: Duke University Press, 2000.

Scream. Dir. Wes Craven. Wr. Kevin Williamson. Dimension Films, 1996.

Sedgwick, Eve Kosofsky. *Between Men: English Literature and Male Homosocial Desire*. New York: Columbia University Press, 1985.

Sedgwick, Eve Kosofsky. *Epistemology of the Closet*. Berkeley: University of California Press, 1990.

Shakespeare, William. *The Norton Shakespeare*. 2nd edn. Ed. Stephen Greenblatt et al. New York: Norton, 2008.

Smith, Patti, and Ivan Kral (lyrics), "Dancing Barefoot." Perf. Patti Smith. *Wave*. Arista, 1979.

Spigel, Lynn. *Welcome to the Dreamhouse: Popular Media and the Postwar Suburbs*. Durham, NC: Duke University Press, 2001.

Spooner, Catherine. *Contemporary Gothic*. London: Reaktion, 2006.

Summers, Montague. *The Gothic Quest: A History of the Gothic Novel*. London: Fortune Press, 1938.

Sunset Blvd. Dir. Billy Wilder. Wr. Billy Wilder, Charles Brackett, and D. M. Marshman Jr. Paramount, 1950.

Supernatural. Created by Eric Kripke. WB, 2005–2006; CW, 2006– .

Taylor, Tosha. "Who's afraid of the Rubber Man? Perversions and subversions of sex and class in *American Horror Story*." *Networked Knowledge*, 5:2 (September 2012): 135–53.

Twisted Nerve. Dir. Ray Boulting. Wr. Ray Boulting, Leo Marks, Roger Marshall et al. Perf. Hywel Bennett and Hayley Mills. Charter Film Productions, 1968.

Walpole, Horace. *The Castle of Otranto: A Gothic Story*. Ed. W. S. Lewis. Intro. E. J. Clery. Oxford: Oxford University Press, 1998.

Wheatley, Helen. *Gothic Television*. Manchester: Manchester University Press, 2006.

Williams, Tennessee. *Where I Live: Selected Essays*. New York: New Directions, 1978.

Winthrop, John. "A model of Christian charity" (1630), http://religiousfreedom.lib.virginia.edu/sacred/charity.html <last date of access: May 10, 2013>.

Wright, Julia M. "The gothic frontier of modernity: the 'invisible hand' of state-formation in *Deadwood*." *The Last Western: Deadwood and the End of American Empire*. Ed. Jennifer Greiman and Paul Stasi. New York: Continuum, 2013, pp. 42–61.

Zimbardo, Rose. "The semiotics of Restoration satire." *Cutting Edges: Postmodern Critical Essays on Eighteenth-Century Satire*. Vol. 37 of Tennessee Studies in Literature. Knoxville: University of Tennessee Press, 1995, pp. 23–42.

Index